CW01660629

Bradford and the Industrial Revolution

Titles of related interest available from Ryburn Publishing:

Victorian Bradford The Living Past
Photographs by Ian Beesley Commentary by David James

The Ryburn Map of Victorian Bradford
Text by Elvira Willmott

Town and City Histories: Bradford
by David James

Bingley in Old Picture Postcards
by Gary Firth

Bradford and the Industrial Revolution

An economic history 1760–1840

Gary Firth B.A. Ph.D.

Ryburn Publishing

First published in 1990
Ryburn Publishing Limited
Krumlin, Halifax, England

A Ryburn Book Production
Jacket designed by Chris Hand
Typeset by Ryburn Typesetting Ltd,
Luddendenfoot, Halifax
Printed by The Amadeus Press, Huddersfield

Bradford and the industrial revolution
ISBN 1-85331-010-7 cased

Contents

For my Mum and Dad

The Publishers gratefully acknowledge
the generous financial assistance of
The Sam Chippindale Foundation
towards publication of this book

List of Figures

List of Tables

Foreword

This book has evolved from research for a doctoral thesis for the University of Bradford (1974) and from years of teaching and research in the fields of regional and local history. In spite of its academic origins I have endeavoured to address this book to the general reader interested in history as something more than antiquarian gleanings of the past. I also trust that professional students of the past as well as history teachers will find some relevance and interest in it.

I owe a particular debt of gratitude to Jack Reynolds, formerly of the University of Bradford, whose vast knowledge, enthusiasm and willingness to help were a source of inspiration for twenty years or more.

I am grateful to Kathleen Head, Elvira Wilmott and Carol Greenwood at Bradford Central Library for innumerable journeys to darkened basements at the library. I am also indebted to David James and his staff at the West Yorkshire Archive Service in Bradford for all their help over many years.

I should like to acknowledge that access to primary source material has also been granted by the following: the Public Record Office, the J.B. Priestley Library at the University of Bradford; Lord Halifax of Garrowby; the Yorkshire Archaeological Society; Messrs. Vint, Hill and Killick, solicitors; the Brotherton Library, University of Leeds; and York Minster Diocesan Library. I thank the University of Manchester Press for permission to use material from an article of mine in *Journal of Transport History* (September 1983). I am grateful to Mrs Bruce and Mr Pratt and Bradford Art Gallery, Museums and Library for permission to reproduce several illustrations in the book and of course to my pal Ian Beesley for contemporary illustrations. Every effort has been made to trace owners of copyright material but in some cases this may not have been possible. The author will be pleased to hear from any further copyright owners.

A serious illness and subsequent disability interrupted work on the book for several years and it is for her help during that bad time that I will owe an eternal debt to my lovely wfe, who played the part of philologist, lexicographer, secretary, filing clerk and counsellor. Thanks also to my children Rachel and Asa for fetching and carrying and thanks in the early stages to little Josie whose frequent visits to my study with numerous playthings have made sure I have kept a proper perspective. I must also thank Hilda Watkinson who made light work of numerous drafts of the manuscript to produce a clear and coherent typescript, and who in the process has become a close family friend. Thanks also to Iain Dick for help with several of the maps reproduced in the book and to Konrad Ronkowski for photographic help. Finally at the publishers, Richard Clark has been helpful and encouraging particularly during the final stages of preparation.

Responsibility for mistakes and shortcomings remains mine alone.

Gary Firth
Wilsden, Bradford
March 1990

1

Introduction: Bradford and the Industrial Revolution 1760–1840

The origins of this book lie in a visit, made by the author many years ago to Cartwright Hall, Bradford, where, displayed in an upper gallery, there is a large landscape oil painting by J.W. Anderson, of 'Bradford in 1835'. This painting of a tranquil rural market town nestling in the Pennine foothills did not resemble the black and noisy mill town of my youth. What a transformation had taken place! But how had it come about and what great causes lay behind it? Later, as a history undergraduate at the University of Leeds some of these questions were answered but Bradford's particular experience of industrialisation continued to intrigue me.

This book is an attempt to explain the transition of an isolated West Riding dale from a remote agricultural backwater into a populous thriving and vibrant nucleus of the English Industrial Revolution. Economically, the principal subject matter of the book is concerned with the great changes which came over the traditional textile industry of worsted manufacture paralleled by the growth of a highly organised and intensively capitalised iron industry. The latter gave a lead to the rapidly changing economic structure of the region and precipitated profound changes to the traditional organisation, technology and financing of Bradford's industrial way of life, particularly in textile production.

The Industrial Revolution was (is) a complete socio-economic process involving a variety of forces: agrarian, technological, demographic, commercial and social which interacted with considerable variation from one region to another. The early chapters of this book consider a number of the more major factors regarded by historians as relevant to the cause of the Industrial Revolution; the prerequisites for the growth of Bradford's regional economy after 1760. They aim to relate, by comparison or contrast, the Bradford experience of industrialisation which, it has been agreed, was preceded and then chaperoned by an agrarian revolution which caused a quantitative increase in the production of food, at the same time as allowing larger numbers of the population employed wholly in manufacturing industries, to become consumers. This was achieved by drastic structural changes in land use and increased specialisation in agricultural production. In Bradford, such changes accompanied industrialisation rather than preceded it, as the local enclosure movement brought about the required economies of scale yet simultaneously accelerated the demise of the small landowner in Bradfordale. The increased demand for food from the growing numbers of people living in the region meant changes to the traditional pattern of food supply and distribution i.e. to Bradford's retailing system (viz Chapter Two).

The stimulus to farming changes was the increased demand for food from an expanding population, matched by a marked shift (particularly after 1800) of people from the countryside into the towns. Demographic increase was both cause and consequence of industrialisation. Certainly in Bradford, population growth (a theme of Chapter Three) became a demand-inducing agent for both agricultural and industrial products – a dynamic force of Bradford's economic change.

The lowering of the age of marriage and a corresponding increase of births to each marriage as well as a slight decline in mortality created a natural demographic increase sufficient to provoke a small growth in Bradford's regional economy before 1800. Thereafter centralised and mechanised textile production made great demands on the town's labour supply and as a result induced massive migration into the town.

If labour is an essential ingredient to industrial 'take off' the availability of investment capital is of no less importance. The dramatic increase in productivity which the Industrial Revolution implies, in turn meant a significant increase in the rate of investment required to sustain it. Many of the achievements of the Industrial Revolution were made and financed by domestic capital, accumulated over many years from property and overseas trade. England, in the eighteenth century was not without capital.

> 'The problem remained much more an institutional one of creating legal procedures, instruments and channels along which savings could flow from those groups receiving them in society to those other groups who needed credit and capital'.

Chapter Three of this book will examine the ways by which Bradford's entrepreneurs, inventive, innovatory, ambitious and socially mobile, were able to manipulate and utilise the accumulation of reserves of capital from land and trade. Eighteenth-century businessmen depended initially on close social networks of family and friends, thereafter, upon a developing system of banking and credit finance.

It has become increasingly apparent that the Industrial Revolution was largely a revolution in transport change. This was particularly true in Bradford's case where geographical disadvantages had handicapped the town's commercial, cultural and economic development for several centuries. The transfer of raw materials and manufactured goods to and from the place of production is an important process of industrialisation. Improved turnpike roads and the cost-reducing innovation of the canal network enabled the Bradford economy, particularly in coal, to function smoothly at a time of important economic change (viz Chapter Four).

The central chapters of the book are concerned with the changes which occurred in the Bradford iron and textile industries. The Victorian 'boom' town of Bradford had its foundations in a prosperous worsted industry but the original initiative to large-scale capitalist enterprise stemmed from the operations of Bradford's local ironworks at Low Moor and Bowling amongst others in the late 1780s, where the scale of capital investment and labour was unprecedented in local industrial and commercial history. Nevertheless it was the transformation of worsted cloth production in terms of methods, organisation and technology which provided the basis for Bradford's transition to large-scale urban status later in the nineteenth century.

The earlier chapters of this book consider the ways by which the people of Bradford achieved wealth and status through commerce and industry. The final section of the book is concerned with the ways in which they used some of that wealth and influence to acquire political power, promote culture and shape a new industrial town – in readiness for its finest hour, the Victorian age and the part of Bradford's history which is best known and which has been told elsewhere.[1]

1. D.G. Wright and A.J. Jowitt, *Victorian Bradford* (1982) and J. Reynolds, *The Great Paternalist* (1983)

2

Land, the Bradford Squirearchy and the Food Supply

We begin our study of Bradford's industrial origins by an examination of the land and the people who worked it prior to large scale industrialisation after 1800. This is no mere coincidence, for long before that acceleration of economic growth, called the Industrial Revolution, the interests and wealth of the law, finance, trade and industry were inextricably entwined with those of the land. In Bradford as in other parts of England there was no schism between the interests of town and country, indeed there existed an extensive overlap between the landed interest and the moneyed interest. Out of Bradford's backward farming economy sprang an enterprise for manufacture and commercial growth. In this chapter it will be necessary to examine the weaknesses in the farming system which prevailed in this Pennine market town during the eighteenth century and which prompted an increased involvement of farmers and landowners into industrial and commercial ventures.

Secondly, once an industrial and commercial momentum had been generated those local farmers, who had remained loyal to their agricultural economy, were able to improve or to modify their farming systems and take advantage of the ready made market of a seething, populous and hungry industrial community like Bradford. By 1760 the town of Bradford was considered to be a well built market town situated at the junction of four small streams three miles south of the River Aire. Although it was considered as a branch of Airedale 'from a remote period it has borne the distinct appelation of Bradfordale'. This long forgotten Yorkshire dale stretched from the moorlands above Thornton and Denholme, down the gentle slopes of Clayton, Heaton and Horton into the ancient manorial township of Bradford which was completely enclosed by high land (except for the valley of the North Brook via Shipley to the River Aire). In 1812 John Bigland described Bradfordale as extremely pleasant,

> 'The country is open and picturesque, the prospects on every side are grand and extensive; the neighbouring hills, though of a very considerable elevation present no abrupt precipices but their gently sloping declivities are in many places adorned with elegant houses and the spacious vales below contribute to form a magnificent landscape'.

Bradford is located upon the north west corner of the Yorkshire Coalfield, more specifically upon the Lower Coal Measures (viz Fig.1). A few miles to the north, the geological features change to the Millstone Grit of the Pennines. This change in the geological strata provides the area with a very mixed soil structure. On the sandstone outcrops of the Lower Coal Measures there is a tendency for the soil to be of a light nature and well drained. Conversely, slates and clays on the Coal Measure give a much heavier and wetter type of soil. Between these extremes, the intermediate type of soil provides easily cultivated sandy loams, which, unfortunately, possess a high acid content.[1]

To the north west of Bradford, following a line along the River Aire, begins the area of the Millstone Grit, with its long dipping slopes which rise again to the table-like hill tops. Much of the higher land is moorland, rising to 1,300 feet above sea level. On the lower slopes of these Grit Uplands the soil is covered with a layer of boulder clay. Still further down, along the Aire valley, there is alluvium present. Essentially, therefore, the geological features do not provide anything more generous than poor to variable soil materials from which the worker of the land might struggle to make himself a living. An agricultural survey of 1798 would seem to confirm this, 'some parts being rich loam and others of a cold watery quality.'[2] The relief and geology of the area do not in any way assist the farmer and the climate also is detrimental and acts as a severe limitation to any intensive scheme of agricultural production. The mean annual rainfall is between thirty and thirty five inches per year which discourages the growth of wheat. The mean annual temperature at sea level is 49°, and most of Bradford is at least 250 feet above. Altitude has an obvious effect on the growth period of any crop, including grass.

These natural limitations on agricultural production are just as great a burden for the modern farmer to bear, as for his counterpart of two centuries ago. Yet the latter was part of an agricultural system, essentially medieval and intrinsically ill-equipped to cope with the growing demand for food from an increasing population.

What can be said of the eighteenth-century Bradford farmer making a living under these restrictive conditions? For several hundred years the enclosure movement had been slowly eroding away the ancient field system of the area, although there were examples of open-field farming surviving into the nineteenth century at Cullingworth, Wibsey and Keighley (viz Fig.2, p.27). However, much of the land around Bradford had been enclosed by 1760.[3] A large proportion of land enclosed before the eighteenth century had shown a conversion from arable to pasture. The dalesmen of the West Riding had little incentive to continue working a soil which was imperfect for arable cultivation and therefore turned increasingly to the rearing of sheep and cattle. Ideal soil for pasture farming was alluvium and marl which were found in the flats and the hollows along the valley of the River Aire. Boulder clay also encouraged pasture farming and such soil is found on the slopes of both the Coal Measures and the Millstone Grit areas. This conversion to pasture had gradually progressed throughout the seventeenth century, after which it underwent a swift acceleration.[4]

Figure 1 Geological Map of the West Riding of Yorkshire

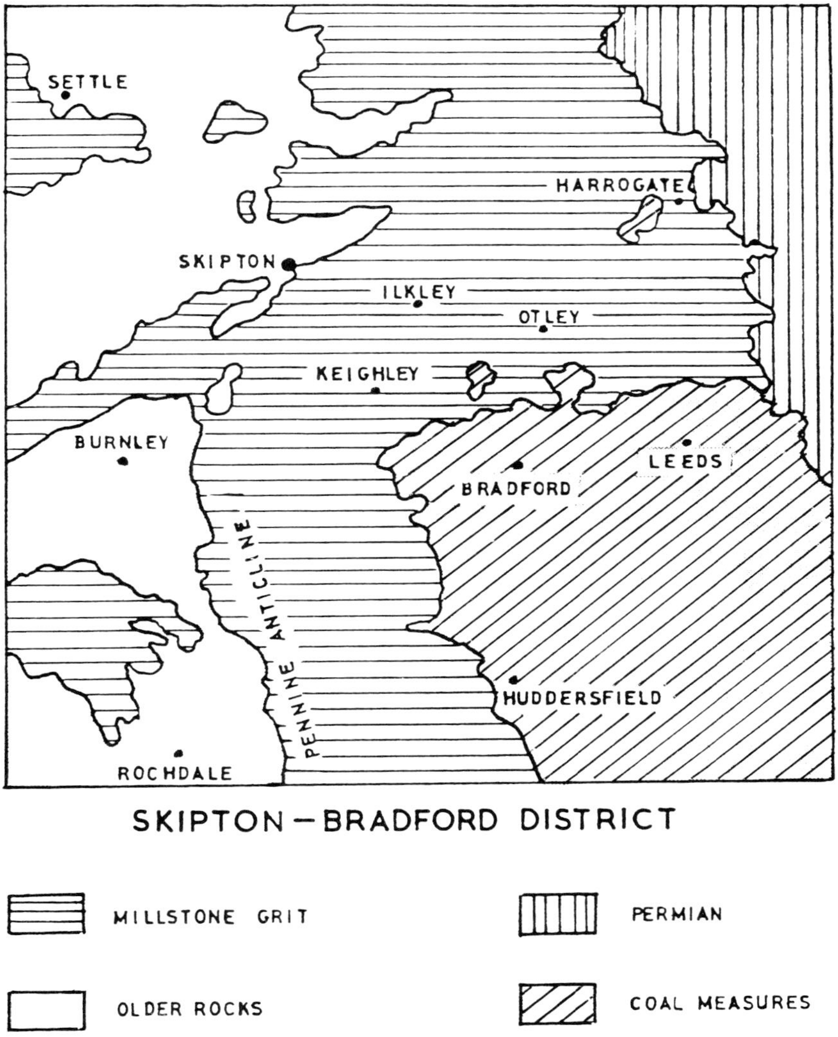

The pre eighteenth-century enclosure movement had not only advanced the transition to pasture farming but had also compounded the number of small farming units in the Bradford region, 'The country is inclosed, inclosures are small, few exceeding six acres but by them, the country has both been enriched and the land improved'.[5]

Thus, small holdings were the norm in Bradford. Land was owned by the small proprietor and occupied by the equally small tenant farmer or manufacturer. There were few estates in the area able to participate in an organised and intensive system of high farming. In an area of poor soil, and in a wet climate, the small farmer seeking alternative economies turned increasingly to weaving and spinning in the domestic textile industry. The West Riding farmer had long been inhibited by the smallness of his farm.[6] From a selection of seventeenth-century inventories, it has been shown that the farmer, in an area such as Bradfordale, possessed an average of only 10.7 cows; cattle being over 40% of his annual valuation.[7] This is directly attributable to the small size of the farmsteads in this area. Many of these small holdings used by the farmer-weaver were, (and still are) to be found on the hillsides close to the water supply with its power and softness. Probably from the fifteenth century these farmsteads had been enclosed from the unwanted wastes of the high moorland.

Restricted then by nature from following a prosperous and reliable living, the small farmer relied more and more on his ability to weave. Thus, by 1775, there was in Bradford 'scarcely a single instance of a man living entirely by farming'.[8] Many of the holdings were no more than fifteen to twenty acres, occupied by men who increasingly considered farming 'only as a matter of convenience'. Consequently the cottage weaving industry was largely responsible for prolonging the fragmentation of the land into small units of agricultural production.

On the eastern slopes of the Millstone Grit and on the adjoining Lower Coal Measure outcrops, these small farm manufacturing units were to be found in abundance. Their occupiers farmed their lands only to provide sufficient food supplies of milk and meat for themselves. A few cattle and perhaps some hens were the only livestock which grazed in the small walled enclosures of five to eight acres (a separate pasture for the packhorse might be owned by the wealthier farmer-clothiers). Although there was considerable regional variation, this type of farming unit was typical of the dipslopes of the West Riding in the eighteenth century. This oft quoted passage from Daniel Defoe's *Tour through the Whole Island of Great Britain* (1724) confirms this pattern of farming,

> 'Then as every clothier must keep a horse, perhaps two, ...so every manufacturer generally keeps a cow or two or more for his family and this employs the two, three and four pieces of enclosed land about his house, for they scarce sow corn enough for their cocks and hens....'[9]

Bradford hill-farms averaged eight acres, many of which were under grass, though more of the fields were cultivated than in the Halifax region where the average farm was only four acres. In the Yorkshire Survey of 1798 Brown remarked that Bradford and the surrounding district produced more corn than he had previously seen on the survey in this part of the Riding. However, he adds that it was all in bad order.

Therefore the presence of the woollen trade had seriously detracted from the agricultural potential of this area. Men who sought their incomes increasingly from the cloth they produced and not the lands on which they lived, could be blamed for the lack of a general agricultural improvement. Furthermore, pastoral farming required less female/child labour and consequently there was more time for them to spin or knit. The owners of the small manufacturing farms 'seldom are farmers beyond the convenience and exigencies of their trade'.[10] What speculation and investment they undertook, was in a new loom or packhorse, rarely in a barn, a plough or a seed drill. Nevertheless livings were made from the local farming system and not all farmers simply catered for their individual needs. There was some farming for the local market in both crops and livestock. A variety of crops were grown but they were always at the mercy of the climate. The high rainfall (as much as forty inches at Thornton) is too great for extensive wheat growing. Perhaps in the sheltered valley bottom, conditions were more conducive to the growth of wheat, but generally it was not a popular crop in this area. Dr. Johnson's maxim that oats is 'a grain which in England is generally given to horses but in Scotland supports the people' might be noted. For oats was the principal crop grown in eighteenth century Bradfordale for both human and animal consumption. As predominant a crop as it was, it had not been raised to any heights of quality by its cultivators. It remained coarse, husky and defective in soil.[11] Apart from this, oats drained away what little goodness the poor soil had to offer. Unlike oats, barley was not as hardy and found difficulty in withstanding bad weather. Although some barley was grown on the uplands, barley and rye were not popular in the dale, particularly on heavy clay soils which badly affected their growth.

The use of legumes and root crops provided a more flexible system of rotation. It also signified an increased fodder supply for the winter feeding of the livestock. The use of turnips and peas was by no means new to the area. At Horsforth, to the north east of Bradford, John Stanhope's tenants made extensive use of legumes and clover in the 1740s.[12] His field books show little evidence of a regular pattern of rotation except for a fallow every fourth year. Soil at Horsforth is more loamy than at Bradford, and consequently more conducive to arable farming. Although peas, beans and turnips were grown, they were not a regular part of the rotation and it would appear that local cultivators did not take full advantage of them. Sown broad cast, they made little profit and often encouraged weeds. To receive full benefit from peas or beans they should have been sown with a drill in rows, 'with sufficient intervals to admit horse hoeing'.[13] Similarly with turnips, which were grown in most parts of the Riding, they too were sown broad cast and infrequently hoed. It was as late as the mid 1760s that the Duke of Rockingham introduced the horse hoe to West Riding farmers. Brown made the caustic comment, 'It may readily be supposed that a people who so lately thought horse hoeing unnecessary will still think an imperfect hoeing sufficient....'[14]

In an area whose association with wool stretched back many centuries, it would be natural to think of the sheep as the most important livestock of this part of the country. This was not so. Before, during and after the Industrial Revolution, cattle played the leading part in the pasture-farming of this district. The breed which was strongly identified with the area in the years before 1800 was the Craven Long Horn, reared for the production of milk, cheese or salted butter. Its ability to withstand the inclement weather made it a favourite with the small and large farmers of this region. Steps taken to cross breed the beast with the East Riding Durham were successful and produced a reliable breed of milkers. Beef cattle in the Riding were not of a very high quality, and consumers usually relied on the Scottish herds being driven down from the north. Nevertheless, the Bradford moorlands and wastes were not without their livestock. Most of the sheep were scraggy, horned and very light in the fore quarters. Of the many interbreedings, the Penistone and Scottish Teviotdale were the most distinct, yet their fleeces weighed no more than three and a half pounds, which compared badly with the twelve pounds of Bakewell's breed. Once again, the West Riding farmer found himself in the rearguard of agricultural progress. It was the most western parts of the Riding which were the last to take up the selective breeding ideas from Dishley. The farmers of the Yorkshire Wolds had reared an improved breed by 1800, having crossed their ewes with a Bakewell ram.[15]

The fragmentation of the land into small enclosures also impeded progress in stock breeding. The sheep of this area were mostly owned by the smaller and poorer farmers, each having no more than twenty head of sheep. To the east, nearer Leeds, the farmers who occupied larger estates kept bigger flocks and consequently, sheep rearing became a worthwhile investment. The smallholder was, however, inhibited by a lack of space from making any significant contribution to stock breeding. This restriction was considerably alleviated by the acceleration, during the Napoleonic Wars, of the enclosure movement.

Small enclosures and the cottage textile industry have been seen as important factors in the backwardness of the agricultural system of Bradfordale. They contributed significantly to the poor livestock, retrograde technology and small scale farming of the region. A further detriment to local agriculture was the reluctance of small tenant farmers to improve their estates and an important reason was the shortness of the tenant's lease. The most common lease employed in this area was the annual lease which accounted for 75% of the land in the West Riding, according to Brown. Farming under yearly leases, with the possibility of being evicted at six months' notice, was not conducive to progressive farming techniques. Short leases, along with the onerous burdens of poor rates and tythes discouraged any inclination to improve. However, extended leases became more popular by the end of the eighteenth century, but even three or eleven year leases could be inhibited by a limiting covenant. For land in Horsforth, Abraham Barrett paid to John Spencer-Stanhope thirty pounds per annum, 'the whole of the land had to be kept in grass the two fields that are now ploughed, the one to be fallowed and cleaned and manured and sown with seeds for grass in July 1833 and the other field to be done in the same way'.[16]

Had Barrett ploughed any land outside the agreement he would have had to pay £10 per acre for it. He was not allowed to remove hay or manure from the lands and finally he was not 'paid for any improvements whatever, he made upon the land or buildings during his occupation'. Restrictions on agricultural practice, such as the covenant and the absence of a sensible leasehold period, held back even further the agricultural progress of this area. Few tenant farmers were willing to invest their small savings in the repair of buildings or the improvement of the soil, in the knowledge that at the end of the year or even three years, their occupancy might be terminated. At the turn of the century a Yorkshire tenant farmer noted how these restrictions affected his profession, 'he must neither think nor act for himself but be forever subject to the whim and caprice of those he lives under'.[17]

Agricultural Improvements and the Bradford Squirearchy 1800–1830

The inadequacies of the farming system of Bradfordale made its inhabitants dependent upon other markets and upon the agricultural producers of the eastern parts of the county. Bradford's farming community continued to work the land as inefficiently as they had done for many generations. Slowly, in the three decades after 1790, several factors were at work which forced the region's farmers into a momentum of improvement and enterprise. Firstly, the small but noticeable population growth expanded the consumer market for both grain and meat. Moreover, supplies of foreign corn were severely reduced in 1793 and wheat prices rose steadily until, in 1795, they reached 90/- per bushel in Bradford. There were bread riots in the town as corn prices rocketed daily at Wilson's, the town's leading grain merchant.[18] Of far greater importance to the Bradford farmer after 1790 was the slow gravitation of the worsted industry towards the towns, away from the isolated farmsteads on the surrounding hillsides. Some of the farmer-weaver small holdings came back into operation as full-time farming concerns. The transition from a domestic to a factory system of textile production further consolidated estates into the hands of those men whose inclination was to farming *per se*. This relocation of the worsted trade and the subsequent growth of Bradford also increased the demand for local agricultural produce and as a result, forced Bradford's farming system into an intensification of crop production and an improvement in the quality of livestock.

Urbanisation and the growth of the Bradford market affected drastically the 'hybrid' nature of local farming and encouraged the Bradford farmer to develop a separate and prosperous existence. By 1800, railways were still a thing of the future and consequently food production had of necessity to be increased by the local farming community. This healthy state of affairs was only brought about by a complex overhaul of the region's farming practices and in the latter decades of the eighteenth century reform and improvement came to several facets of the local agricultural scene.

A positive lead was given by the local squirearchy, or their stewards, in the agricultural improvements which occurred after 1790.[19] Firstly, strict covenants were drawn up in order to protect land from the hands of a neglectful tenantry. For instance, Francis Wood, principal landowner at Monk Bretton near Barnsley, advised his younger brother Charles Wood, on the treatment of his tenants at the latter's estate at Bowling,

> 'we thought of letting some of them remain till your return, as tenants-at-will, but your Lady said you wished to get entirely rid of them. They deserve no sort of encouragement, their grounds and fences being in most shameful disorder. There is next to no fence towards the turnpike road.... I entirely disapprove of obliging the tenants by their leases... or indeed to do anything but look after their farm....'[20]

When tenants allowed their lands and farms to fall into such disrepair, it was not too difficult to understand the harsh views expressed by the same Francis Wood, when he wrote to his sister-in-law, Caroline Wood,

> 'in letting four farms which I would not advise you doing but from year to year or for 3 years at most specifying each acre which should be sowed with wheat...what quantity of lime and other manure...and to forbid under great penalty breaking up of one acre of grassland or touching the bough of a tree....'[21]

Propagandists like Marshall and Young were complaining of the rigidity which strict covenants of this kind imposed upon good farming practice. Although local landowners continued to employ them to protect their estates, covenants ceased to be as rigorous, and provided more flexibility for the tenant during, and after, the Napoleonic wars.

A second improving practice which was popularised in the area during these years was the intensification of soil improvement. The benefits of renourishing the soil had been fully realised by Bradford farmers in the eighteenth century. Folding and manuring had become established farming practices. An initiative was given by the local squirearchy in this field. The Spencer-Stanhope's insistence of liming in their lease covenants is confirmed many times, as indeed it was by numerous leasors of land in the Bradford region in this period.

In 1809, Joshua Crompton assumed the title of Lord of the Manor of Idle from Mr. Rookes. The Crompton family promoted several experiments in agriculture. They also understood the need to manure the land which they worked. Crompton, on his estates at Idle, had constructed several tanks for holding liquid-manure from his fold yard.[22] Pumping the manure onto the land had proved beneficial but he found that the liquid corroded both copper and cast iron pumps. His carpenter designed and built a wooden pump which solved the problem immediately. Although a clear example of trial and error, this is how many of the new ideas emerged, 'The novelty lay not in the innovations, but in the readiness of practical men to put their minds to using the science and technology which had long been available and within reach'.[23] Although Crompton did not occupy all his lands at Idle, his innovations were nevertheless taken up by the tenants of his estates and promulgated by his local land steward.

Others even went so far as to conduct their own folding experiments with various raw materials. A few miles south west of Bradford, at Lightcliffe, Mr. D. Carter, fertilised his lands with cheap Dewsbury shoddy. It proved successful, particularly on grass lands, but he warned that 'it should be well mixed with soil as the wool is a long time decomposing'.[24] The properties of waste wool were already known to refurbish soil chemicals. Nitrogen found its way into the plant as ammonia; processed wool provided carbonic acid. When experiments of this kind doubled the amount of hay to each field, then others were encouraged to follow.

One of the most difficult problems facing the Bradford farmer was that of land drainage. This was particularly serious on the soils overlying the Coal Measures, which were badly drained. Again the local squirearchy gave some kind of lead in alleviating the problem. Land belonging to Mr. Paley at Bowling was described as 'sufficient during one half of the year to produce an ague fit, the other half resembled a demi-burnt brick'.[25] With some care and expense the land was thoroughly drained and within five years was employing a regular rotation of turnips/wheat/clover/wheat. Similarly, Joshua Crompton dedicated himself for ten years to drainage experimentation on his estates at Idle. Commencing with an unsuccessful combination of stones and tiles in 1798 he finally used only the latter. By 1812 his lands were well drained and produced the finest grass for his dairy herds.

An important obstacle to farming improvement had been the length and conditions of tenures. The local squirearchy was fully to blame for this. However, in a period of rising prices (as were the years after 1760), the rent originally charged on a long-term lease remained fixed and consequently was undervalued. It was customary for the landlord to await the termination of the lease before he raised the rent. A case in point occurred in May 1805. James Hardy reported to his employer that the Bradford surveyor had revalued the Horsforth land and farm of Robert Emersley at £175-7s-0d, the existing rent for the eighty nine acres being £117. Hardy believed this sum was far too small and estimated the value at £150. 'I have heard Robert Emersley will not give what it is valued at, nor do I think it will let for it'.[26] However, the tenant himself did not always prefer a long lease. For a time, depression would mean his annual rent would be too much for him. In the Napoleonic wars, the 'boom-slump' recurrences deterred both sides from negotiating long-term leases.

In spite of this, long-term leases were required by the better tenant farmers. Without a long lease, the Bradford farmer was not prepared to invest his hard-earned savings into improving land which he might lose the following year. He saw the improvement of his lands simply as the amelioration of the 'owners fee simple in perpetuity'. The stewards of the Spencer-Stanhope estates foresaw the advantages of long leases on good farming land. John Hardy in a letter of December 1777, refers to his letting, for eleven years, of thirty acres 'of new land for £21 a year nett rent and before Mayday I doubt not but having another part of it let for £16 a year'.[27] The letter refers to Stanhope's Thornton estate. Five years earlier, Stanhope had received approximately 140 acres in the enclosure of Thornton Moor and the 'new land' may refer to that acquisition. It would probably have taken that number of years to convert the waste ground into good farming soil.

Not all tenancies were held on such a long-term basis. In fact, many of the small tenants continued to work their lands from year to year and were quite content to do so. Their families had been tenant farmers on the same lands for hundreds of years and, as long as they remained good and reliable tenants, they would probably stay there. Although the number of long leases was increasing, normal practice continued to be the annual lease. It was the proprietor, therefore, who was responsible for any improvements that might be made. New farms, extensions to old farms, stables, fencing and the general improvement of the tenement was left to the landlord. In return for the money invested, he rightly increased the rental value. This compensation equivalent did not always apply and rent was assessed in excess of the money laid out.

There were some improvements in farming technology, though by and large, the Bradford farmer of 1830 continued to use those implements employed by his forefathers for generations before. Several of the new mechanical ideas had, however, received some kind of acceptance. The drill was slowly replacing broadcast sowing in the Eastern Pennines. Improvements were made in ploughshares, scarifiers and grubbers. The importance of turnips and straw was acknowledged by the introduction of a new cutter for those crops. The steam machine was first adapted to the threshing of harvest crops as early as 1796.[28]

The Enclosure Movement

Finally, the major expression of agricultural improvement for Bradford and its out-townships (after 1780), was the enclosure of uncultivated waste. It was estimated that 100,000 acres of new arable land were brought into cultivation in West Yorkshire between 1790 and 1840.[29] Once again leading landowners of the locality played an important part in investment and improvement of unenclosed land in this period. Unlike many areas, Bradford had long since seen the decline of the ancient open-field system, although vestiges of it still prevailed. To the north-west of Bradford, on the high ground at Cullingworth, the open fields had mostly disappeared, yet by 1809 the whole village had retained its medieval character. The large fields of former years had slowly given way to individual tenures, although some land continued to be worked in strips alongside the enclosed lands. In 1809 'a survey and admeasurement has also been made of the common field called the Royd and Royd Wood'.

Adjoining this was the old pinfold easily accessible at the junction of the main Halifax Road and the smaller Nook Road. The village itself was central to the fields around and had continued its medieval settlement pattern [30] (viz Fig.2).

Figure 2 Cullingworth prior to Enclosure 1809

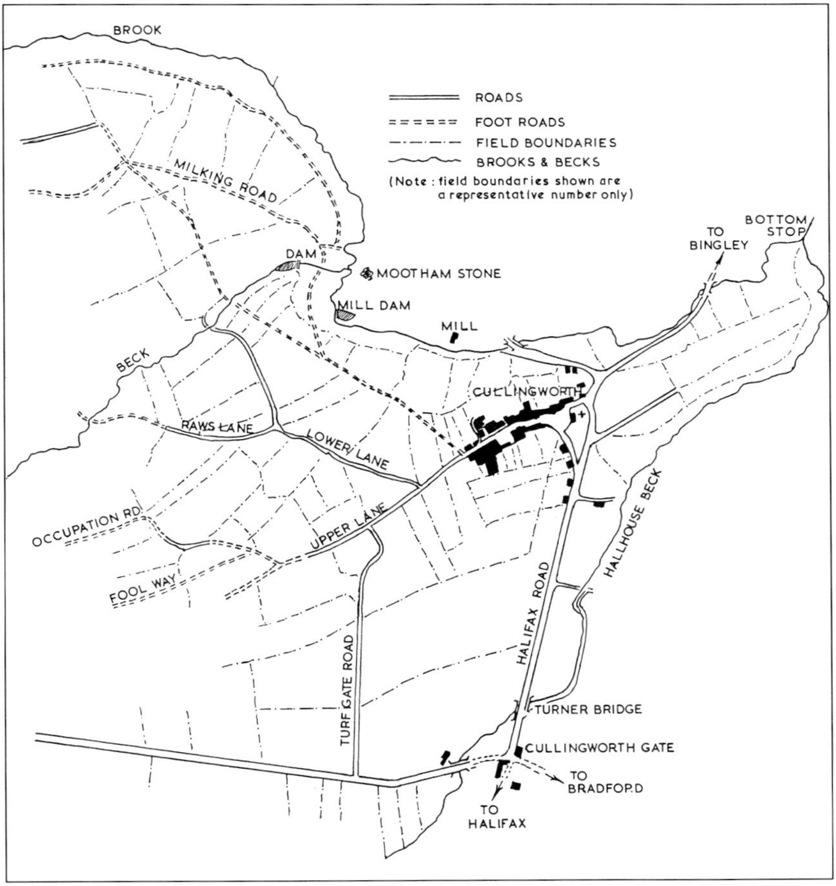

However, since the sixteenth century a redistribution of the land into small private enclosures had reduced the large open fields of Bradfordale to nothing but husks of their former selves.[31] Before 1760, enclosure by exchange or by private commission, had reduced the number of small landowners and had consolidated the estates of the larger proprietors. By that year, the increased numbers of people in the county meant even greater competition for the occupation of lands. The rise of both prices and profits accelerated the process of enclosure which had been going on for almost two centuries. William Marshall shrewdly observed that, 'It may be taken for granted that the first mover to an enclosure is private interest rather than public spirit'.[32]

Even Defoe, as early as 1725, observed that the rents of enclosed lands were many times more valuable than the rents of open lands. Consequently, proprietors were not dissuaded from enclosure by the cost, for increased rents would quickly meet their expenditure. The expansion and consolidation of estates caused increased rentals. In Bradford the rents probably did not rise too sharply because of the poor quality of the land, but generally, Brown estimated rentals were lifted by 25% after enclosure. As a result, the initiative for enclosure usually originated with the largest land-owner, in most cases the Lord of the Manor. With a further few hundred acres of land under pasture or corn, enclosure also increased the remuneration of the holder of the manorial tithes. Such a lead was given by the local squirearchy at Thornton in 1770. The manor lord, Walter Stanhope, had for some time been trying to persuade the freeholders of the town to enclose the large tract of waste on Thornton Moor. His arguments prevailed and it was proposed that two commissioners be appointed by the Lord of the Manor and a further two by the freeholders.[33]

Enthusiasm to enclose the lands and raise the rents was only one of many causes of enclosure.[34] Each enclosure had some degree of individuality. In the case of Thornton, it was the size of the commons rather than the quality of the soil. Elsewhere it was the number of open fields or the need to improve standards of cultivation. Sometimes, it was the wealth and enterprise of the small freeholder whose numbers were large and who needed more land. This probably happened at Idle in 1809. Although the manor lord, Joshua Crompton, was a progressive and esteemed farmer, it seems that pressure from below for land rather than Crompton's eye for improvement brought about the enclosure of the waste land there. There were 144 recipients of only 332 acres of land though Crompton himself received over ninety acres.

For the smaller freeholders the expense of enclosure initially proved inhibitive but the long-term consequences were to their advantage.[35] At Thornton in 1770, Stanhope estimated the costs at 15/- per acre. Eventually the legal costs for the Thornton enclosure reached £840. Taking the Board of Trade average of 9/6 per acre for fencing and drainage, the final expenditure was approximately £1,600. Assuming each freeholder mortgaged or borrowed the capital, an interest rate of five per cent would have meant an increase of a shilling or less per acre of his total costs.[36] The freeholders of Wyke in 1813 shrewdly overcame the problem by deciding that the commissioner should 'sell by public auction to the best bidder such parts of the several commons etc. as...should be most eligible for that purpose....'[37] However by the 1790s, costs per acre had increased, largely owing to the higher expenses of the enclosure commissioners. Their pay was sometimes given them in a lump sum, but more often they were paid by the day, 'one guinea each and no more for every day they shall respectively travel or attend for the purposes of this act, over and besides all their reasonable expenses at the time of such their journeys and attendances'.[38]

This was the rate paid to Thomas Chippendale and Miles Dawson, commissioners for the enclosure of Heaton in 1780. The fee might vary from ten shillings to two guineas per day and by 1820 it had risen to three and a half guineas per day. A well known enclosure commissioner in the Bradford region in the late eighteenth century was Nathan Jowett of Clockhouse, Mannigham (present Bradford G.S site) who supervised several local enclosures including Idle, Thwaites (Keighley) and Riddlesden. Men like Jowett held a great responsibility, for they had to be completely impartial in their decisions. They held in their hands the welfare and security of hundreds of lives. Often, when enclosure awards like those at Shipley and Yeadon took up to ten years to complete, they were also responsible for the course of farming on the lands with which they were dealing. This was done, not only during the passing of the act, but also after its completion. At Heaton in 1780, Chippendale and Dawson were quite explicit in their stipulations that,

> 'no sheep or lambs shall be kept in any of the new enclosures (except such are not fenced by Quicksets) during the space of 9 years from the execution of the award; unless the Person keeping such sheep or lambs do, at their own expense, fence their neighbours Quicksets adjoining the enclosures which such sheep or lambs shall be kept....'[39]

In exercising their rights the enclosure commissioners of the eighteenth century could exert an extensive influence on the course of husbandry of the area in which they were employed.

Throughout the period 1755 to 1825 there were sixteen parliamentary acts of enclosure relating to lands in and around Bradford[40] (viz Fig.3).

Table 1 Enclosure Acts in the Bradford District 1755–1825

Township	*Date*	*Acreage*	*Type of Land*
Calverley	1755–8	855	Waste
Thornton	1770–2	1,600	Waste
Oxenhope	1771–7	2,500	Waste
Thwaites	1780–2	5,000	Open Fields & Waste
Heaton	1780–1	675	Waste
Riddlesden	1788–90	2,254	Waste
Cleckheaton (i)	1795–7	200	Open Fields
Guiseley	1796–1801	–	Waste
Cleckheaton (ii)	1802–6	–	Waste
Yeadon	1803–13	321	Waste
Idle	1809–14	332	Waste
Cullingworth	1809–17	379	Waste
Pudsey	1811–20	180	Waste
Wyke	1813–21	200	Waste
Shipley	1815–25	277	Waste
Bolton	1819–24	23	Waste
Total =		14,796 acres (av. 1,057 acres)	

Source: *West Yorkshire County Record Office, Enclosure Statutes*

Figure 3 Local Enclosure Acts 1755–1825

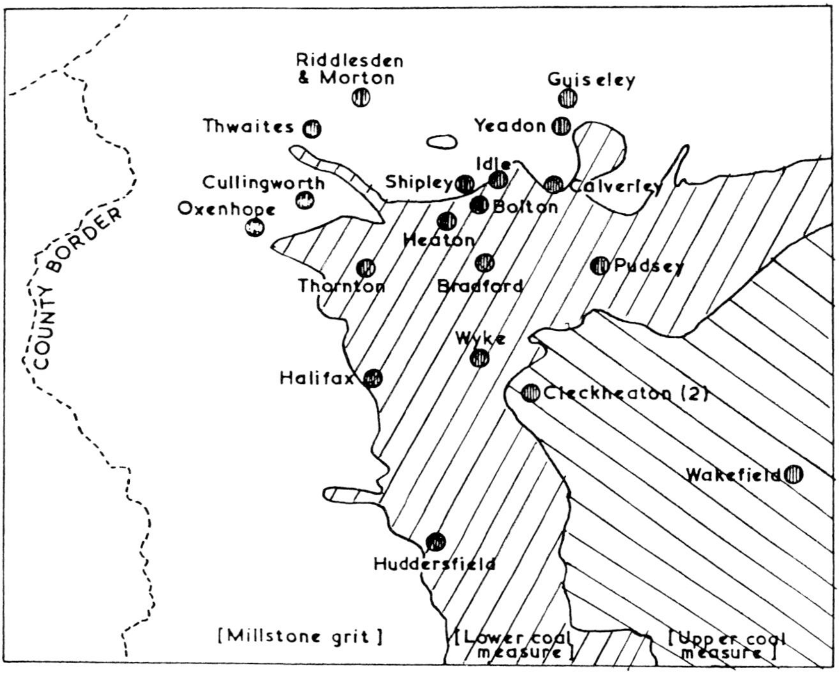

The majority of these enclosure awards brought under cultivation tracts of waste or common land varying from the 5,000 acres at Keighley to the relatively negligible twenty three acres at Bolton. There were several instances of one locality reacting to its neighbour's enclosure and within a short time enclosing its own waste lands. Riddlesden in a little less than six years, followed the example of Thwaites and enclosed almost half as much land again. Idle, Shipley and Bolton with their adjacent boundaries, enclosed their wastes in a sequence of years, as did Guiseley and Yeadon at the turn of the century.

Over the whole period all but four of the sixteen local enclosures surrounding Bradford, occurred to the north and north west of the town (viz Fig.3). Of these, ten formed a chain along the edges of the geological strata of Millstone Grit and the Lower Coal Measures. It is on these escarpements and the lower dip slopes that boulder clay, intermixed with alluvium, were to be found. This type of soil was difficult to work for arable purposes but made good pasture and meadow land for cattle and sheep. This is suggestive, although not conclusive, of a very strong response to the dietary needs of the developing urban market of Bradford, i.e. dairy products. From the acts above, this response really accelerated after 1790 when Bradford began its unprecedented growth. The demands of its growing number of inhabitants for milk and meat is expressed in the increased enclosure activity in these ideal pasture lands. Like Leeds and the Wolds, Bradford was developing its immediate agricultural frontiers upon which it could depend for its farming produce. In the late eighteenth century Bradford township's population increased from about 4,000 to 6,393 in 1801. This growth was not significant compared with that which followed, yet the whole farming economy became geared to it. By 1800 local farmers had realised the potential of the town's urban market and had begun to adjust to it, by the better organisation of holdings and the further application of improved techniques, but more importantly, by the direct appropriation of more land for farming.

As in other areas, the enclosure movement in Bradford had been a response to the needs of an increasing consumer population. This had shown a particular acceleration in the war years when prices were high, but also when the Bradford farmer had the extra stimulation of a new and growing urban market. The demand for milk and meat meant the enclosure of waste lands and commons, and their conversion into good pasture land. Enclosure was, perhaps, the greatest single agricultural improvement and certainly the one in which local farmers invested much of their capital, in their attempts to accommodate the needs of a growing and expanding regional economy.

The positive response from Bradford's farming community to the urban growth of Bradford as an expansive market had materialised through a number of important agricultural improvements. Such a reformation of the local farming system resulted in the specialisation of dairy farming. The West Riding has been described as 'probably the oldest centre of intensive milk production in the country'.[41] The demographic shifts to the region's urban centres after 1780 assured the regional farming community of a constant demand for its milk and dairy goods, 'In the vicinity of the manufacturing towns, great numbers of milk cows are kept, and there is a constant demand, not only in those places but over the whole West Riding for milk and the articles of cheese and butter....'[42]

Bradford was surrounded by farm holdings of ten to twenty acres many of which were located on the Millstone Grit. The majority of the farmland in this area was given over to permanent grass and devoted to pasture for dairy cattle. The hay grown on the upper slopes of the Pennines was dragged down by the ancient hay sled, drawn by enormous shire horses. It has been estimated that many of the Pennine hill farmers by 1870 possessed an average of six cows whose milk went to the city consumers.[43] The dairy products of cheese and butter were mainly taken by the local market, although some of the butter found its way to London with that from the Vale of Pickering. As early as 1786, Arthur Young had been informed that Yorkshire headed the list in the quantity of butter it sent each year to London, with a total of 100,000 firkins. Cheese production never matched that of other counties and, in fact, much cheese was imported via the Staffordshire Canal and Manchester into the West Riding.

The area also became an important poultry centre, many of the farmers combining their retail milk concerns with eggs and poultry. Towards the end of the 1830s vegetables were becoming a popular product and, although there was some market gardening around Bradford, its main area of cultivation came to be that area south of Leeds. Thus, farming in and around Bradford after 1800 was more diverse than was that of the neighbourhood around Halifax and Huddersfield. Dairy cattle and the retail milkround had become the mainstay of the Bradford farming system by 1830.[44]

Industry and the Bradford Squirearchy – Abraham Balme

The role played by English squirearchy in the agricultural improvement of their estates, has been considered in some recent studies to have been matched by their contribution to industrial development in the same period. The aristocracy and gentry had undoubtedly a reputation for non-agricultural involvement stretching back to the sixteenth century.[45] Sir Richard Shireburn, for example, made profit from his timber at Esholt in 1567, and the inferior wood he used in an iron bloomery at Esholt Wood, mining local deposits of both ironstone and coal.[46] This commitment to alternative economies was by no means a general feature of the landed classes. Interest and investment in non-agricultural economies was determined by available resources and by the social and political values of individual landowners, 'Their economic behaviour is often only explicable in terms of the concept of their social and political leadership'.[47]

Certainly Henry Fielding's archetype of Squire Western prevailed in many English counties. For some landowners, increased incomes from industrial and commercial schemes were simply fortuitous increments to their estate receipts. Yet for many more, industrial development was a deliberate and actively followed policy of promoting economic growth. Capital was invested, often at considerable risk, in a variety of transport, financial and industrial schemes. Several landowners risked and lost everything in their pursuit of commercial and industrial success. Edward Leedes' ambitious and single-handed plans for his Low Moor estates in the 1770s brought him £60,000 of debts and ultimate ruin. As his estate came under the hammer in 1785 Leedes cut his own throat on a journey to North Milford.[48]

Leedes could have off-loaded the risk onto others and acted the role of rentier but, for reasons difficult for the historian to determine, he and many others chose to fulfil the entrepreneurial role with its attendant risks. The limited rewards and natural handicaps of the local farming system motivated several Bradford landowners into the capacity of entrepreneur. Many of the small gentry in the Bradford region were able to maintain their position after 1650 by developing interests in industry and commerce. Their adjacency to expanding coal and woollen industries enabled them to increase their incomes and simultaneously sustain their roles as landowners. Within the confines of this book it is possible to examine the activities of but one local landowner who undertook a wide range of business schemes.

Abraham Balme was born in 1706 the eldest son of a yeoman farmer of Thornton. During his lifetime of ninety years Balme observed profound changes in the economic framework of his native region. For the greater part of his life Balme continued the tradition of his dissenting forefathers. He farmed and leased his estates, which had increased as a result of two marriages and by direct purchase of lands at Bowling and Oxenhope. Balme also functioned as a stapler of raw wool and in the 1750s was active in the marked-wool controversy. By 1760 he had acquired a considerable estate in Bowling. In fact Balme resided at Bolling Hall between 1753 and 1766 when he acted as land steward to Thomas Pigot, lord of the manor there.[49]

It was during his stewardship of the Bowling manor that Balme realised the potential of raw materials other than wool. That estate was rich in both Black and Better Bed coal as well as ironstone and consequently Balme was responsible for the mineral development of the estate. Apart from leasing mines to others, he organised Pigot's labourers into a colliery gang and worked the coals on Pigot's behalf. Furthermore Balme worked incessantly to extend his own estates at Bowling. In 1756 he purchased a large tract of land from Robert Stansfield and two years later acquired the mineral rights of Okes Hold farm and six other closes.[50] After his second marriage his personal estate included lands in Tong, Horton, Bowling, Birstall and Hopton. His successful participation in the local coal trade prompted his interest in the improvement of Bradford's transport system. He became a trustee of several turnpike trusts including the Leeds–Halifax turnpike. Like Edward Leedes, John Jarratt and several other local landowners, Balme was involved with the coal-limestone trade in the Craven area. His close involvement with the Leeds–Liverpool and Bradford canals will be discussed elsewhere in this book. Both companies drew upon his expertise as a land valuer and he was responsible for the purchase of lands requisite to both canals. Subsequently he was appointed to the management committee of both canals and for many years handled the financial affairs of the Bradford Canal. His daybook provides evidence of his paying contractors, labourers, shareholders and also suggests a very busy involvement with several of the local and national banks and the financial system in general, 'I think there is a bill for £14...if it comes to hand it will speak for itself. I was so busy paying wages it hath slipt my memory'.[51]

As work on the shorter Bradford canal was completed in 1774, it transformed the landscape of the old market town with its locks, wharves and coal staithes. Another feature to impose itself upon the Bradford landscape was the lime works at Northbrook which had opened at the same time as the canal. The provision of the main canal from Skipton to Shipley and the completion of the Bradford Canal, coincided with the founding of the Bradford Lime Kiln Company in 1774. Balme and seven other local landowners including Joshua Field and John Preston formed a joint-stock company to build eight lime kilns alongside the canal.[52] Balme's daybook makes frequent reference to visits to the lime kilns and to business on the company's behalf. When the kilns commenced in March 1774 Abraham Balme was the principal supplier of both coal and limestone to the company. The achievements of the Lime Kiln company will be examined elsewhere.

The anchor to all Balme's industrial schemes however, remained his landed estates. From these came much of the capital for his commercial and industrial undertakings. He was therefore, a keen advocate of enclosure and, holding a moiety of the manor of Oxenhope, was anxious to enclose the 2,500 acres of moorland adjoining his estates there. His good friend and partner in the Lime Kiln Company, John Smith was one of the three commissioners appointed to deal with the enclosure in 1771. From the enclosure act it appeared that Balme possessed an attractive estate of forty five acres with several buildings and a parcel of privately enclosed lands.[53] The number of claimants was so many that the act took several years to complete. In his daybook Balme mentions several visits 'settling with the commissioners about the Oxenhope enclosures', where he was forced to stay overnight with his friends, the Greenwood brothers of Oxenhope. After six years the act was completed and Balme received over seventy acres of land, very close to, but not adjoining, his original estate. He benefitted equally well in 1772 when his estate at Thornton, between Wilsden Common and Denholme Park was consolidated by approximately twenty four acres bounded by highways on both sides. By marriage (twice), inheritance, purchase and finally enclosure, Abraham Balme had brought together a large and profitable estate.

Balme also had responsibility for the lands of others. For many years he acted as trustee to Mary Hodgson, a distant relation and good friend. He put out income from her Manningham rental as favourable loans. As well as acting as money scrivener for Miss Hodgson, Balme cashed and held bills of exchange on his own behalf. These basic banking activities were intensively carried out during 1774 to 1780, the period which his bill-book covers. Most of his financial business was carried on with Leach, Pollard and Hardcastle, owners of the first Bradford bank and his main central bank was that of Smith, Payne & Smith in London. However, his dealings were fairly widespread as his letterbooks reveal.[54]

Balme's banking and money lending scheme seems to have ended abruptly in 1780. At least the bill book shows no further entries after that year when the local economy was hit hard by recession brought on by the colonial war. In the following year Leach, Pollard and Hardcastle, Bradford's only official bank, was declared bankrupt along with several leading local farmers and tradesmen. Thus, Abraham Balme had made a direct contribution to the nascent industrial economy of the region from his base as landowner and manor lord. In other ways he had confirmed his enthusiasm for the shifting economic emphasis. His appointment as commissioner to the Piece Hall, his support for friendly societies and his long service in parochial office to the Bradford Parish church, all served to reaffirm his faith in industrialisation. The positive attitude to industry, shown by men like Abraham Balme, created the ideal context for economic change. Balme was but one of many Bradford landowners whose social attitude and economic ambition were formulated to produce a distinct change of economic pace in the second half of the eighteenth century. Several months before his death Balme chaired a meeting of the Bradford vestry to discuss the recruitment of local men to fight against Napoleon. Born in the era of the French Sun King, Balme's life had thus spanned an ascendant age. He had made a significant contribution to the industrial framework of Bradford but his origins were in Bradfordale, in the farming system and lands at Thornton, Tong and Allerton. He was typical of the small West Riding landowner whose agricultural, commercial and industrial interests were mutually informing and integral to the nature of squirearchy in this region.

Figure 4 Balme Monument. This memorial tablet of white marble can be found on the north wall of the chancel of Bradford Parish Church. Sculpted by John Flaxman, it recognises the public service of Abraham Balme (1706–1796) a man prominent in the early industrial history of Bradford. *From an engraving*

The Food Supply of Industrial Bradford

In his *Phases of Bradford Life* (1871) James Burnley begins a chapter on the town's market life thus,

'Market life must always be a noticeable feature in the existence of a nation of shopkeepers. Nowhere are the evidences of our nationality more visible than in the market. It is the pivot upon which all our social machinery turns...'[55]

The centrality of urban marketing and the ways by which people bought food and other essentials of life have not been acknowledged by historians of the period, who have tended to concentrate their researches in other areas of urban history. Nevertheless there has been some academic debate on the roles of markets and fixed shop retailing in the early development of industrial towns like Bradford.[56] Recent research has revised early suggestions that urban markets provided for the working classes and specialist retailers catered for the better-off.[57] The transition to fixed-shop retailing by the lower classes as complementary to market trading has been located further back into the nineteenth century than early writers on the subject originally suggested.[58] In this section of the book our concern is with the changing pattern of food provision in Bradford before 1835. This will necessitate an evaluation of the role of markets in the town's network of food distribution and may enlighten our understanding of how, and when, fixed shops became important to Bradford's retailing system.

In 1251 Edmund de Laci and his heirs were allowed by the crown to hold 'one market every week on Thursday at the Manor of Bradford'. Since the town served as both a commercial and religious centre for an extensive parish, market day was held each Sunday close to the parish church. By 1760 the location of the market was in Westgate and was held each Thursday. In addition to the weekly market, local farmers and craftsmen had found an outlet for their produce at the ancient fairs, granted in a second market charter in 1294.[59] By 1780 Bradford township held three fairs each year. The first was held in early March; the second was a midsummer fair in Bridge Street when cattle, horses and furniture were the primary items for sale (viz Fig.5). A large fair was held in early December each year when pig sales dominated trading. Abraham Balme attended this fair in 1774 'was at the fair at Bradford, a Great many fat beasts and Swine, a very bad show day and a poor market'.[60] Adwalton, eight miles from Bradford, was also renowned for its fortnightly horse and cattle fairs.[61]

The steady growth of population after 1780, and the cumulative expansion of Bradford's trade and industry, strained the town's traditional marketing and retailing facilities. By 1780 the need for larger and more convenient markets was all too apparent to contemporaries. 'The town of Bradford, by the extension of its trade and manufactures has of late years become very populous and its market is resorted to by all the neighbouring towns and villages'.[62]

In 1760 Bradford's market place was located in the triangular opening at the top of Ivegate and Kirkgate. Two sides of this central market place were occupied by butchers' stalls with a slaughterhouse nearby. The butter market occupied the ground floor of the toll-booth in Ivegate. It was the traders in meat, however, who were the first to feel the pressures of increased demand and suffer from the lack of space, which their expanding trade required. The

Figure 5 Bridge Street Horse Fair and Market. Bradford's ancient horse-fair was traditionally held in Bridge Street on the day of St Andrew the Apostle. By 1800 it had become a market of general commerce although horses were still bought and sold there. This print is of a time shortly before the corporation closure of all street fairs in 1866. In the far distance is the home trade warehouse of Milligan and Forbes close to the railway station.

market rights of the absentee lord of the manor John Marsden 'were not much attended to, and as the population and importance of Bradford was at that time very trifling, their profits were not much regarded'.[63] Marsden's lack of concern provoked a number of the town's traders to purchase land in Bower Croft in 1782 for the erection of a new market house. When work began on the building, Marsden intervened and his manorial privilege was upheld. Eight years later he refused once again to approve the New Street market.[64]

In 1795 Marsden sold the Bradford manor to Benjamin Rawson for £2,100 and within a short time the new lord of the manor was pressed by Messrs. Hustler, Aked and Fletcher for improved marketing facilities. The butchers, with their not inconsiderable stock and their public slaughter of beasts, had occupied the greater part of the market area.

> 'The Old Market place in Westgate not being sufficient for the Butchers and others who brought flesh, meat and other provisions for sale nor for the convenience of the people who attended....'[65]

In February 1798 Rawson accepted the traders' petition to provide a larger market. He purchased the site of the projected private market of 1782 and added to it a plot of land which he had bought from Edmund Peckover in 1796. On this site, fronting Bank Street, Rawson went to great pains to erect a market hall of some splendour.[66] This building copied the Italian style and comprised of almost fifty butchers' stalls and the shambles. The stalls were arranged in a single row and were leased from Rawson at one shilling per session.

Formerly, Bradford butchers had paid from five to seven shillings to the lord of the manor several times per year for their wooden stalls on the Westgate highway. The town's leading butchers, Thomas Ackroyd, Richard Blackburn and Thomas Pullan seemed well pleased with the new arrangement. So too, were those whose 'carts were laden with potatoes, apples, greens and other provisions'. With the removal of the old market cross to the junction of Bank Street and Hustlergate, the New Street Market was opened on 1 October, 1801, and held every Thursday and Saturday thereafter.[67] The new market was dominated by a hall of Italianate design which contrasted sharply with the ancient inns and houses surrounding it. Its upper floors later served Bradford as a Sunday School and Assembly Room. The lower half was occupied by butchers and greengrocers and nearby was 'the Butter Cross and two bazaars filled with miscellaneous stalls'. Although this new market had increased retailing facilities it perpetuated the unpalatable practice of public slaughter of livestock. One of the earliest meetings of the Bradford Improvement Commission in August 1803 referred to 'the appalling state of Benjamin Rawson's slaughterhouse'[68] and by December the commissioners had noted:

> 'It being very dangerous to the Public that cattle should be exposed to sale in the public street. Resolved that Mr. Hustler and Mr. Hailstone be requested to apply to the Lord of the Manor to appoint a proper place for the sale of cattle'.[69]

Many of the original lessees of the new market were farmers from the neighbouring townships who brought their livestock into the town and killed them in the slaughterhouse adjoining the new meat market. However, this direct supply from producer to consumer, via the Bradford market, began to change as the urban demand increased and, as the farmer paid more attention to his role as producer.[70] Gradually, the urban butcher, as retailer, purchased his meat from local farms or from the live-cattle market in the town, for as Brown had noted of Bradford in 1791 'from the extent of the population there is a constant demand for all that can be fed'.[71] By 1825 Dr. John Simpson also noted in his diary,

> 'Some years ago the lower class people ate very little animal food.... Now when trade is good...the call for animal food is much greater, for all now can partake of that article of diet....'[72]

As improvements were made to the marketing facilities in Bradford, and as the town continued to grow, a greater specialisation developed in the butchery trade. By 1823 Rawson's market hall was woefully inadequate and several butchers continued to trade from wooden stalls in a narrow street leading to Westgate, called the Straits.[73]

Figure 6 Market Locations in Early Victorian Bradford

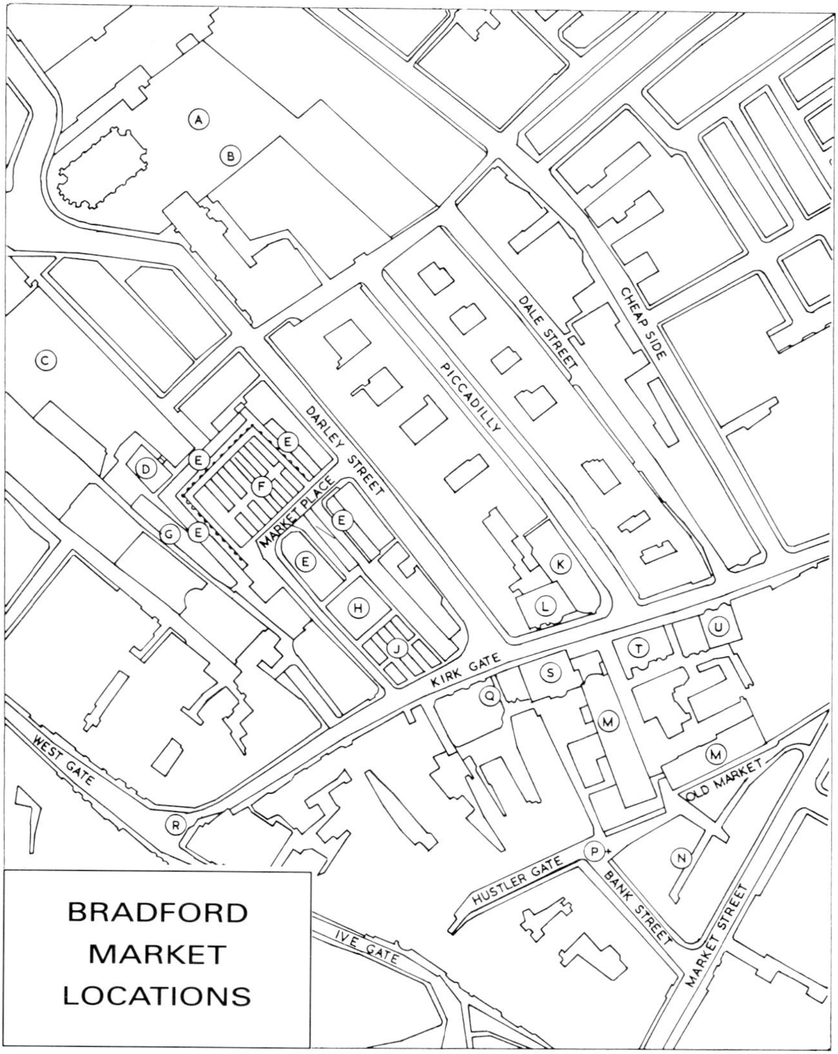

A Fair Ground
B Poultry Market
C Green Market
D Market Tavern
E The Shambles
F Fruit & Veg Market
G Slaughterhouse
H Manor House
J Fruit & Delf Market
K The Exchange
L Bradford Banking Co.
M Piece Halls
N New Piece Hall
P Remains of Old Market Cross
Q Post Office
R Old Market Place
S Talbot Inn
T Nags Head Inn
U White Lion Hotel

In October 1824 Rev. Godfrey Wright opened a new shambles of thirty butchers' shops and an abattoir in Hall Ings. This clashed with William Rawson's plans, for he had recently completed the erection of a large new market area to the rear of the Manor House on the west side of Darley Street.[74] The litigation which followed throws light on the specialisation which had developed in the town's meat trading by 1825, 'the growing divisions within the trade which proved necessary as business expanded. It became increasingly difficult for one man to combine two or more functions in the production and distribution of meat'.[75]

The original market place in lower Westgate had developed as the main live cattle market of the town, though it had doubtless moved from the main highway, probably to Fair Gap. In Westgate could be found the farmer who was no longer able to both produce and distribute his meat. The New Street Market and its environs had become the main slaughtering precinct of the town,

> 'If anyone should doubt this statement let him pass down Ivegate and along New Street, at any time...oxen and cattle of all descriptions are openly slaughtered and the footpaths covered with blood and garbage'.[76]

Reverend Wright sensibly moved his slaughterhouse from the town centre to a site alongside the Bradford Beck. Yet this was hardly the answer to a problem in which an increasing number of butchers simply outstripped the facilities available for the retail of meat.

The final division of the trade was the retail sector which, by 1825, functioned in the New Darley Street Market, and for a short time, at Wright's Hall Ings Market. Specialisation had brought about the middleman and the extension of the producer-consumer gap. With the coming of the railways and the continuing expansion of industrial Bradford, the price power of the retailer was gradually undermined by the wholesale butcher. Thus, the most important effect of the increased demand on the market facilities was an increase in the number of intermediaries between producer and consumer. In Ibbetson's *Directory of Bradford* for 1845 only two of the town's 126 butchers are also identified as farmers or cowkeepers. By the mid-nineteenth century the farmer-butcher was in decline in Bradford and those butchers who bought from local farmers were also beginning to retail their meat from their own premises as opposed to market stalls.

This trend can be identified by an examination of local trade directories and the town's ratebooks for the corresponding years. There are drawbacks in this method but the general trend may be established.

The increased market facilities between 1798 and 1825 were taken up largely by the butchering fraternity, the majority of whom resided within the town and therefore were unlikely to be both producer and retailer. Moreover, the sale of meat was increasingly achieved from fixed retailing locations as Bradford's butchers sought to keep pace with the demands of the growing population. 'Butchers...sold their meat at their own homes where they had shops for the purpose'. Therefore, the inability of the manorial authority to

Table II Outlets for the Retail of Meat in Bradford 1805–1845

	Butchers' Stalls/ Shambles	*Butchers' Shops*	*Butchers with both Stalls and Shops*
1805	19	3*	nd
1822	35	10	nd
1827	39	33	9
1834	43	42	14
1845	55	71	40

*incomplete

Source: *B.C.L. Various Directories*

provide sufficient market accommodation for the butchers after 1825 forced many to establish their own private and fixed shopping premises. Despite the contemporary attitude that market trading was more fair and less profiteering,

> 'The reluctance of butchers to stay on the markets and the relative failure of what appeared to be the most convenient sites, must put a large question-mark against the assumption that markets were intrinsically more attractive than shops to the working classes'.[77]

The transition from market shopping to fixed location retailing was well under way in the butchering business in Bradford by 1830. How far this switch was applicable to the other sectors of the town's retail economy is less clear.

Certainly by 1830 a number of smaller markets continued to offer outlets for general sales and specialised trading in fruit, vegetables and earthenware (viz Fig.6). A fruit and pottery market was located in Kirkgate in front of the ancient manor house. Fruit and vegetables were sold on the higher side of Market Place which also housed the overspill from the central meat market. Canvas covered butchers' stalls surrounded the Hall. The Green Market was located on the site of the present Rawson Place Market and on the higher ground, behind Christ Church, was the fair ground and open poultry market (viz Fig.7).[78] The sale of fruit and vegetables from the market stalls continued throughout the period. In 1871 James Burnley wrote of the Bradford Green Market,

> 'carts and waggons with the growth and freshness of the country upon them are closely ranged. These are owned by market gardeners, many of them having come from Wakefield and other outlying districts'.[79]

The farmers and market gardeners were supplemented by costermongers whose donkey carts carried the goods to streets and homes each day. The numbers of these casual traders are impossible to assess for they have no regular stalls. Women, with no menfolk to provide for them, also resorted to the casual selling trade, either as keepers of small shops or by carrying their goods by hand. Central market retailing therefore continued to dominate the fruit and vegetable trade in Bradford before 1835 although there was a move in the direction of fixed shop retailing by 1845. Those provisions, like fruit and vegetables, purchased irregularly did not require localised and specific retail outlets. In Bradford,

Figure 7 Green Market and Fairground. This open market for fruit and vegetables grew up around the disused Manor Hall and alongside Christ Church (1815) which was demolished in 1879 to make way for a road linking Darley Street, Rawson Square and North Parade. In the centre rehearsals are in progress, at the Old Theatre Royal in nearby Duke Street. Here, distinguished thespians like Macready, Kean and Helen Fawcett trod the boards.

> 'the town and neighbourhood and partly the several ironworks where the work people received their wages on Saturday, a market had been held on Saturday whereat these people bought their meat and vegetables for the Sunday and following week....'[80]

Thus the central market site continued to be favoured by most fruit and vegetable dealers in Bradford before 1850.

The shift towards fixed-shop retailing may have been insignificant in the fruit and vegetable trade but elsewhere in Bradford's retailing system it was manifest by 1835. Commercial directories do not always provide reliable data in this respect and tend to suggest that few small general shops existed in this period. The Bradford ratebooks suggest otherwise as the 'corner-shop' or 'house-shop' was as important a feature of working class life in 1820 as it was in 1920.[81]

William Scruton remarked in 1890 'It is only within the past twenty years or so that Bradford has redeemed its character as a town of good shops. Formerly a shop was little else than a portion of the tenement in which resided its proprietor....'[82]

Table III Retail Outlets in Bradford

	1792	*1809*	*1822*	*1834*	*1845*
Shopkeepers	–	–	–	77	270
Grocers	19	21	27	32	48
Tea Dealers	2	1	7	21	20
Confectioners	–	–	2	7	11
Fruiterers	2	–	–	–	28
Provision Dealers	–	–	7	5	23
Flour Dealers	3	2	6	25	–

Source: 1792 *Universal British Directory*; 1809–11 Holden's *Triennial Directory*; E. Baines: *History, Directory & Gazeteer of West Riding of Yorkshire*; 1834 Pigot's *National Commercial Directory*; 1845 T. Ibbetson's *Directory of Bradford*

As early as 1783 it was reported in the Leeds newspapers that the new shopping precinct in New Street 'would affect the market trade unless the shops sold corn for only one and a half hours a day'.[83] Increasingly these new shops sold a diversity of provisions and by 1845 the day of the general dealer had arrived in Bradford. Many of them took advantage of the town's newspapers to advertise their services.

> 'Thomas Parkinson, Grocer & Tea Dealer, Kirkgate. Has just received an abundant supply of TEA, COFFEE, FRUITS and GROCERIES of every description. As these goods were purchased at the best markets, he feels confident that both price and quality will give general satisfaction. Thomas Parkinson takes this opportunity to acknowledge with gratitude, the liberal patronage bestowed upon him and to assure his friends that no effort shall be wanting on his part to deserve its continuance'.[84]

Bradford's earliest shopping zone had been located in Westgate where there was Mr. Wyvill's ironmongers and Thomas Cure's grocery store.[85] Opposite the old Court House was Judy Barrrett's spice shop and Lund's book shop. In 1836 Manoah Rhodes commenced business in Westgate as watchmaker and jeweller. Ivegate housed Crossley's, the Quaker tea dealer, John Wilton the clothes broker and next door to the Unicorn Inn was Mrs. Cousen's drapery which later became George Thorpe's emporium and one of the largest department stores in Victorian Bradford. The completion of the Bradford Canal in 1774 transformed the residential character of Kirkgate and a whole colony of shops was established as a result. Most of them were alongside the Broadstones. The relocation of the market in the New Street (later Market Street) deterred shopkeepers from taking premises in that quarter. Gradually several respectable establishments were opened, including Blackburn's the music seller, Messrs. Nelson, hop merchants, Allison the bootmaker and John Dale the printer and stationer. Nearby and next to the Hope and Anchor Inn was Henry Brown's store. Begun in 1817 by his mother, the business mirrored the retailing revolution in Bradford through the nineteenth century. In 1845 Brown took into partnership Mr. Muff, a milliner in Westgate, and created a household name in Bradford's shopping history.

These are but a sample of the increasing number of fixed shop retailing outlets in Bradford before 1840. Retailers of general provisions, meat, and to a lesser extent, fruit and vegetables were beginning to move away from central markets and towards retailing from their personal premises. Population growth and Bradford's urban sprawl encouraged localised retail outlets in preference to the central markets. Nevertheless Bradford's Saturday markets continued to play an important role in the retailing system of the town, particularly for the working classes, whose Saturday night visits to the markets, with their quacks, cheap jacks and hot pies, became an essential part of their urban way of life.

1. J.V. Stephen, *Geology of the Country between Bradford and Skipton* (1953) and S.H. Beaver, *Land Utilisation Survey* (1942)
2. R. Brown *et al. A General View of Agriculture of the West Riding of Yorkshire* (London 1794) pp.9–72
3. B.C.L. Bradford Manor Court Rolls, 12 Henry IV 3rd August and W. Cudworth, Courts Baron and Leet, *Bradford Antiquary* Vol. II (1895) pp.185–9
4. W. Harwood-Long, *A Survey of the Agriculture of Yorkshire* (London 1969) p.60
5. R. Brown, op. cit. p.115
6. Ibid.
7. W. Harwood-Long, Regional Farming in Seventeenth-Century Yorkshire, *Agricultural History Review*, Vol. 8 No.2 pp.103–114
8. R. Brown, op. cit. p.13
9. D. Defoe, *A Tour Through the Whole Island of Great Britain* (1971 edition) p.493
10. R. Brown, op. cit. p.39
11. R. Brown, op. cit. p.19
12. Bradford Central Library (hereafter B.C.L.) Spencer-Stanhope Mss 911
13. R. Brown, op. cit. Appendix
14. Ibid.
15. W. Marshall, *The Rural Economy of Yorkshire* (1778) Vol.1 p.48
16. B.C.L. Spencer-Stanhope Ms 2446
17. R. Brown, op. cit. Appendix
18. W. Scruton, *Pen and Pencil Pictures of Old Bradford* (1891) p.225
19. J.H. Charnock, Farming in the West Riding of Yorkshire, *Journal of the Royal Agricultural Society*, Vol. IX 1849 p.293 and G. Firth, The Roles of a West Riding Land Steward 1773–1803 *Yorkshire Archaeological Journal* Vol.51 1979
20. York Minster Library (hereafter Y.M.L) Hickleton Papers A2/24 29 December 1782
21. Ibid A2/6/3 12 November 1781
22. J.H. Charnock, op. cit. p.293
23. E.J. Hobsbawm, *Industry and Empire* (1969) p.60
24. J. Hannan, The Economy of Wastage Manure, *Transactions of the Yorkshire Agricultural Society* Vol.6 (1843) pp.86–88

25. J.H. Charnock, op. cit. p.307
26. B.C.L. Spencer-Stanhope Mss 2168 10 May 1805
27. Ibid Ms 1308
28. J. Charnock op. cit. p.305
29. Ibid.
30. West Yorkshire County Record Office (hereafter W.Y.C.R.O.), Cullingworth Enclosure Award 1809–17
31. C. Richardson, *The Geography of Bradford* (Bradford 1976) pp.35–39
32. W. Marshall, op. cit. p.53 and H.G. Hunt, Landownership & Enclosure 1750–1830, *Economic History Review*, Vol. XI (1958–9) p.497
33. W.Y.C.R.O. Thornton Enclosure Award 1770 and Spencer-Stanhope Ms 1309 c1768
34. E.K.K. Garner, *Common Land and Enclosure* (1912) and G.E. Mingay, *Enclosure and the Small Farmer in the Age of the Industrial Revolution* (1968)
35. J.D. Chambers and G.E. Mingay, *The Agricultural Revolution 1750–1880* (1966) pp.77–105; W.E. Tate, The Cost of Parliamentary Enclosure in England, *Economic History Review* Vol. V (1952) pp.258–265; M. Turner, Cost, Finance and Parliamentary Enclosure, *Economic History Review* Vol. XXXIV No.2 (1981) pp.236–248
36. W.E. Tate, op. cit. p.260 and *The English Village Community and the Enclosure Movement* (1967)
37. W.Y.C.R.O. Wyke Enclosure Award 1813–21
38. B.C.L. Miscellaneous Ms.B346 H.S. Rodgers, West Riding Commissioners of Enclosure 1729–1850, *Yorkshire Archaeological Journal* Vol.40 (1962) pp.401–419
39. W.Y.C.R.O. Heaton Enclosure Award 1780
40. Details of all these awards and the respective maps can be found in the West Yorkshire County Record Office
41. W. Patterson, The New Pennine Dairy Farming, *Agriculture*, Vol.66 (1959–60) pp.340–342
42. R. Brown, op. cit. p.39
43. J.B. Butler, *Small Farms of Industrial Yorkshire* (Leeds Unversity) Oct. 1958)
44. W. Harwood-Long, Report of the Land Utilisation Survey p.174
45. G.E. Mingay, *English Landed Society in the Eighteenth Century* (1963), J.T. Ward and R.G. Wilson, *Land and Industry – the Landed Estate and the Industrial Revolution* (1971)
46. B.G. Auty, Sir Richard Shireburn's Esholt Ironworks, *Bradford Antiquary* 1960, pp.243–57
47. J.T. Ward and R.G. Wilson, op. cit. p.11
48. J. Parker, *Illustrated History: From Hipperholme to Tong* (1904) p.15
49. W. Cudworth, *History of Bolton and Bowling* (1891) pp.285–293
50. B.C.L. Miscellaneous Mss. Unclassified 25 March 1758
51. B.C.L. Bradford Canal Mss. Minute Book 1774
52. B.C.L. Bradford Limekiln Company Mss. & G. Firth, Bradford Limekiln Company 1774–1800 *Bradford Antiquary* XLVII 1982, pp.129–134
53. W.Y.C.R.O. Oxenhope Enclosure Award 1771
54. B.C.L. Balme Mss. Daybook & Accounts 1771–76
55. J. Burnley, *Phases of Bradford Life* (Bradford 1871) p.64
56. J.B. Jeffreys, *Retail Trading in Britain 1850–1950* (Cambridge 1954), and D. Davis,

History of Shopping (1966)

57. D. Alexander, *Retailing in England During the Industrial Revolution* (1970)
58. J. Blackman, The Food Supply of an Industrial Town, *Business History*, Vol. V (1963) p.96
59. W. Scruton, *Pen and Pencil Pictures of Old Bradford*, p.5
60. B.C.L. Ms 6/1 Daybook of Abraham Balme, 9 December 1774
61. R. Brown, *Survey of Agriculture of West Riding* (1794) p.31
62. Y.M.L. Hailstone Ms 1/1/62
63. Ibid.
64. B.C.L. Misc. Ms 11/2
65. Ibid.
66. W. Hustwick, The Old Market House, *Journal of Bradford Textile Society* (1953–54) pp.81–3
67. Hailstone Ms 1/1/62
68. B.C.L. Bradford. Improvement Commission Minutes 17 August 1803
69. Ibid, 30 December 1803
70. J. Blackman, op. cit. pp.88–9
71. R. Brown, op. cit. p.32
72. B.C.L. *Diary of John Simpson*, op. cit. 17 March 1825
73. W. Scruton, op. cit. p.229
74. *Bradford Courier*, 2 July 1825
75. J. Blackman, op. cit. pp.229
76. Y.M.L. Hailstone Ms G3 1825
77. R. Scola, Food Markets and Shops in Manchester 1770–1870, *Journal of Historical Geography*, Vol. 1 No.2 (1975) p.165
78. Hailstone Ms 1/1/62
79. J. Burnley, op. cit. p.66
80. B.C.L. Ms 11/2
81. M.T. Wild & G. Shaw, Locational Behaviour of Urban Retailing in the Nineteenth Century – the Example of Kingston upon Hull. *Transactions of the Institute of British Geographers* 61 (1974) pp.101–117
82. W. Scruton, op. cit. p.223
83. *Leeds Intelligencer* 11 November 1783
84. *Bradford Observer* 17 April 1834
85. W. Scruton, op. cit. pp.224–32

3

Of Men and Money – Factors for Industrial Growth

Introduction

We turn now to look at some of the elements which helped to convert Bradford from a small and remote Pennine market town into a bustling populous industrial city. There was no formal recipe of these ingredients, no magic formula for industrial success. Certain factors within Britain's particular social, political and financial structure all came together to make profound social and economic changes for which we use the shorthand term of 'Industrial Revolution'. These factors varied considerably from one region of the country to another and in this chapter we consider *three* of the major causes of Bradford's move towards industrialisation. Already we have seen how a profitable and go-ahead system of farming (requiring fewer labourers) produced the necessary food and growing profits for landowners to invest elsewhere. In this chapter we shall discover how an expanding *population* meant a larger domestic market for goods and provoked a search for new methods of producing them. Secondly, economic growth requires *capital* investment and this chapter will examine how Bradfordians developed an unprecedented system of banking to channel money at low interest rates into their commercial and industrial schemes. Finally, in the chapter following there was a revolution in local *transport* facilities which improved the movement of goods from one region to another.

Population Change

Between 1780 and 1850 there occurred a dramatic change in the number of people living in the Bradford township. Population of the township increased from 4,506 to 52,493 – a rise of 1,064 per cent. In the borough the growth of population was equally rapid, soaring from 8,525 in 1780 to 103,778 in 1851 (1,170 per cent increase). The nature of this massive transformation of the town's demographic structure stems from the general rise in population throughout England and Wales in these years. National figures rose from about nine millions in 1801 to twenty one millions in 1851 which represents an increase of 130 per cent. Yet Bradford's growth was almost ten times that.

A second demographic trend, the emergence of urban living on an unprecedented scale, was particularly appropriate to Bradford in the first half of the nineteenth century. The urban population of England and Wales in 1801 has been estimated as 33.8 per cent of the whole. By 1851 it had become 54.0 per cent and by 1901 had risen to 78.0 per cent.[1] The nineteenth century has been viewed by many as the age of great cities and Bradford's contribution was not inconsiderable.

Unlike Leeds, Bradford had no pre-industrial claims to important urban status. In the eighteenth century it was a small market township, the centre of a vast and thinly settled parish. Economic devastation, resulting from the Civil War, and the ravages of persistent epidemics of plague in the seventeenth century, had taken their toll on the regional population. John James, using the parish registers, noted Bradford's inability to recover.

Table IV Baptisms, Marriages and Burials 1639, 1659 and 1739[2]

	Baptisms	*Marriages*	*Burials*
1639	209	61	183
1659	113	38	117
1739	182	94	134

In 1743, Archbishop Herring ordered a visitation return for the whole of his bishopric. This included the diocesan church of Bradford and the parochial chapels of Haworth, Thornton and Wibsey. The Reverend B. Kennett estimated 4,500 communicants in the parish of Bradford, half of which are in the district of the church. These figures are suspiciously 'round' and the so-called church district is impossible to define. Children under the age of fifteen were excluded from the return. However, of the 335 Dissenting families in the Parish, there was a heavy concentration of them in the 'district' (about 600 in all). The vagueness of these figures does not allow us to reach any accurate conclusions as to the population of Bradford in 1743.[3]

A more precise analysis of the history of population in pre-industrial England has been achieved through nominative analysis of parish registers and the development of the 'family reconstitution' method.[4] The application of this method of historical demography is, however, more problematic with larger communities like Bradford. Consequently, using the parish registers, a more aggregative analysis will be undertaken here. Even so, parish registers have their pitfalls as Eden observed when he visited Bradford in 1795,

> 'It is impossible at Bradford and Halifax to form any conclusions respecting the population from the number of births and burials in the parish registers. There are many dissenters, some of whom bury and christen in their own chapels and churches. The names of baptisms and burials from outlying districts are inserted at random – so that it is impossible to disentangle Bradford itself from the outlying districts'.[5]

Baptismal and burial registers are, therefore, usually an underestimate of the number of births and deaths and are employed in this chapter to indicate no more than broad trends.

Population Change in Bradford 1750–1800

Before the first official census in 1801, a local census of 1780 provides a useful indication of Bradford's population on the eve of intensive industrialisation. A detailed but unofficial census was taken for a law suit involving the Soke Mill. John Hardy, John Hustler and Samuel Lister quarreled with Marsden, the manor lord. As part of their case, they hired Christopher Dibb of Shipley to take a census on 2nd December 1780.[6] Though their case was dismissed, their survey, taking in the area within two miles of the soke mills, has survived:

Table V Unofficial Census of 2nd December 1780

Bradford	4,506 persons
Horton	1,964 persons
Bowling	1,119 persons
Manningham	936 persons
Total	8,525 persons

These four townships were to constitute the future borough of Bradford and provide a useful pre-census baseline. Twenty years later the first national census attributed to Bradford township 6,393 persons (Eden had estimated 5,000 persons in Bradford in April 1795). It would seem from these surveys that Bradford's population had increased at an undramatic but consistent rate throughout the later eighteenth century.

This suggestion can be confirmed by the annual totals of the parish baptisms and burial registers for the years 1760 to 1800. The vital index (dividing burials into baptisms) is a long-term measure of growth and is probably on the low side owing to baptismal evasion[7] (viz Table VI).

Table VI Vital Index* of Bradford 1760–1799 Quinquennial Averages

	Vital Index		*Vital Index*
1760–64	1.5	1780–84	1.4
1765–69	1.2	1785–89	1.4
1770–74	1.3	1790–94	1.7
1775–79	1.3	1795–99	1.9

*Baptisms divided by burials

Source: *Bradford Cathedral Library, Parish Church Mss Parish Registers 1760–1800*

With a few exceptions, the vital index remains fairly consistent up to 1783. From that year it took an upward course which found its ultimate maturation in the middle decades of the following century. Why then, did this index rise? It is clear from the evidence of the registers (Table VII) that baptisms began to outstrip the number of burials in these years. One must also remember that both burials and baptisms increased in direct terms. It is to the increased birth rate, rather than the declining death rate, that we must attribute this expansion in the number of parishioners. The burial registers reveal no acute decrease. Burials over the long term remained moderately low. The dramatic death tolls caused by the epidemics of the seventeenth century no longer applied. A medical practitioner like William Maude whose father had been a surgeon in Westgate, was one of the first to practise vaccination in the town in 1794, and thus contributed to the decline of large scale epidemics.[8] However, there were still occasions when epidemics of influenza and cholera did claim an abnormally high number of victims. This occurred in 1773, when the number of burials outnumbered baptisms by almost one hundred. This was the only occasion, throughout the period under review, when such an imbalance occurred.

Table VII Quinquennial Averages of Baptisms, Marriages and Burials from Bradford Parish Register 1700–1800

	Baptisms	*Marriages*	*Burials*
1760–1764	270	138	208
1765–1769	290	134	243
1770–1774	322	169	259
1775–1779	398	181	285
1780–1784	417	193	296
1785–1789	466	209	327
1790–1794	559	225	314
1795–1799	621	232	322

Source: *as Table VI*

Apart from such exceptional occurrences the mortality rate in Bradford before 1800 seemed consistent. Over the whole period there was no dramatic change in the mortality of the area. Recorded infant deaths remained constantly low for the size of the parish, but there is good reason to assume here that evasion or inefficient recording has occurred in the registers.[9] The natural increase of baptisms over burials was aided to some extent by the steady mortality rate in the Bradford parish before 1800. A much more dramatic contribution however, was made by the steady increase of parochial baptisms. The baptismal registers show a healthy and substantial increase in the number of children christened in the Bradford parish each year. This is a continuous process through all four decades after 1760. Moreover, because of the evasion of baptisms, the figures are probably underestimated.

In comparison, the number of marriages shows only a small increase over the whole period. The marriage figures are perhaps the most reliable of the three accounts, and they show a constant rate of nuptuality.[10] Unfortunately, the Bradford marriage registers do not indicate the age of those concerned. Consequently, they obscure important information regarding earlier marriages which automatically extended womens' fertility periods and which tended to increase the size of families. From the figures one can only assume that earlier marriages became the general practice in this area. These in turn brought larger families. Early marriages and an apparent decline in the number of deaths of chrisom children and infants, meant a greater potential in the women for child bearing before the menopause. It must be remembered, however, that the population was rising throughout the period, and the number of infant deaths to total population is low in proportion. Thus it would seem that the baptism and marriage rates, and increased fertility were the main factors behind the steady population growth of Bradford parish in the latter half of the eighteenth century.

The numbers of those migrating into the region before 1800 are difficult to assess. The steady surplus suggested from the parish registers might account for the moderate 6393 persons of the 1801 census that is, by natural increase alone. The work of Cole and Deane might be cited at this point.[11] They have postulated that migration played only a minor role in the demographic change of the West Riding before 1800, and that growth was due 'to the greater fecundity of their population' seems appropriate to Bradford's steady population increase in that period. Within the general economic climate of the late eighteenth century the farmer-weaver of the worsted trade benefitted from the cheapness of his own cultivation and from the regular wages of his textile work. The domestic system under which he laboured, encouraged the introduction of children as wage earners. Moreover the lax approach to apprenticeship in the woollen and worsted trades enabled a young man to receive maximum wages at an early age. All these factors prompted earlier marriages and consequently longer fertility periods. Population growth through natural increase could not meet the needs of domestic production but the time would come when centralised and mechanised production would make greater demands on the supply of labour and induce urban immigration of some magnitude.

This is not to completely discount migration as an influence on population change in Bradford before 1800. The spatial association of population change and intensive industrialisation has more meaning in the nineteenth century but at Bowling and Bierley after 1788 there was doubtless in-migration on some scale as the ironworks in both townships expanded and recruited accordingly. There is evidence of Cornish tin workers being brought to Low Moor; of Midlands foundryworkers coming to Bowling but these were regional variations to a pattern of unprecedented industrial activity, planned and achieved largely by means of the *native* labour force.[12] The industrial expansion in the Bradford region between 1770 and 1790 was not sufficient for its entrepreneurs to demand a greater labour force than that provided by the locality. Once industrialisation was under way, it reinforced the growth of population within the town by its demand for labour and also on consumers. A feature that was quite apparent to contemporaries, 'Formerly the market was of trifling importance in consequence of the thin population but since the year 1790 and later, the population both of town and surrounding country has increased in an extra-ordinary manner'.[13]

In Bradford, industrial expansion reinforced an upward moving population. This had probably been caused by the increased number of births to each marriage and to a lesser extent, by a consistently moderate burial rate. The steady increase in the rate of baptisms was the major long term factor in Bradford's population growth before 1810.

Population Change in Bradford 1800–1830

However, in the very early years of the new century, population movement in Bradford was more directly influenced by the important factor of immigration. As the town prospered and its industry expanded, immigrants came in from the surrounding area and beyond. Immigration contributed to demographic growth in two ways. The immigrants themselves automatically increased the numbers, but of greater significance was their potential as child-producers in subsequent years. They reinforced the natural increase which Bradford had already experienced before 1800. At any time, the people most likely to travel in search of work are independent individuals and young persons not rooted to an area for a lifetime. It was this class of people, the reproductive age-group, which contributed to this acceleration of the town's population after 1810.[14] The census figures between 1801 and 1851 (viz Table VIII) demonstrate the immense contribution to Bradford's demographic growth made by the immigration of thousands in search of work in the new industrial century.

Table VIII Census Returns for the Parish, Borough and Township of Bradford 1801–1851

	Bradford Parish	*Bradford Borough*	*Bradford Township*
1801	29,848	13,264	6,393
1811	36,358	16,012	7,767
1821	52,954	26,309	13,064
1831	76,996	43,537	23,223
1841	105,257	66,718	34,560
1851	149,563	103,778	52,493

Source: *BCL Census Enumeration Extract; 1801–1851*

Natural increase of births over deaths inadequately explains the mean annual increase of over five per cent during these years. Between 1821–31 the annual rate of increase actually reached six per cent. A gazeteer of 1851 remarked; 'The rate of increase from excess of births over deaths is less than

2% p.a. so that the percentage of immigration into the borough must have been at least 3%.'[15]

Between one and two per cent of the annual growth rate can be attributed to natural increase, the rest is down to migration. Bradford like any other nineteenth-century city had its share of 'comers and goers' but a majority came into the town to stay. Men like Thomas Wood of Bingley were frequently on the move in search of work within and without the town,

> 'I left home in search of work in the beginning of March and returned in the beginning of April. Having walked through Lancashire in search of work I saw hundreds out of work.... I remember getting home quite exhausted.... The skin was off my thighs with my wet clothes clinging to me and walking so far.... I had been at home about a week when meeting my old master of Bradford he asked me to go and do a piece of work. This was in April 1843'.[16]

It is not possible to obtain a clear picture of the patterns of Bradford's in-migration until the census returns of 1841 which reveal that twelve per cent of the Bradford borough were born outside Yorkshire and that 1 in 8 of the people living in the township of Bradford were born beyond its boundaries.[17]

These trends are substantiated by the parish registers for baptisms and burials. In the latter, there is an irregular trough between the years 1801 and 1820, within which the baptism rate took an unprecedented leap of almost 50%, explicable only in terms of in-migration. It was during these years that the migration into the town escalated, particularly after 1810, when it caused such rapid increases in the town's vital index (viz Table IX). This kind of advance continued throughout the third decade.

Table IX Vital Index* of Bradford 1800–1829 Quinquennial Averages

	Vital Index
1800–1804	2.5
1805–1809	3.1
1810–1814	3.5
1815–1819	3.7
1820–1824	3.4
1825–1829	3.4

* Baptisms divided by burials

Source: *Calculated from Bradford Parish Registers 1800–1830*

This great influx of migrants coincided with the centralisation of mechanised spinning in the manufacture of worsteds. As the town expanded, first as a centre of manufacture then as a worsted market, greater was the intake of migrants. Since the eighteenth century there had been a steady flow of merchants, manufacturers and artisans from Norfolk as that area continued to abdicate as the principal centre of worsted cloth production. By 1851 there was also the nucleus (244 in all) of a German colony in Bradford. Families like Behrens, Moser, Delius and Rothenstein were to make an important contribution to the social and cultural development of Victorian Bradford over and above their commercial and industrial commitments.

The immigrant group which has received the closest scrutiny is the Irish community of nineteenth century Bradford. They were the largest ethnic group and, along with the Germans, made Bradford 'at once one of the most provincial and yet one of the most cosmopolitan of English provincial cities'. By 1851 the Irish settlers constituted over eight per cent of the borough population (8,677 in all). There had been a recognised Irish colony in Bradford as early as 1825 as a result of Irish land eviction. The pace of Irish immigration quickened after 1829 with the heaviest migration occurring between 1835 and 1846. Richardson, in his study of the Irish in Bradford, estimated that 'A proportion of the Irish migrants came from cloth-making towns in Ireland, notably in Queen's County though the majority came from largely peasant environments – western Ireland'.[18]

In addition to the Irish, a very large number of those families who migrated to Bradford in these years came with an expertise in the manual methods of cloth production. They were drawn to the industrial expansion of the worsted trade which continued to dominate the economic and social structure of the region. In 1780, 53 per cent of the future borough's populace lived in the Bradford township and by 1851 it had dropped only slightly to 51 per cent, after seven decades of rapid demographic expansion. Thus, it was to the central township that the greater number of immigrants were drawn after 1810. Other industrial townships experienced similar demographic growth (viz Table X). Bowling and Bierley continued to attract migrants to their expanding ironworks and collieries. The latter was second only to Bradford until 1821 when Horton became the largest of the out-townships. Horton's growth was determined by the industrial overspill of Bradford. The increasing number of textile mills there, required a new work discipline and a punctuality which tied their work-force to living near their places of work.

Those townships still committed to a farming economy, Allerton, Thornton and Eccleshill grew at a much slower rate. Although Manningham was to become part of the borough in 1847 and was situated close to the central township, its growth was significantly slower than other townships adjoining Bradford. Manningham adjoined, to the west, a semi-agricultural sector including Heaton, Bolton and Shipley, and therefore its position marked it out as an early Victorian middle-class suburb for the smaller gentry, manufacturer and merchant of the central township.

As early as 1831 Bradford township provided for 1,065 manufacturing employers and a further 339 capitalists, bankers or professional men. Industrial capitalism and the mechanisation of worsted manufacture had stimulated unprecedented demographic change. The decade 1821–31 placed Bradford second only to Brighton as the city with a maximum rate of growth, ie. 65.5% (Leeds 47.3, Sheffield 40.5, Manchester 44.9). Those ten years saw the rise of

Table X Population of Townships in Bradford Parish 1780–1851

	1780	*1801*	*1811*	*1821*	*1831*	*1841*	*1851*
Bradford	4,506	6,393	7,767	13,064	23,223	34,560	52,493
Bowling	1,119	2,055	2,226	3,579	5,958	8,918	13,538
Horton	1,964	3,439	4,423	7,192	10,782	17,615	28,143
Manningham	936	1,357	1,596	2,474	3,564	5,622	9,604
Allerton	n.d.	809	1,093	1,488	1,733	1,219	2,041
Bierley	"	3,820	4,766	6,070	7,254	9,512	11,710
Clayton	"	2,040	2,469	3,609	4,469	4,347	5,052
Eccleshill	"	1,351	1,608	2,176	2,570	3,008	3,720
Haworth	"	3,164	3,971	4,668	5,835	6,303	6,348
Heaton	"	951	1,088	1,217	1,452	1,573	1,637
Shipley	"	1,008	1,214	1,606	1,926	2,413	3,272
Thornton	"	2,474	3,016	4,100	5,968	6,788	8,051
Wilsden	"	913	1,121	1,711	2,252	2,684	3,454

Source: *As in Table VIII*

the twelve great Victorian cities of 1871 and half of them experienced their highest growth rate in that decade. Of them, seven were situated in the manufacturing regions of the North.[19] It was the period after the Napoleonic Wars, when the northern textile industries showed their true potential. There can be no doubt that Bradford's demographic growth after 1810 was very largely influenced by the processes of industrialisation and immigration. Before the new century there had been a steady growth of population through natural increases of births and deaths. The region had experienced some industrial activity in the 1770s but insufficient for its industries to require a greater labour force than could be provided by the locality. Demographic growth of the town and parish before 1810 antedated any substantial increase of large scale industrial capitalism (with the exceptions of local ironworks). As the manufacturers of worsteds geared their capital and productivity to the factory system, they strained the resources of the local labour supply and consequently Bradford's natural population growth was boosted by immigration. Henceforth, the twin forces of population and industrialisation interacted and reinforced each other. During the third decade population went at too fast a rate for the town's under-capitalised industry to cope. However, with the mechanisation of weaving, new sources of capital and healthy markets, industry caught up and the twin forces pushed Bradford on to her greatest age.

The Financial Framework and Capital Accumulation

The acceleration of economic growth in the eighteenth century required an unprecedented accumulation of capital, both fixed and circulating. This necessitated a corresponding increase in the efficiency and organisation of the channels through which that capital could pass. How capital was diverted from traditional uses and channelled into new enterprise is an important development in our understanding of the economic growth at that time. Where surplus resources were tapped and how that excess capital was manoeuvred into the hands of the eager Bradford businessman will be considered in this section.

By 1760 the national facilities for a fluid money market were minimal and often restrictive. The most important financial institution was the Bank of England which controlled a monopoly of joint-stock banking. Acting primarily as an 'ex officio' department of the government, the Bank held large amounts of capital but restricted its circulation of notes to the area immediate to the metropolis.[20] Secondly, there were a number of private banks, again mainly centred around London. This category was subdivided into the West End bankers and several smaller concerns. The former, like Hoares & Coutts, dealt mainly through bills of exchange and a greater part of their business was done by acting as financial agents to the larger landed gentry. Neither the Bank of England nor the metropolitan private banks, had any direct influence on the financial system of small towns like Bradford. However a number of the smaller private banks did influence the provinces, for their main business was in discounting bills of exchange, providing short term loans 'on call' and financing commercial exploits with circulating, rather than long-term, capital. Their most important function was to supply gold and silver to the country bankers. By acting as agents between London and the provinces these banks built up a very sound business, although at greater risk than their counterparts in the West End. Their number increased from thirty in 1750 to seventy in 1800.[21] To the provincial man, the country bank had more relevance than any of those distant metropolitan institutions. Country-banking accelerated in response to the needs of localities and, consequently, their number sharply increased during the period of rapid industrial growth. In 1750, there were only twelve such banks but by 1800 their number had expanded to 350.

Country banking usually developed as a sideline to a more important occupation. Bradford's first bank was formed in 1777 when three local gentlemen formed a partnership.[22] Thomas Leach lived at West Riddlesden Hall, near Keighley and owned considerable estates at Morton and Halifax. He was already making good use of the minerals on his estates and was an early coal supplier to the Bradford Lime-Kiln Company. The second partner was William Pollard of Halifax. Little is known about Pollard apart from the fact that he was a wool-stapler whose sister, in 1760, had married the third partner, William Hardcastle. Hardcastle was also a wool stapler but there is good evidence to suggest that he had carried on the business of banking before 1777. The point, however, seems adequately made. Country banking emerged as a secondary occupation to a more profitable commercial enterprise, its main objective being the manipulation of idle and surplus funds.

The firm of Leach, Pollard and Hardcastle was the Bradford region's first official bank and began business on the £1,000 which they had each subscribed.[23] They operated from a small apartment adjoining Hardcastle's

Figure 8 The First Bradford Bank. The premises of Leach, Pollard and Hardcastle, proprietors of Bradford's first bank. The building was in Well Street.

warehouse in Well Street near to the old Broadstones. Like all country banks, they had their London agent – in this case, Mildred, Masterman & Walker. The amount of bullion which a company retained depended on several factors. The status of the bank, the condition of trade and local trust and confidence were all important prerequisites for a flourishing country bank. After issuing notes, Leach & Company were no doubt able to tempt local investors into releasing their surplus capital. From thereon, they became deposit bankers and more important, were able to supply local credit facilities. The Leeds–Liverpool Canal scheme and the local coal and worsted industries had already boosted commerce in the area. Such credit facilities as Leach & Company provided, acted as a further stimulus to that kind of expansion. The bank created an incentive to the thrifty and an organised system, through which to divert savings into profitable investments. The fluctuating economy of the years 1779 and 1780 finally accounted for their demise and the company fell into bankruptcy in 1781. Some have attributed their failure to the decline of the primary occupations. An entry in Abraham Balme's Diary for 1771 notes that Bradford was an 'Ill fated town for failures lately formed both Bank and stocks – justly blamed to traid'.[24]

It would appear however that they suffered more in consequence of the American War. This affected all trades in the area, ended construction of various projects and closed a valuable market of woollen and worsted exports. Furthermore, panic led to runs on the banks and the government began to offer higher and more attractive interest rates. Although this was the last genuine bank in Bradford until 1803 there were several other credit facilities available of a less official nature. A number of the local gentry and merchants found themselves at the nexus of several sources of incoming capital. Land agents, attorneys and trustees are good examples. Abraham Balme, whose entrepreneurial activities have already been examined in this book, exemplified this kind of money scrivener. Balme's daybook provides ample evidence of the range and scope of exchange bills which passed through his hands. The bill was the principal means of purchase and sale, particularly in provincial towns like Bradford. It was discounted by the creditor at an interest rate, in order to turn his sale into cash before the time settled upon, for the bill to mature. Consequently, it could quite easily be held as an investment, for there was a reasonable increase in its value between discount and maturity. Balme, as landlord, trustee, steward and treasurer to two joint-stock commercial companies, had the opportunity to accumulate bills and release them when it pleased him.

Joshua Firth, of Thornton, a friend and neighbour of Balme's, began operations as a banker and money lender sometime after 1781. Using bills of exchange he eventually issued his own notes, one of which has recently come to light. Firth worked in conjunction with a London Bank which paid him interest when his account was in credit and vice versa when in debt. In some areas, a commission system developed. Details of Firth's banking activities have yet to appear. He doubtless operated for almost twenty years, helping to nourish the periods of high economic activity in 1789–93 and after 1797.[25] However, his banking days came to an end in the early months of 1800 when he was declared bankrupt. Having practised as 'merchant banker, dealer and chapman, using and exercising the trade of merchandise by way of bargaining, exchange and bartering', he was found to be £700 in debt.

Another source of credit at this time, was the collection of public revenues which were often held over long periods of time.[26] The officers either kept the money themselves and forwarded it in instalments or they sent it by bills on London private banks. Either way, time was on their side. The banks could use it for private credit. The collectors left it with the country banks or acted as bankers themselves. Again it meant an expansion of the credit facilities of a locality. It was not an inconsiderable amount. After 1750, taxation increased extensively. The Land Tax was particularly appropriate in this respect.[27] The government appointed area Receiver-Generals who selected three or four deputies. These latter officers received a low salary and as a result were encouraged to hold money and gain interest in order to substantiate their stipend. William Stanhope of Leeds and Horsforth was Receiver-General for the West Riding until 1772 when Walter Stanhope succeeded him. Both men complained of the arrears of their subordinates. On his election to the post in 1765 William Stanhope appointed John Blayds, Richard Lee and Jeremiah Dixon as his receivers. Within months he was compelled to reprimand them,

> 'Bills to ye amount of ye publick monies shall be regularly remitted to ye Bank at certain stated times and ye cash produced by such bills shall not be applied to any other purpose than that of being paid into ye Exchequer....'

Lee owed almost £6,000 and his colleague Blayds £3,900; both became bankers in their own right at this time. Stanhope was ultimately responsible for something like £60,000 and therefore he had to keep a wary eye on his deputies. Lee's arrears rose to £18,700 and prompted Stanhope to write,

> 'Now where is this money? In whose hands is it? Or where is the Fund to pay it? I can find no pretence for having always £10,000 of the Government's money'.[28]

Stanhope was forced into brow-beating Lee for the money, for his own position and personal honour were at stake when he received the following reprimand from the Treasury.

> 'The Lord Commissioners of His Majesty's Treasury were yesterday pleased to postpone your appointment for the present years Land Tax on account of ye large sums of publick money now in your hands. Therefore you will reduce ye balance as fast as possible that we may report the same to their lordships'.[29]

These were considerable sums of money to accumulate and hold over. Whether paid tardily or even by instalments, it meant local country banks were holding substantial amounts of usable capital for long periods of time. Loans were invariably short-term and consequently were quite easily accommodated from this source. This practice boosted the local circulation of notes, and simultaneously increased the availability of credit for commercial expansion of all kinds. In this way, Central Government unwittingly contributed to the capital investment of industrialisation. The continuing complaints of the Stanhopes and others bear witness that the abuse functioned in the distant foothills of the Pennines as well as in the more fashionable business arena of London.

The next official Bradford banking institution after Leach & Company came from the closely integrated ranks of the Quakers. Renowned for their close personal family ties, the Quakers were not without roots in the small town of Bradford. An assessment of the actual contribution which this tiny group made to the economic growth of the town, has been made elsewhere. The most prominent of that group was the Hustler family. Wool staplers for most of the eighteenth century, the family had risen to prosperity and high repute largely through the efforts of John Hustler (1715–1790).[30] After a successful commercial career, he had purchased ninety acres of land at Eccleshill and erected Undercliffe House. This he mortgaged in 1778 with Daniel Mildred and Samuel Hoare, both merchant bankers of London.[31] Mildred and Hoare were both Quakers and became good friends of Hustler, whose second son, John, eventually married Mary Mildred in 1815. This second John Hustler (1771–1842) succeeded his father as a wool stapler, a trade which frequently took him to the wool markets of Lincolnshire and Norfolk. It was there, no doubt, that he met other great Quaker families like the Gurneys and Pease, (his first wife was Elizabeth, sister of Edward Pease of Darlington). His travels to Lincolnshire also brought him a new business partner, Edmund Peckover who was one of three very enterprising sons of Richard Peckover, an East Anglian Quaker. Edmund's brothers, Joseph and Jonathan, both owned general stores at Fakenham and Wisbech respectively. Both saw the possibility of successful banking activities within their towns but they lacked sufficient capital to go ahead. Jonathan contacted the great Norwich banking house, the Gurneys, who obliged with a loan and by 1782 the first ledger was opened.[32] Edmund Peckover had for many years been a wool stapler and before 1786 had spotted the necessity of moving into the vital economy of the West Riding. About that time, his partnership with the younger John Hustler began. Peckover, like his brothers, had gained the confidence and trust of his customers, and prior to 1790 was acting as a banker. A letter from Samuel Hailstone to Bartlett Gurney at Norwich in February 1790, certainly confirms Peckover as some kind of financial intermediary. 'On Thursday last Mr. Brooke paid £507 to Mr. Peckover which with £2,400 to be secured on the interest will be in full for his purchase money'.

Throughout the 1790s John Hustler was at the centre of market controversies, canal administration and a variety of commercial and industrial schemes. In 1803 Peckover became treasurer for the £3,000 subscription opened for the acquisition of an Act of Improvement for Bradford. Within a matter of weeks of its collection, and in somewhat dubious circumstances, Peckover gave up the wool-stapling business, and the premises in Canal Road and in March 1803 gave notice to the public of a new Bradford bank. Drafts on London banks show Peckover to have done some banking business with his nephew, Charles Harris previous to 1792. It was Harris, another Quaker, who partnered Peckover in 1803.[33] Before the bank was opened, Peckover had consulted his friend and fellow Quaker, William Birkbeck, partner in the Craven Bank. Birkbeck gave the scheme little chance and thought the Leeds banks sufficient for Bradford's needs. Peckover ignored his advice and trusted his own judgement beginning business at the end of 1803.

At a time of industrial expansion, capital investments meant risks and Peckover & Harris in their new premises in Bank Street had to be wary of applicants for loans and credit. The Butlers of Kirkstall Forge had prospered from the iron trade's growth and began a new concern at Mirfield in the autumn of 1804. Peckover, eager for trade, agreed with Thomas Butler for the company to open their new cash account with Peckover and Harris. Hard bargaining came with the question of what security could be given. The Butlers wanted to draw upon the bank, 'by weekly payment of about £50 for wages to the amount of £1,000 in your own notes which will be paid at Mirfield and we think may be in circulation a good while before they are brought back to you'.[34] By the new year they hoped the new firm would be complete and remittances could be sent to obtain the balance. What the iron company required was a short-term credit loan to get their new enterprise off the ground. Once an income was forthcoming, then the account would go 'into due bounds and can then go upon your regular Banking System'. Several shares and a £700 loan of the Leeds–Liverpool Canal Company were finally given as security and doubtless Peckover & Company supplied the required circulating capital which bridged a precarious period for any new concern.

This type of transaction was a considerably important part of the bank's business in the early years. The national financial structure provided an inadequate supply of currency for payment of wages and raw materials. Industrial expansion at home, symbolised by the canal mania, exhausted the currency supplies of the land. After the Suspension of Cash Payments Act the country banks were no longer discouraged from issuing notes as low as £1. Even so, some of the new industrial companies were forced to issue their own tokens and notes. At Bowling Ironworks the weekly wage bill rose from £192 in 1799 to £429 within ten years. John Sturges & Company were forced into issuing their own guinea notes and £5 notes as late as 1830. Between 1803 and 1826 the Low Moor Company also had a currency of its own, using notes of a guinea and one pound. The ironworks at Birkenshaw were owned by Aydon & Elwell but these two banked with Swaine & Ramsbotham and managed to survive the latter's bankruptcy in 1807. The demise of this bank meant that Peckover & Harris monopolised banking in Bradford during the French Wars.

The success of Peckover's banking venture, and of Bradford banks in general, was noted by the Reverend William Atkinson of Bradford in his *Political Works* in 1816. He reminisced of the time when every man was his own banker, handling gold. Since 1770 gold had disappeared and had been replaced by provincial notes,

> 'till at length, almost every farmer, as well as commercial men and every man of money transactions had his bank. It is the banker's policy in the regular course of trade, to keep the money market well supplied; because in this he obtains interest for all the currency he has in circulation'.[35]

Edmund Peckover enjoyed only a few years of his successful banking venture for he died in 1810. Henry Harris was brought into the company to take his place. The company continued to attract valuable members of the local squirearchy into investing large amounts of capital into various national and local commercial schemes. In addition to individual clients, the firm dealt with the accounts of several turnpike trusts, the Bradford Navigation Company, the Bradford Improvement Commission and also invested local capital into government stock.[36]

The Peckover & Harris monopoly of Bradford banking was broken in 1819 when the Wakefield company, Wentworth, Chaloner & Rishworth opened a branch bank in Bradford. The country as a whole was still adjusting to a peace-time economy following the French wars. Recovery seemed well on the way by 1823, but over-confident speculators invested money in foreign funds. An increase in imports and a glut of joint-stock companies, led to a high proportion of money being withdrawn from circulation. Prices rose and investors began to demand back their money. The boom broke in the late summer of 1825 and by December the editor of the new *Bradford Courier* declared, 'money seems to have vanished'. The Bank of England did nothing to mitigate the crisis and continued to discount bills at the usual rate. By the time any preventive action was taken, it was too late for Wentworth, Chaloner & Rishworth who duly crashed in the first week of December 1825.[37] Shortly afterwards, Dobson's Bank failed at Huddersfield and the panic was well and truly on. 'Runs almost unprecedented in their continuance and severity have assailed every banking house in the district'.

This did not exclude Harris & Company who suspended their Saturday payments, hoping for a weekend reprieve. Pound notes changed hands for fifteen shillings and a partial 'run' on the company occurred on the following Monday. However, the sensible townsfolk of Bradford expressed their faith in the bank by a declaration of, 'entire confidence in the perfect stability of the Bank of C-H & H. Harris of this town and are not only ready to accept in payment any of their notes but offer our united guarantee of the safety and responsibility of the firm'.[38]

This joint security was estimated at two million pounds, which came from more than forty Bradfordians (30% of whom were from the landowning class). This public statement of support was sufficient to save the company, but not to save many of the small workshops and artisans who had banked with Wentworth & Company. They came to ruin and aggravated an already serious unemployment crisis in the town. Thus, Harris & Company survived their worst crisis and lived to prosper, finally going public in 1864.

Shortly after the act freeing joint-stock banking in 1826, talk of a new bank quickly circulated the town. At first, it was associated with the political interest of the Whig party. It finally appeared in March 1827 (with a capital of £500,000) as the Bradford Banking Company. After Wentworth's failure, public opinion in Bradford had come out strongly against branch banks and called for the townsmen of Bradford to form their own company. Subscribers of the £100 shares were from the new industrialist class. Led by self-made ironmasters, J.G. Paley and Henry Leah, other subscribers included most of the town's leading textiles manufacturers. However, the man largely behind its formation had been former manager to the Wentworth Company, Samuel

Laycock. Aided by an enthusiastic committee Laycock soon doubled the bank's capital and the company moved to new premises in Kirkgate. In the 1830s, two more banks came to the town, the Bradford Commercial Joint-Stock Banking Company and a branch of the Yorkshire District Banking Company.[39]

This brief account of the capital supply system in Bradford after 1760 has, to a very great extent, been concerned with an awkwardly linked complex of financial agencies. At times of depression, over-speculation and panic, this structure was often shaky and unreliable. At best the country banks were able to provide short-term loans to develop fixed capital in well established businesses. Evidence of banks providing initial fixed capital for completely new enterprises is limited. Where then did Bradford's entrepreneurs obtain their capital and credit for the new ventures which they established in these years?

The remainder of this chapter will consider a number of the methods utilised by local businessmen in the raising of finance and initial fixed capital for their businesses. Perhaps the most popular of sources for long-term loans was the mortgage of property and land, which remained the best security throughout this period.[40] The importance of mortgages to the general capital market is demonstrated in the business records of Jonas Jowett, corn miller of Oxenhope, who purchased the Hewenden Mill estate at Wilsden. Jowett was typical of many local traders and industrialists who resorted to this effective means of raising capital, 'Freehold property remained the best security extant in eighteenth century England and the mortgage market was one of the most efficiently organised sides of the capital market'.[41]

Many of the early entrepreneurs like Jowett relied on mortgages to get them into industry and, once there, to keep them in. Robert Heaton, cotton spinner, whose commercial affairs are examined elsewhere in this book, experienced a severe trading loss in the years 1806–9. His creditors in the cotton trade lost faith,

> 'they came so clamorous for the money I owed them that I was obliged to sell an estate to discharge my debts and if I had got no other income than that what I derived from trade I should have been before now in the same poor situation with a considerable number of cotton spinners in the parishes of Keighley and Bingley who have become bankrupts within the last 3 years'.[42]

In May 1808 he had sold the Kildwick estates left to him by his brother Michael Heaton. A farm at Ling Crofts Gill and two closes brought him £3,500 which cleared his debts and established his credit status once more. Freehold property had made him and saved him.

Property and the mortgage market enabled the first proprietors of the Low Moor Iron Company to accumulate initial capital in 1788. However, having made the original purchase of the estate at £34,000 the new owners spent almost fifteen years building up the plant and machinery. This was done by the most popular of methods of capital accumulation, the 'plough-back' of profits.[43] Like many other local businesses the Low Moor Company pulled themselves up by their own bootlaces. A more detailed analysis of the company's financial structure will be given in Chapter Five, but it might serve our purpose here to examine the Low Moor proprietor's handling of the 'plough-back' system. It can be seen from the Table XII that the partners advanced capital into the firm until 1805. Over fifteen years this amounted to £62,937 which went into the construction of various buildings and the installation of new machinery. In addition, profits in the years 1793 to 1797 were not touched but retained for the company's use. During this period, the 'proprietors agreed to pay themselves small salaries, restrict their household expenses and put their profits to reserve'. This was the practice followed at Low Moor, a practice often ignored in the contemporary business world.

Money was taken out of the business in small amounts but was mainly used for installation of fixed-capital assets like steam engines, forges and rolling mills. However, the fixed capital was often minimal in proportion to the Company's requirements of circulating capital for wages, raw materials and general trading. The following are stock-takes at Low Moor at quinquennial periods during these years 1795 to 1835.

Table XI Quinquennial Stock Accounts of Low Moor Ironworks 1795–1835

Year	*Property & Estates* £	*Fixed Capital* £	*Stock & Utensils* £	*Book Debts* £
1795	23,086	22,030	20,890	25,585
1800	28,405	30,800	35,290	58,849
1805	39,578	46,700	66,972	86,866
1810	65,975	42,000	67,511	83,862
1815	64,789	38,000	92,072	85,363
1820	80,837	32,500	55,507	80,713
1825	84,774	29,000	132,184	109,161
1830	100,965	23,000	104,520	80,958
1835	108,464	47,173	138,770	98,024

Source: *BCL Low Moor Ironworks Mss 1795–1835*

The figures show the proportion of fixed capital to circulating capital. In 1795, the original fixed-capital assets are 24% of the total capital value of the firm, whereas at the end of the period in 1830, they are fractionally over 7%. However, this was increased between 1832 and 1835 when over £30,000 was added to the fixed capital account, lifting it to 12% of the total capital value.

The West Yorkshire worsted industry in the eighteenth century differed significantly from the local ironworks in terms of capital requirements. Domestic textile production had never been a heavily capitalised industry. Even the Yorkshire worsted trade's 'small number of big men' required little more than short-term credit for buying wool and paying wages.[44] According to the ledgers of Robert Heaton of Oxenhope and Stanbury, his short-term needs were best met through the bill of exchange.[45] The credit finance of exchange bills allowed a small manufacturer like Heaton to operate without using large amounts of currency. There were other ways of economising on currency. Under the putting-out system Heaton employed weavers who were also tenants of his lands. They were paid by a redemption of their annual rent. Richard Nichols, a Wilsden clothier, made use of his brother 'who was in the practice of sending a great part of the produce of his farm to the mills where a market was found him amongst the workpeople'. Through the truck system Nichols gave goods in exchange for labour and thus reduced his weekly needs of cash.[46]

Table XII Financial Structure of Low Moor Ironworks 1790–1819

Year	*Total Advanced* £	*Total Taken Out* £	*Profit* £	*Capital Employed* £	*Depreciation Fixed Capital* £
1790	16,755	–	–	–	–
1791	7,678	–	–	–	–
1792	10,307	–	–	–	–
1793	3,265	–	14,258	52,265	–
1794	4,042	–	11,806	68,113	–
1795	335	–	9,249	77,698	–
1796	–	–	15,400	93,137	–
1797	13,933	–	16,278	123,349	–
1798	–	5,010	15,458	133,796	–
1799	–	14,271	18,078	137,602	1,043
1800	–	10,999	15,828	142,431	1,000
1801	5,811	1,045	26,408	173,604	1,000
1802	–	8,495	20,347	185,456	–
1803	–	1,108	11,310	195,658	–
1804	607	–	14,650	210,917	–
1805	204	11,121	10,569	210,568	–
1806	*	16,568	18,236	218,236	2,200
1807	*	18,236	11,860	211,859	–
1808	*	11,859	5,552	205,551	–
1809	*	9,551	19,655	215,655	3,000
1810	*	11,655	18,290	222,290	1,000
1811	*	18,290	17,430	221,430	1,521
1812	*	17,430	18,000	220,000	1,000
1813	*	18,000	16,200	220,200	1,000
1814	*	16,200	23,200	227,200	1,000
1815	*	11,200	23,200	239,200	1,000
1816	*	12,000	16,000	243,200	1,000
1817	*	16,000	14,000	241,200	1,000
1818	*	14,000	22,800	250,000	1,000
1819	*	22,800	34,500	233,680	1,000

*No Further Advances Made

Source: *BCL Low Moor Ironworks Mss C33*

Even when the transition to mills took place, the worsted textile producer required surprisingly small amounts of fixed capital. As J. Swift remarked in 1825, a man who employed a hundred weavers could be a considerable manufacturer but not necessarily a large capitalist. 'No we do not consider him so, a man may have many weavers and yet not have a large capital'.[47]

Recent research of insurance company records has shed new light on fixed capital valuations of early mills. From a sample of twenty mills in the Bradford parish before 1805, the Sun Fire Company records revealed an average fixed capital valuation of £950 per mill.[48] This modest figure was inevitably increased with the introduction of steam driven machinery and purpose-built mills. By 1820 the average valuation for the same sample of mills had risen to £2,300. D.T. Jenkins has confirmed this trend for the West Yorkshire region as a whole.

Table XIII Estimates of Total Value of Fixed Capital in Mills of West Riding Wool Textile Industry

	No. of Mills	*Average Value of Mills (£)*	*Total Value of Fixed Capital (£)*
1800	243	1,657	402,651
1810	276	2,510	692,760
1820	326	4,305	1,403,430
1835	610	5,803	3,539,830

Source: D.T. Jenkins *The West Riding Wool Textile Industry 1770–1835* (1975) p.151

Many of the early millowners in the worsted trade were already established master manufacturers under the domestic system. They had substantial businesses from which to develop and sufficient credit facilities to draw upon, including the banks. A large proportion of the financing of fixed capital came from the entrepreneurs themselves and their social and family networks. E.M. Sigsworth has examined in considerable detail the financial origins and progress of John Foster's Black Dyke Mills at Queensbury.[49]

The Marriner enterprise at Greengate Mill in Keighley also typifies the financial organisation of West Yorkshire's early worsted mills. The mill was constructed in 1775 for employment in the expanding cotton trade.[50] The Marriners were not original partners in that mill; these partners had included five small woollen clothiers and one James Greenwood who brought no capital into the concern, but was 'possessed of a plan in respect to other mills of a similar nature...and a genius well adapted for constructing the machines and other works'.[51] The mill, driven by water, stood opposite a house built by William Marriner, a manufacturer and landowner formerly of Kirby Lonsdale. Marriner's first interest in the mill came via his marriage to a Miss Fletcher, a niece and heiress to Abraham Smith, an original partner of the mill. By 1785 the firm rested in the hands of Thomas Blakey and William Marriner. Greengate Mill continued to produce only cotton twist and, utilising the six month bill of exchange, prospered in the cotton trade until the depression of 1813. By that time William Marriner had been succeeded by his sons Benjamin and William jnr. In 1817 John Blakey relinquished his share of the mill for £450. The firm's fixed capital until that time rested largely on reinvestment as this extract from William Marriner's accounts demonstrates,[52]

Table XIV Extract from William Marriner's Accounts

		£	s.	d
1802	Profits to Declare	853	2	0
1803	Profits to Declare	97	18	0
1804	Profits to Declare	437	18	0
	Total	1388	18	0
	Average	462	19	4
	Mill assessed at	126	0	0
	1/3 share =	336	19	4
		112	6	6
	From Illingworth & Marriner	70	0	0
		£182	6	6

Of the £462 profit, approximately 25% was assessed for the mill. By 1807, this had accumulated in the form of thirty six spinning frames (£1,400), fifteen cards (£275), and other machinery to the total value of £2,143. When the two brothers began business in their own right in 1818 the mill was valued at £4,900 but this was immediately increased by the setting-up of a combing shop, as the mill was converted to the spinning of worsted yarn. The main source of power continued to be the river Worth but, also in 1818, some 'steam apparatus' was purchased. The thriving trade done by the Marriners is reflected in the physical growth of the mill also in the stock accounts for the years after 1819.[53]

Table XV Annual Stock Accounts of Marriner Brothers 1819–1832

1819	£2,295	1826	£3,627
1820	£2,332	1827	£5,260
1821	£2,332	1828	£5,180
1822	£2,374	1829	£4,710
1823	£3,171	1830	£5,688
1824	£3,661	1831	£7,376
1825	£3,722	1832	£7,324

Source: *Brotherton Library Marriner Mss 146 Box 8*

The steps taken by William Marriner and his sons at Greengate Mill in the nascent factory system highlight some of the methods by which a firm might be financially launched and consolidated. The original mill had been constructed and financed through mortgages (although Greenwood's technical talents obviated these). William Marriner had become a partner through marriage and by the liquidation of other assets. His holdings had been consolidated by the plough-back of profits, gained by means of an accepted credit system. On his death, his sons had inherited the mill and geared it to the expanding worsted trade. No doubt, their profits were reinvested to boost the overall capital of the firm thereafter. It can be suggested with some certainty that Bradford families like the Rands, Fawcetts and Thompsons launched their early mills and realised their entrepreneurial ambition through an admixture of similar financial facilities.

There were numerous local mills built and financed by persons outside the worsted trade, seeking only a profitable return on their investment. Local landowners, many of whom were absentee landlords, built mills as a means of estate development. Joshua Crompton of Esholt Hall was responsible for Buck Mill, Wilkinson's Mill, Vincent Mill and Whitfield Mill all in and around Idle. Walter Spencer-Stanhope was informed by his steward in July 1800,

> 'The Mill tenants at Wood Bottom are going on with their new engine and a large addition to the mill, with great spirit.... I am glad to find that they have withdrawn themselves from every other mill concern so that they may apply all their capital and ability to yours'.[54]

Companies not directly concerned with the textile trade were prepared to finance and construct worsted mills. Bowling Ironworks and the Bradford Navigation Company built mills at Bowling and Frizinghall respectively.[55]

As the banking system expanded and matured, local banks were more willing to commit themselves to loans over a longer term, though these were not always direct. Trade credit finance can be viewed as something more than short-term credit. Deficit balances and short-term loans were extended over several years and were used continuously. John Foster of Queensbury had this kind of arrangement with the Bradford Banking Company during the 1830s when he commenced work on his own mill at Black Dyke.

Table XVI Financial Position of John Foster, Queensbury, 1824–1838

	Capital (£)	*Addition to Capital (£)*	*Money Owed on Current Transactions (£)*	*Cash in Hand(£)*	*Bank Position (£)*
1824	11,185	Nil	3,899	30	-1,436
1837	15,781	4,596	3,363	243	-2,576
1838	19,294	3,512	7,548	Nil	-3,436

Source: *E.M. Sigsworth: Black Dyke Mills (1958)*

Finally, the personal loan was an important source of obtaining fixed capital particularly amongst families and religious groups. Before the age of mail, telegrams and railways, business was done person to person and the value of personal contact saved many a needy business.

The provision of fixed and circulating capital was an integral part of Bradford's shift to a large scale industrial economy. This section has attempted to show how early entrepreneurs in the region obtained their initial capital and what sources and credit structures they utilised to provide the working capital which they required to run their businesses effectively.

The importance of money for these early industrial capitalists is summed up perfectly in the poetic talent of Robert Heaton, an early Pennine mill owner. Inside the cover of one of his stock books can be found this literary masterpiece written in the spring of 1789 at a time when there was great uncertainty in the world, particularly across the Channel. Heaton penned this little piece 'Oh Money'.

"Oh Money! Money! – I too plainly see
That in good earnest I'm in love with thee
When I alone they beauteous form survey,
Do not my eyes my tender thoughts betray?
Does not my trembling hand thy person seize?
And eager grasp thee with an amorous squeeze
No lover can more grievously repine
At Myras absence than I do at thine
And well I may, for when deprived of thee
I can enjoy no other company".[56]

1. M.W. Flinn, British Population Growth 1700–1850 and H.J. Habbakuk. English Population in the Eighteenth Century, *Economic History Review* VI 1953 pp.269–84
2. J. James, *History of Bradford*, p.144
3. Yorkshire Archaelogical Society (hereafter Y.A.S.) Local Record Series 1928, *Archbishop Herring's Visitation Return 1743* pp.58–60
4. E.A. Wrigley (ed.) *Introduction to English Historical Demography* (1966)
5. F.M. Eden, *State of the Poor*, (1795) p.810
6. B.C.L. Scruton Collection Ms 27/16 and Misc. Ms 10/18/13. Also W. Cudworth, The Bradford Soke, *Bradford Antiquary* Vol. 1 (1888) pp.77–8
7. J.T. Krause, Aspects of Population Change 1690–1790, in E.L. Jones & G.E. Mingay (eds), *Land, Labour and Population in the Industrial Revolution*, (1967) pp.187–205. 'The reliability of this method is not complete but errors over a period are relatively constant and therefore erase themselves'
8. J.D. Chambers. Population Change in a Provincial Town: Nottingham 1700–1800 in L.S. Presnell (ed.) *Studies in the Industrial Revolution* (1960) pp.97–124
9. B.C.L. Bradford Cathedral Mss Vestry Registers
10. F. Beckwith, The Population of Leeds During the Industrial Revolution, *Thoresby Society Publications*, XLI, (1943–51)
11. P. Deane & W.A. Cole, *British Economic Growth* 1688–1959, (Cambridge 1962)
12. W. Cudworth, *Round about Bradford*, p.48
13. B.C.L. Hailstone Ms. 11/2
14. J.T. Krause, Changes in English Fertility and Mortality 1780–1850, *Economic History Review*, XI, (1958), pp.52–70
15. J. Lund, *Directory & Gazeteer of Bradford* (1858)
16. T. Wood, *An Autobiography 1822–1880* (1956)
17. C. Richardson, The Irish Settlement in Mid-Nineteenth Century Bradford, *Yorkshire Bulletin of Economic and Social Research* Vol. 20, (1968)

18. Ibid p.46
19. A. Briggs, *Victorian Cities* (1971) p.27
20. L.S. Pressnell, *Country Banking in the Industrial Revolution* (Oxford, 1956) and R.E. Cameron, *Banking in the Early Stages of Industrialisation* (N. York 1967)
21. P. Mathias, *The First Industrial Nation*, (1969), pp.165–9
22. W. Cudworth, The First Bradford Bank, *Bradford Antiquary* N.S. Vol. II (1901–3) p.232
23. B.C.L. Misc. Ms. 5.40 (a)
24. B.C.L. Balme Mss. 6/1 p.84 c.1771
25. W. Cudworth, *History of Manningham* etc. (Bradford 1896), p.328; W. Robertshaw, *Bradford's Banks*, (Bradford 1956)
26. L.S. Pressnell, Public Monies and the Development of English Banking, *Economic History Review*, Vol. 5 (1953), pp.378–97 and E.B. Schumpeter, English Prices and Public Finance 1660–1822, *Review of Economic Statistics*, XX (1938), pp.21–37
27. W.R. Ward, *The English Land Tax in the Eighteenth Century*, (Oxford 1953)
28. B.C.L. Spencer-Stanhope Ms 1138 16 September 1767
29. Ibid Ms 2186
30. A. Raistrick, *Quakers in Science and Industry* (Newton Abbott 1968) pp.78–80
31. B.C.L. Misc. Ms. 5.40 (a)
32. W.H. Bidwell, *Annals of an East Anglian Bank*, (Norwich 1899)
33. *Bradford Old Bank, Centenary Souvenir* (Bradford 1903)
34. R. Butler, *A History of Kirkstall Forge* (Leeds 1945) p.70 26 October 1804
35. York Minster Library (hereafter Y.M.L.). Hailstone Ms G3 1816
36. B.C.L. Misc. Ms 1/16/21
37. H.C.J.B. W/39/13 19 December 1825
38. Souvenir (1903) op. cit.
39. W.C.E. Hartley, Banking Development in Bradford, *Bankers Magazine* 1302 (1952), pp.210–215
40. S. Pollard, Fixed Capital and the Industrial Revolution in Britain, *Journal of Economic History* Vol. XXIV No. 3 (1964), pp.299–314 and S. Pollard, Investment, Consumption and the Industrial Revolution, *Economic History Review*, 2nd series XV (1958/9) pp.215–226
41. P. Mathias, *The First Industrial Nation*, (1969) p.150 and H. Heaton, Financing the Industrial Revolution, *Bulletin of Business History Society*, II (1937)
42. B.C.L. Heaton Ms A520
43. T.S. Ashton, *Iron and Steel in the Industrial Revolution* (Manchester 1924), pp.158–9
44. H. Heaton, op. cit. p.298 and D.T. Jenkins, *The West Riding Wool Textile Industry, 1770–1835* (Pasold 1975)
45. B.C.L. Heaton Ms B.156
46. B.C.C. Misc. Ms A.385
47. P.P. No. 25 (417) IV p.130
48. D.T. Jenkins, op. cit. and Sun Fire Office County Registers 11937/116/119
49. E.M. Sigsworth, *Black Dyke Mills*, (Liverpool 1958), Chapters 4 & 5
50. J. Hodgson, *Textile Manufacture and other Industries in Keighley* (Keighley 1879) pp.52–54
51. Brotherton Library, University of Leeds (hereafter BLU.L) Marriner Ms 13

52. Ibid Marriner Ms 199
53. Ibid Ms 148 Ledger 1814–29
54. B.C.L. Spencer-Stanhope Ms 2168. 22 July 1800
55. Sun C.R. 37/713369/1801 quoted in D.T. Jenkins op. cit. p.200
56. B.C.L. Heaton Ms Stock Book March 1789

4

Bradford and the Transport Revolution 1760–1830

The relevance of transport change to economic growth, and to industrialisation in particular, is a keenly contested historical debate. What is undisputed however is that transport developments inevitably influenced the spatial structure of economic change. As population distribution and commercial activity were decidedly marked in the mid-eighteenth century, the intensity of interaction between places was equally affected. Current transport networks were unable to meet the strain of demographic and economic expansion. Contemporaries responded by increasing the transport capacity; by creating new routes or by developing alternative transport methods.[1]

In the second half of the eighteenth century Bradford's land-owners and men of commerce were confronted with this problem. Bradford lies within a basin-like depression on the eastern side of the Pennines, surrounded largely by hills rising to 1,200 feet above sea level. John James described it thus,

> 'The town lies in a valley which may justly be considered a branch of Airedale, though from a remote period it has borne the distinct appellation of Bradfordale. This valley, stretching from the moorlands above Thornton to the Aire at Shipley, forms at Bradford a considerable bend....'[2]

Cut off from the central arteries of transport and communication by its own location, Bradford had remained a small regional market town incapable of significant commercial and economic progress.

By 1850 Bradford had developed into an important regional centre of road, navigational and railway communications. C. Richardson has described this transformation as a 'remarkable change from its position as an economic backwater to that of a major manufacturing city, owing much to its emergence as a man-made node....'[3]

The primary stimulus to this change came in the second half of the eighteenth century with the growing regional demand for Bradford's relatively untapped mineral resources and with the improved intra-regional trade in wool and agricultural produce. The strain which was imposed upon the traditional transport network by these economic forces compelled Bradford's men of enterprise to respond with capital and technology and to transform the local transport network. Only with cost-effective improvements in transport and communication, could the businessmen of late eighteenth-century Bradford realise the vast potential of raw materials, capital and their own entrepreneurial talents.

Roads and Highways

Daniel Defoe in 1745 had remarked that road carriage and English roads were 'the very medium of our inland trade'. The importance of road transport in pre-industrial times has been obscured by numerous exaggerated accounts of the poor quality of English roads. As a result the utility of road transport has been seriously underestimated.[4] Bradford for example, in the absence of a navigable river, was entirely dependent upon the regional highway system and the numerous scattered tracks and pack-horse trails around it.

The maintenance of these highways had rested with the parishes since the statute of 1555. This system relied heavily upon 'parochial service' and was consequently much neglected. This voluntary scheme along with the decline of central government control after the Interregnum, led to a severe deterioration in the condition of the country's roads. In many parishes the position of surveyor was abused and disregarded, and certainly by 1730 the Bradford vestry had proved an ineffective administrative body in respect of its highways. As the inter- and intra-regional commodity flows increased their volume in the eighteenth century, the condition of West Yorkshire roads was called into question by the primary users, the gentry and the merchants of both town and country.

The parochial inability to keep pace with the increased road traffic led to an entirely new initiative from the private sector, the introduction of the turnpike trust. Each trust had statutory powers to charge tolls and reinvest capital in road maintenance and improvement. The system has been maligned for its parochial and sectionalised nature. Many turnpikes were conceived as linkages between two localised end-points or as products of inter-regional commercial rivalry.[5] Consequently turnpikes were largely the results of local initiatives. Bradford was first linked to the turnpike network in 1734 largely as a result of the ambition of Leeds and Manchester merchants. In that year the first Yorkshire turnpike act was implemented between Manchester–Halifax–Leeds via Great Horton and Bradford. This was followed in 1740 by the Selby–Halifax road which passed through Bradford and Leeds[6] (viz Fig.9). It was prompted by the commercial competition between Leeds and Wakefield merchants in the Yorkshire cloth trade. Several Bradford manufacturers subscribed to the trust including Abraham Balme, John Hustler and William Preston. Equally, several of Bradford's squirearchy supported the scheme, Henry Wickham, Walter Stanhope, Edward Leedes and Jeremiah Rawson, all of whom were local lords of the manor.

The turnpike roads were not popular with everyone. A branch of the Leeds–Halifax line was extended to Wibsey and Bankfoot in 1752 and on 18th June 1753:

Figure 9 The Turnpike Road System around Bradford 1750–1820

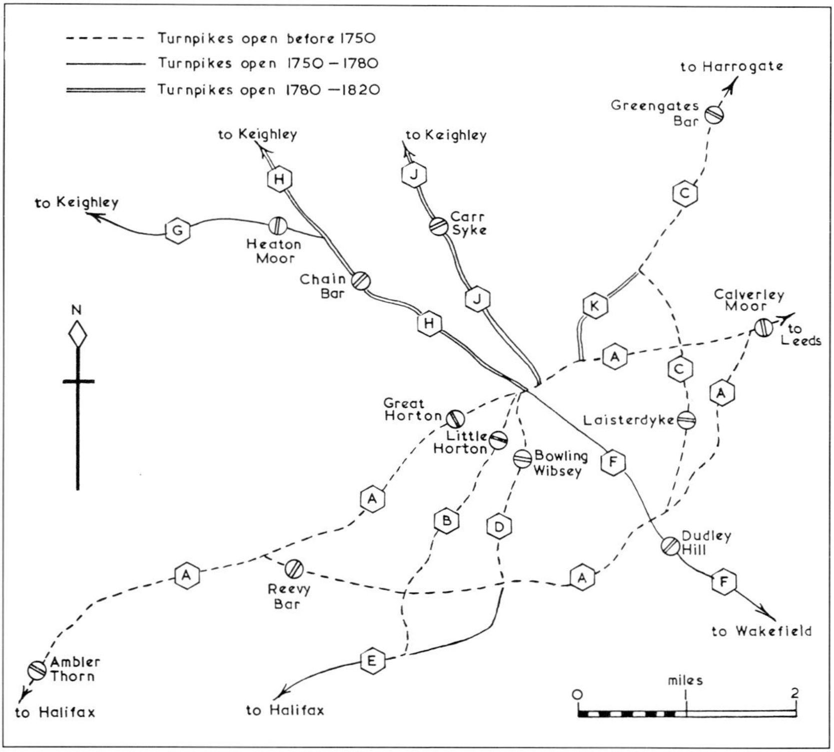

Turnpike Company and Date of Act

A	Leeds and Halifax Trust	(1734)
B	Little Horton Branch of Leeds and Halifax Trust	(1734)
C	Dudley Hill, Killinghall and Harrogate Trust	(1736)
D	Bowling Lane Branch of Leeds and Halifax Trust	(1740)
E	Wibsey, Bank Foot and Lidget Branch of Leeds and Halifax Trust	(1752)
F	Bradford and Wakefield Trust	(1753)
G	Toller Lane, Howarth and Blue Bell Trust	(1755)
H	Keighley and Bradford Trust	(1794)
J	Keighley and Bradford Trust	(1815)
K	Dudley Hill, Killinghall and Harrogate Trust	(1816)

'a mob arose from several parts, but chiefly from Yeadon and Otley, and the adjacent places, and pulled down a turnpike at Bradford Moor end, and afterwards attempted to destroy Bradford turnpike: the same day, they destroyed one at Apperley Bridge. On the 22nd, they assembled again, and were joined by many hundreds of people, from most parts of Bradford parish, when they tore down a turnpike at Tyresal Moor end and burnt it and the house together; the same day, they burnt one at Newil Hall, and Wibsey Bank Foot turnpike house, and Bradford turnpike shared the same fate. At last, they beset Mr. Balme's house, and behaved in a very irregular and unseemly manner'.[7]

In spite of such temporary setbacks, by 1750, the regional centres of trade and industry in West Yorkshire were well served by the turnpike system both internally and with their external connections with the metropolis and the open sea. Bradford was linked to Halifax, Wakefield, Leeds, Keighley and Harrogate by an effective network of turnpike roads. The road building innovations of John Metcalfe were taken up by West Yorkshire trusts in the 1750s although they were not popularised nationally until the new century. The turnpikes permitted the development of important services like the Royal Mail, stage-coaching and long distance haulage. By 1825 there were fourteen coaches running daily between Leeds and Bradford carrying upwards of two hundred people. There were daily connections from Bradford to Liverpool, Manchester, Hull and London as well as the Royal Mail which posted at the Bowling Green Hotel, one of several coaching houses in the town.[8]

Understanding the nature of the turnpike system might best be achieved by examination of a particular trust. The Toller Lane, Haworth and Blue Bell Trust was commenced in 1755 and stretched from Heaton in Bradford to the Bluebell Inn at Two Laws near Colne.[9] It was originally promoted by a large number of gentlemen from the locality which included John Field of Heaton, Samuel Lister of Horton, William Lamplugh of Cottingley and the ubiquitous Abraham Balme. Another important subscriber was Robert Heaton of Ponden and Haworth who remained a trustee of the road until his death in 1795. Bradford's commercial interests were represented by John Hustler, Thomas Hardcastle and Thomas Leach. The previous mentioned gentlemen, all became trustees of the road and were empowered to raise money for its improvement. Such capital was usually raised by public subscription and interest was offered at the rate of 4 or 5%. Slow economic growth between 1750 and 1770 meant that paying this interest was difficult and redeeming the original debt impossible. The trustees employed William Chapman as surveyor and he estimated that the cost of repairing the road over Cottingley Moor through Cullingworth and Haworth would cost £1,400. Tenders were put out and the trustees accepted the tender of £1,250 from John Gott, Thomas and Abraham Rhodes. They promised completion of the repaired road in two years including the new bridge at Ponden. It was also their responsibility to erect all toll bars and side bars along the route like those at the Black Bull in Haworth and at Hewenden Brow near Wilsden. The annual rents were let to the toll farmers. A very important source of toll was the coal from Denholme taken through Haworth to the west.[10] The carts of the Horsfalls and Andertons were charged six pence per wagon and many of the colliery proprietors found it easier to compound their tolls at a yearly rate. John

Greenwood, another Denholme carrier, used as many as twenty four horses on the coal/lime trade along this road. The completion of the Leeds to Skipton section of the canal in 1777, badly affected the road traffic in these materials, although local demands for coal helped to continue part of that trade along this particular turnpike. The tolls were inconsistent from one trust to another but in 1803 the Bradford–Colne Trust increased their levy to:

3d for horse and cart at 1st Bar
3/- for herd of cows at 1st Bar
7d for score of sheep at 1st Bar
6 Horse coach of any kind = 2/6
4 Horse coach of any kind = 1/8
Coals: Wagon & 5 Horses = 1/- at 1st Bar
Wagon & 3–4 Horses = 8d at 1st Bar
Wagon & 2 Horses = 4d at 1st Bar
Wagon & 1 Horse = 2d at 1st Bar

These revised tolls reflect the increased powers of the trusts and their improved financial situation by 1800. The accounts of this particular turnpike demonstrate a precarious existence before 1790 (Table XVII). Thereafter, the quickening momentum of economic growth in the district and an increase in passenger traffic contributed to an upswing in the trust's accounts and a favourable balance of payments. However, by 1818, the trust committee called for 'the utmost economy' in the application of funds because of the high outstanding interest due to creditors. In addition they had paid nothing to the local townships and a costly act of renewal was imminent. There had been no provision for the gradual redemption of the original debt. Finally, the trustees lost the money loaned and the trust wound up its affairs in 1878.

Table XVII Accounts of the Blue Bell Turnpike Trust 1759–1803

Year	*Income (£ s. d)*			*Expenditure (£ s. d)*			*Balance (£ s. d)*			*Annual Average Gain*
1759/60	240	10	06	210	05	01	+30	05	05	£30
1763/67	747	01	04	830	05	08	-83	04	03	Loss
1767/75	1130	12	05	1310	07	02	-179	14	00	Loss
1775/6	133	19	06	187	03	06	-53	04	00	Loss
1776/79	562	02	00	562	15	11		13	11	Loss
1779/87	710	17	10	676	00	06	+34	16	06	£4
1787/1803	2225	08	00	2098	07	08	+127	06	03	£8

Source: *W.Y.C.R.C. Turnpike Records Box 50*

This trust was typical of the smaller turnpike ventures, many of which were second-rate 'ad hoc' affairs whose administration was narrow and blundered. Leasing of the tolls was tantamount to an admission of mismanagement and ineffective administration, 'they stood moreover in the main stream of English amateurism applied to public affairs'. More important, the turnpike roads around Bradford had done little to reduce carrying costs of goods in bulk. They were a response to the increased economic activity in textiles and farming but the problem of moving and realising Bradford's mineral resources remained unsolved. The exploitation of local coal, iron and limestone was the flashpoint in Bradford's economic development in the late eighteenth century. By 1770, after the turnpike boom, Bradford's mineral wealth had yet to be realised and would only be so, by means of an alternative, superior transport form. It came in the shape of the canal system.

Bradford and the Canal Age

Bradford's geographical position had long hindered the town's growth. The undulating plateaux surrounding the town had restricted highway development and limited Bradford's connections with other regional markets, and even further afield, with overseas trade. By the middle of the eighteenth century, a very large part of West Yorkshire's commerce was carried on with the German and Dutch states. However, the Aire–Calder Navigation Company had, to a large extent, provided reasonable transport links between the Pennine towns and the east coast of Yorkshire. To the West, was the growing cotton trade of Lancashire and beyond the sea, the expanding markets of North America. Increasing and extending the Bradford trade to such distant horizons was doubtless the ambition of many contemporaries. Yet it was upon more local markets that the Bradford businessman pinned his hopes and aspirations in the eighteenth century. By the 1760s coal was becoming the main domestic fuel, in addition to the increasing supplies being consumed by industry. Bradford, standing on the extreme north west corner of the great Yorkshire coal-field, was eager to help satisfy that demand. It was the stimulus of coal which provoked Bradford men to emulate the success of Sankey Brook and the Bridgewater canal both of which were built to cheapen coal costs.[11] So too with the Leeds–Liverpool canal whose origins lay in the needs of Bradford colliery owners to cut costs and find better markets for their coal, iron and limestone.

Several learned studies of transport history, and of canals in particular have made reference to the close association of the Leeds and Liverpool canal scheme with the town of Bradford. The seed of this idea probably originates in Joseph Priestley's *Historical Account of the Navigable rivers, canals etc.* (1831).[12] Priestley's father was clerk of works to the canal company for almost fifty years. Bradford's strong ties with the project were also confirmed in 1900 by another employee, H.F. Killick, who was law clerk to the company.[13] Both writers emphasised the substantial Bradford influence on the affairs of the Leeds & Liverpool canal from its beginnings in the 1760s. The remainder of this chapter will examine why Bradford took such a close promotional interest in the canal and also in the building of a branch canal from Bradford to Shipley.

Coal mining was central to the history of the British industrial revolution, and in particular to the early industrialisation of the Bradford region. The north-west corner of the Yorkshire coalfield has two distinct types of coal, the Black Bed and the more famous Better Bed coal. To the south of Bradford the latter seam had an average thickness of twenty-five inches. Its coal was described as a 'bright burning bituminous coal' which was sulphur-free and ideally suited to the iron trade. A third type, the Hard Bed coal, was close to the surface and was for many years an important source of domestic fuel.[14] As the town is located on the edge of the coalfield, the seams to the north began to peter out quickly and early mining schemes were quickly exhausted.

Simple digging at the outcrops of coal had occurred since the fourteenth century, but by 1700 there was a proliferation of small-scale mining schemes to the south and south-west of Bradford. Local lords of the manor and leading estate owners in this area had a long tradition of non-agricultural involvement. As far back as 1568 Sir Richard Shireburn had profited from timber on his Esholt estates. The inferior wood he burnt in an iron bloomery at Esholt Wood.[15] By 1750 several of the leading Bradford gentry were actively taking up the role of industrial entrepreneurs, involving themselves directly in capital investment and entrepreneurial risk; the exchange trade of Bradford coal and Craven limestone was a major element in this activity.[16] Edward Leedes, of Low Moor and North Bierley, is a typical example of the Bradford gentry in those years. His activities in the field of mineral extraction were extensive and included an eighth share in a lead mine on Grassington Moor, as well as numerous collieries at North Bierley and Wibsey.[17] By 1760 he had planned for his mineral estates something more than a scratching at the surface coals. He had conceived an enormous colliery network at Low Moor linked by railroads, to provide for wider markets and even exports. There was talk of a 'great plan of improvement'. However, he failed in his attempt to raise capital and realise the full potential of this scheme: money was scarce, and the American war affected interest rates. In August 1781 he was declared bankrupt, but continued to believe in his plan. 'The small Wood Colliery,' he wrote after his bankruptcy, 'will bring in £3,000 a year if there was a Newcastle Waggonway made to Brighouse and £1,000 a year if it was only made to Lightcliff'.[18]

Had Leedes continued to live the life of the landed squire, drawing his income from yearly rentals, there was every possibility that his family name would have survived. He chose, however, to risk borrowed capital in the exploitation of his subterranean estates. After 1775 he drew annually upon persons in London for large sums of money amounting to £20,000 and more.[19] His single-handed efforts to finance the collieries, as well as carry the burden of a heavily mortgaged estate, ultimately ruined him, and in August 1785 he took his own life. It has been said of Edward Leedes, "To him the mineral wealth of his vast estates was an unknown quantity; he lacked the energy to reap the rich harvest which subsequently fell to the lot of the Low Moor Iron Company."[20] This is an undeserved comment, for he was one of the many landowners who risked and lost everything in the pursuit of commercial and industrial success. Here, it is important to recognise that the ambition and foresight of Leedes, and his 'great plan', were built upon the growing regional trade of Bradford coal for Craven limestone.

The use of calcinated limestone for building purposes had been known for many years, and by 1700 lime was being put to a wider use in the West Riding as a fertiliser.[21] Much of the limestone in mid-Airedale was found around Skipton and Bingley, where it was burnt in rectangular 'pye-kilnes' close to the quarries. Throughout the eighteenth century several Bradford colliery owners like Leedes increasingly moved their coal up the dale towards Skipton and in return received lime or limestone which was burnt in the limekilns at Bingley.[22] Edward Leedes was joined in this local trade by Abraham Balme of Bowling, John Hustler of Undercliffe, John Stanhope of Thornton, John Jarratt, John Preston and several others. These men took advantage of the increasing potential of coal as a domestic fuel where the transport system allowed, but the movement of large quantities of minerals exposed severe limitations in the region's existing transport network. Heavy but cheap commodities like coal and limestone could have their price raised to a disproportionate extent by transport costs. The carriage of minerals by packhorse through Airedale was painfully slow, inhibited output and sustained high prices.[23] In spite of such restraints the Bradford coal dealers carried on a sound business in the middle decades of the eighteenth century. The trade in coal and limestone was one of the most prominent features of Airedale's market economy at that time but the demand for coal as a domestic fuel, and the needs of Bradford farmers and builders for high-quality lime, strained the local transport system more than any other commercial traffic during this vital economic period.

As early as 1744 there had been a proposal to make the river Aire navigable from Inghay Bridge to Cottingley Bridge in order to accelerate the movement of coal between Bradford and Skipton. The final estimated cost of £5,500 proved prohibitive, and the scheme was dropped.[24] In consequence, the Bradford colliery owners fell back upon improving the local road network. As the inter-regional commodity flows increased in volume in the eighteenth century the condition of West Yorkshire roads was called into question by their primary users, the gentry and merchants. Between 1734 and 1760 Bradford as we have already seen was drawn into a network of turnpike roads, whose trustees included the familiar local names of Balme, Leedes, Hustler, Preston and Stanhope.[25] The close involvement in road improvements of these Bradford colliery owners did little to affect 'the prodigious expense of land carriage'. John Hustler, like the petitioners of 1744, acknowledged this as a primary problem in his propaganda pamphlet for the Leeds–Liverpool canal:

> 'The price of land carriage at present is on an average one shilling per mile per ton, the price proposed to be taken by water...for merchandise two pence per ton per mile, for coals a penny half penny per ton per mile, or one eighth part of the land carriage'.[26]

In a private survey of 1768 the Bradford canal promoters found that 46,880 horseloads of Bradford coals were consumed in the Skipton district at a cost of tenpence per load. It was calculated that the delivery of coal by navigation could be made at a maximum of eightpence per load and the cost of limestone could be cut by half. These preparatory calculations estimated an annual profit margin of £21,132 of which £7,200 would come from the carriage of merchandise and £13,932 (65 per cent) from coal and limestone.[27] As early as August 1764 there appeared a newspaper comment that:

> 'As the Rivers Aire and Ribble may be so easily joined at different places and rendered navigable between Leeds and Preston at an expense which gentlemen who have estates on the banks may readily supply, it is thought proper to mention it to the public at this juncture.'[28]

At that time the economic benefits of the Sankey brook and the Bridgwater Canals were generally known. Early canals tended to be local schemes, financed and organised by those who had a direct interest in the results.[29] The Leeds and Liverpool Canal was initially conceived to meet the specific needs of a small group of Bradford colliery owners, keen to cut costs and accelerate distribution to the traditional regional markets of the Yorkshire dales. Most secondary works have credited John Hustler, the Bradford woolstapler and coal merchant, with the original idea of a trans-Pennine canal. Two writers have gone so far as to dedicate their work to his memory.[30] Certainly the initiative came from within the cabal of Bradford colliery owners, but another candidate deserves mention in this context, namely John Stanhope of Horsforth and Thornton. Stanhope's career and those of his brothers, Walter and William, have been examined elsewhere.[31] As an attorney John had made a name for himself in the woollen cloth disputes of the 1760s, representing the case of the Leeds clothiers. Having inherited the Horsforth estate, he purchased the manor of Thornton in 1746. John Stanhope then encouraged local men to lease his Thornton lands and invest in mining schemes. In June 1765 he received a letter from his nephew, Walter, who had recently visited the impressive Bridgewater Canal. Walter observed:

> 'We went in a pleasure boat down ye navigation, sailed over rivers and highroads and at last arrived at ye banks of ye Styx where we embarked on board Charon's boat and sailed 1,000 yards underground by ye twinkling of a few farthing candles. We then arrived at a highroad leading to ye infernal regions where we met one of ye Furies of Darkness as black as ye Devil: by him we were conducted, having left our boats, 100 yards almost upon our hands and knees till we came to ye Coal....'[32]

Thus, the idea of connecting the east and west coasts by canal was firmly in Stanhope's mind by the autumn of 1765, when he hired John Longbotham of Halifax (assistant to John Smeaton) to survey the lands on both sides of the Pennines. The Yorkshire side posed few problems, as Longbotham proposed a route from the end of the Aire & Calder Navigation at Leeds through Airedale to Gargrave. The Lancashire terrain proved more difficult, but in late December 1765 Longbotham promised Stanhope a completed preliminary survey by the following February. Several writers have suggested that the initiative for the canal came from the surveyor, who proposed the scheme to the energetic Quaker John Hustler. However, John Stanhope was committed to the canal before either of them, and several letters confirm his early interest and enthusiasm. Lowther at Preston described him as 'the great encourager of the intended Navigation', and Tempest of Tong Hall, Bradford, wrote to him, 'It is highly reasonable that the thanks of all whose property or dealings are interested in the intended navigation should be given to you as its author....'[33]

Stanhope headed an early subscription list and addressed the merchants of Lancaster as early as the spring of 1766. He made several journeys to Liverpool that summer in order to influence the town's corporation and was asked by the committee to personally enlist the support of the Duke of Devonshire and the Earl of Thanet.[34] When the main subscription for the Leeds & Liverpool Canal was finally opened at Bradford in January 1769, John Stanhope headed the list with £4,000. Many of the West Yorkshire gentry and Bradford colliery owners contributed, but none put up more than a thousand pounds.[35] The Spencer-Stanhope family archive provides ample testimony to John Stanhope's close involvement and commitment to the scheme during the early promotional stage. Unfortunately he died in 1770.

The illness which ultimately caused his death forced Stanhope to relinquish his initiative in the canal as early as 1769. It was John Hustler who replaced him as the leading promoter. Hustler had become actively involved in the scheme in August 1766, having failed to attend the first official public meeting at the Sun Inn, Bradford, in July of that year.[36] Also in attendance, however, were many of the principal landowners of Leeds and Bradford. Of those from Bradford no fewer than ten were working collieries on their estates at that time. The meeting approved Longbotham's plan and opened a subscription to cover initial costs.[37] Stanhope and Hustler were eager to obtain an Act of Parliament for the canal, for several other trans-Pennine schemes had been mooted. Respective county committees were formed, based at Liverpool and Bradford. The Yorkshire group included the Bradford colliery owners John Stanhope, Benjamin Ferrand and Henry Wickham. All parties spent the year 1767 mustering support for the Bill and, in particular, wooing the great landowners through whose land the canal was to pass.

Longbotham's survey (following the Ribble valley to near Preston and via Ormskirk to Liverpool) was sent to James Brindley for his criticisms and comment. In fact the work was done by Brindley's assistant, Robert Whitworth, in the summer months of 1768. Brindley's final report confirmed the route proposed by Longbotham, and it was accepted by the Yorkshire committee. A joint meeting was arranged for August that year, and Hustler, Balme and Buck were in attendance.[38] By this time the promoters of the canal in Lancashire were having second thoughts and serious doubts about the proposed route. As J.R. Harris has commented, 'The Yorkshire subscribers, for their part, wanted the speediest communication with Liverpool consistent with cheapness'.[39] Longbotham's plan had followed the Ribble valley and had not touched emerging industrial towns like Blackburn and Burnley (viz Fig.10).

Figure 10 Original Line of the Leeds–Liverpool Canal

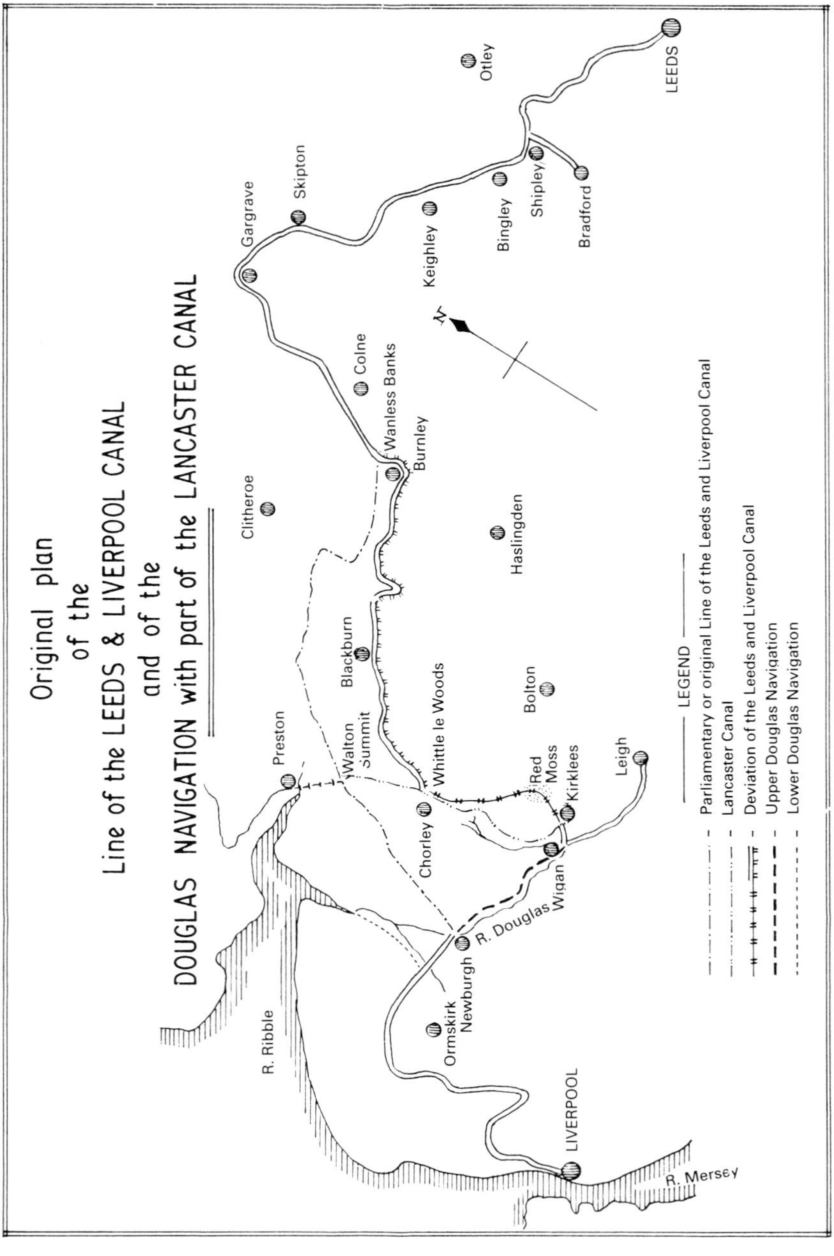

The Wigan coalfield could be penetrated only by the acquisition of the Douglas navigation, and Lancashire industrialists were not to be fobbed off with branch canals.[40] As a result they quarrelled with the leading promoters, and this schism threatened the project. However, Hustler, Balme and William Thornton temporarily pacified the Lancashire committee, and at Burnley on 19 December 1768 the two committees agreed to apply for an Act of Parliament. At this Burnley meeting the promoters accepted Brindley's estimated cost of £259,777 and opened a capital of £260,000 in £100 shares (with interest at 5 per cent). To open the subscription lists it was proposed to hold 'two great meetings', which took place simultaneously at Bradford and Liverpool on 9 January 1769.[41] Within a short time £150,000 had been subscribed, and it was decided to appoint Thomas Hardcastle, Thomas Leach and William Birkbeck as treasurers (all three were local bankers). Not long after these meetings Hustler informed Stanhope that people 'are generally desirous of better information', and he immediately drafted a pamphlet entitled *A Summary View of the Proposed Canal*.

Throughout 1769 Hustler had the difficult task of keeping the two county committees in harness. The Lancastrians renewed their complaint that the route went too far north and employed John Eyres and Richard Melling to plan a line that would meet their needs. Stanhope noted the growing dissent on all sides. He was informed that Hustler 'has lost his influence and others have taken up the lead which... will make confusion'.[42] Hustler asked Brindley to make a further report in the hope that it would placate dissidents. Again it was Whitworth who resurveyed the line, and he found errors in the survey completed by Eyres and Melling. The Bradford group then rejected the Liverpool alternative and insisted 'that the present association and subscription was entered into upon the plan produced at the meeting at Bradford and therefore this committee think they are not at liberty to depart from it....'[43] Henceforth, no other surveys were to be financed from the subscription. The Lancashire faction had meanwhile ordered another survey. It was awaiting P.P. Burdett's report when, at a general meeting summoned at the Sun Inn, Bradford, in October 1769, Hustler and Balme on behalf of the Yorkshire committee agreed that Brindley should consider both schemes. When Brindley confirmed Longbotham's route the Lancashire and Liverpool contingents withdrew their subscription, a decision confirmed at a meeting at Burnley on 11 December. Fearing further defections, Hustler chose to promote the bill in London, and when a number of the Liverpool men surprisingly rejoined the committee in January 1770 Parliament was finally petitioned. The canal bill became law in May 1770.[44] At the first general meeting a committee of twenty-three was elected, including Balme, Leach, Garforth, Walter Stanhope (John Stanhope was already dead) and Hustler, who was nominated treasurer. James Brindley was appointed chief engineer at £400 p.a., assisted by Longbotham as clerk of works at £160 p.a. Brindley was unable to accept the post (he died in 1772), and consequently Longbotham fulfilled both roles.[45]

Work began immediately on the three sections which it was thought would provide the swiftest return on investment: Liverpool to the River Douglas, Skipton to Shipley and Shipley to Leeds. By early 1774 the canal from Skipton to Thackley, near Shipley, was finished, together with the difficult stretch from Bingley to Shipley, and by 1777 the navigation was complete from Gargrave to Leeds. However, Brindley had seriously underestimated the cost, for by 1775 the company had already spent £232,000 in building only fifty-five miles of canal. It was forced to borrow £2,000 to pay contractors and meet the interest due to the proprietors. Hustler estimated that the remainder of the canal would cost £800,000, but he did not anticipate the economic recession that followed the colonial war in America. War debts needed funding, and consequently private credit was hard to come by as interest rates rose. For over a decade, from 1781, work stopped on the canal, which had been completed between Leeds and Skipton on the Yorkshire side and between Liverpool and Newburgh in Lancashire. The importance of this coalfield link to Liverpool has been stressed elsewhere. Coal from the Douglas valley 'became the lifeblood of this important and profitable waterway'.[46] However, the completion of the canal from Leeds to the Yorkshire dales was equally important for Bradford's economic development. While there was evidence of strong local support – after London, Bradford was the largest source of subscribed capital – Bradford colliery owners had been able to utilise a national subscription to promote and finance trading connections within their own regional economy. In particular, John Hustler had been able to exploit his connection with the Quaker communities in London and Norwich to Bradford's advantage.[47] Certainly, in the canal's early years, its affairs were run very much in the interests of Bradford. Joseph Priestley of Bradford was appointed accountant and clerk of works. The company's law clerk was John Eagles, who practised in Bradford, where the company's head office was located until 1850. John Hustler became sole treasurer of the company and controlled its finances until his death in 1790.

The influence of the Bradford colliery entrepreneurs spilled over the Pennines into the Lancashire coal industry. Several of the mid-Lancashire collieries, opened in the decade after 1774, were leased by John Hustler, Thomas Hardcastle, John Jarratt, Joseph Dawson, John Hardy and Edmund Peckover. For one writer the Bradford–Liverpool caucus significantly transformed the capitalisation of Lancashire collieries:

> 'Local finance was dominant in the 1770s on the Leeds and Liverpool Canal when the industry grew slowly but large injections of capital from Liverpool and Bradford were associated with the more rapid growth of the last two decades of the century'.[48]

John Hustler, who ran several collieries in Orrell and Up Holland as well as those around Bradford, dominated the affairs of the canal until his death. He and his clique of Bradford colliery owners were able to control the supply and distribution of coal at both ends of the canal as well as direct and manipulate company policy.

The business records of the Leeds–Liverpool Canal Company for the late eighteenth century show a steady growth of income on the Yorkshire side of the canal, a large share of which came from coal and limestone.[49] The importance of that trade to the business of the canal can be assessed from the income on tolls. In 1792 coal and limestone accounted for 40.7 per cent of the gross income from tolls along the whole of the canal. By 1820, when the canal was completed, it had increased to 50.2 per cent, and by the 1830s remained at least 40 per cent of the income (viz Table XVIII).

Table XVIII Leeds–Liverpool Canal Company Accounts, 1772–1800 (quinquennial averages)

Period	*Total gross income (£)*	*Income from Yorkshire side (£)*	*%total*
1772–75	1,633	932*	–
1776–80	6,292	2,561	40
1781–85	9,746	2,745	28
1786–90	16,892	3,943	23
1791–95	25,160	5,350	21
1796–1800	36,298	8,813	24

* 1773–75

Source: *Statistical History of the Leeds & Liverpool Canal* (1898), in Rail 846/124, P.R.O.

Trade of this kind was realised by the Bradford colliery owners only after the town had been linked directly into the main canal. There can be no doubt that this was their intention all along, although to Hustler's credit he continuously urged the proprietors to complete the main canal to Liverpool. Throughout the 1780s canal companies had difficulty in attracting capital investment as government funds of one kind or another proved more lucrative. In 1790 an act was passed authorising extra capital to implement the Burdett survey which took the line further south than originally planned. The canal reached Burnley in 1796 and Blackburn in 1810 but was not complete until 1816. The great canal of 127 miles had taken almost half a century to complete and at a cost of £1.2 million.[50]

However, the importance of the Leeds–Liverpool Canal and the ambition of the Bradford coal traders was only realised when Bradford itself was interlocked into a waterway system which eventually connected it to the ports of the Humber and the Mersey (viz Fig.11). This was achieved between 1771 and 1774 with the construction of the small branch line, the Bradford Canal which ran between Windhill and Bradford.[51] Brindley visited the town in 1770 and proposed a route from Hoppy Bridge, past the parish church, along the bottom of the valley northwards through Frizinghall to Windhill. Within the three mile stretch there was a fall of eighty six feet which was to be

Figure 11 Canals in West Yorkshire 1750–1800

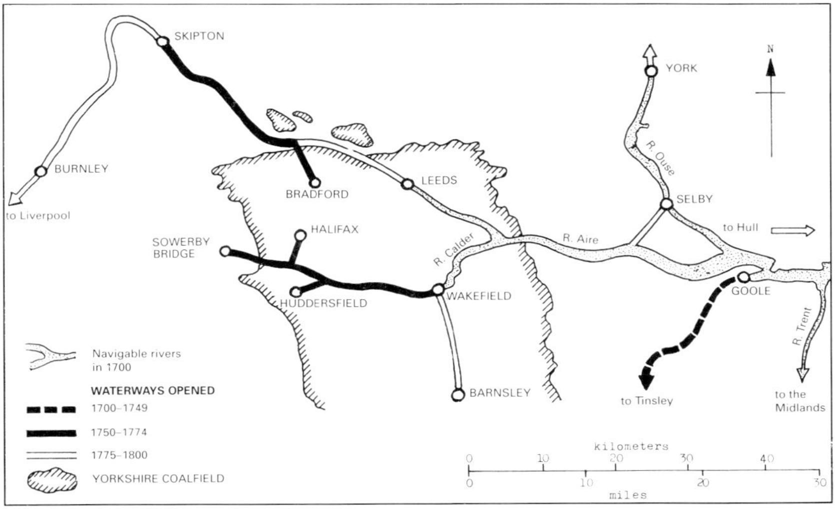

accommodated by five sets of locks (ten in all). There were twenty eight original subscribers including all the local colliery owners like Leach, Balme, Hustler, Leedes and John Preston. Hustler once again played a prominent part in raising the requisite £6,000 for the completion of the canal.

Balme handled most of the company's finances and paid the salaries and wages of the employees. The other elected clerks were William Hardcastle and Nathan Jowett. The latter was very active, along with Balme, in the land purchasing department of the company. The first purchase was made 30 December 1771 when the company got the go-ahead to cut through the lands of Messrs. Dawson & Redshaw at Frizinghall. Having acquired the land, tenders had to be negotiated. The company received four tenders and accepted the cheapest, that of John Knowles at '£4 per yard for cutting the ashlar that may be found from digging the lock'. Knowles had submitted this for the company's approval in July 1771. He had promised to dig 'the lock pits and getting loading and dressing the stones and directing all the locks' and have the work completed by 1st June 1773.[52] Knowles was as good as his word for the canal was open for trade by 1774 as Abraham Balme's journal confirms, '1774 7th Sept. Was at home all day loading the Good Intent took 150 load of the Better Coal and 100 load of the worse'.[53]

Balme continued to give good service to the company as treasurer until 1778, when the company was leased. Even the Leeds–Liverpool proprietors had discussed this idea of tenancy. 'There are some proprietors who think if the canal was lett it would be more advantage to the Undertaking. The Salary, wages etc are monstrous at present...'[54] The practice was adopted by the

Figure 12 Bradford Canal Basin. The canal, completed in 1774, ran into the very heart of the town with its basin just below the Parish Church. This unhealthy place was described in 1844 as giving off such gases 'that watch cases of silver become black in the pockets of workmen employed on the canal'. *From an engraving*

Bradford Canal Company in October 1778, when the canal was leased to Preston, Hird & Jarratt trading as the Bradford Limekiln Company but soon to be future owners of the Low Moor Ironworks. For a nine year lease they paid £834 10/- per annum and in 1797 the lease was renewed at an increased rent of £1222 10s. 0d per annum. The records of the Limekiln Company demonstrate the nature of early trading along the Bradford Canal which ran into the very heart of the town.[55] Coal and limestone were the early staple materials but, as the town grew, the ironworks 'may be said to have been founded, or at least greatly enlarged, in consequence of the favours which this canal afforded...for the conveyance of their castings to all parts of the kingdom'.[56] Flagstones from Spinkwell quarry on the eastern bank and vitriol from the Northbrook chemical works of Benjamin Rawson, were other important commodities which left the town as agricultural goods from Craven flowed in.

The sudden demise of the Bradford canal came with the town's great expansion in the period after the French Wars and is a story that must be told elsewhere. When it was first constructed, 'there was neither a foundry, worsted mill nor (as far as exportation is concerned) a stone quarry'.[57] These three provided the town's main exports yet the commercial expansion of Bradford was of such magnitude that the canal became inadequate to handle the increasing volume of trade. Around the canal basin, there was an acute shortage of warehouse space and wharves. In addition to this, the canal did not receive a sufficient supply of water. It was continuously too shallow, muddy and neglected. Consequently, the canal lost its trade, firstly to the turnpikes and later to the railways, although as late as 1910 the Bradford canal carried 102,000 tons of coal and stone. By 1920 this had dropped dramatically to 28,000 tons and in 1922 the canal company was wound up.[58]

The Bradford Canal and the Leeds–Liverpool Canal provided a solution for Bradford businessmen to low cost carriage of heavy bulky raw materials like coal and limestone. Canals facilitated the growth of inland coalfields like Bradford through the cheap and effective transportation of minerals and through the increased capacity of carriage (Bradford barges each carried 40–60 tons). Yorkshire colliery owners eagerly benefitted from the low-cost facility.

Table XIX Coal Carried on the Yorkshire Side of the Leeds–Liverpool Canal 1784–1834[58]

1784	17,503 tons	1814	106,314 tons
1794	32,800 tons	1824	100,807 tons
1804	58,127 tons	1834	100,726 tons

The Leeds and Bradford canal companies charged 1½d–2d respectively per ton per mile, a rate with which road hauliers could not compete. In 1797 Joseph Dawson of Low Moor Ironworks confirmed that 'low duties and freight rates encouraged the coal trade on their canal and that gave vigour to the coal owners and proved an abundant source of wealth to both'. Samuel Hailstone announced increased duties in 1815 which caused a public outcry and accusations of profiteering were directed at the proprietors. Inevitably, income and profits increased dramatically after 1780, a £3054 profit in 1780 rising to £10,605 in 1811 and £22,539 in 1831.[59] Irrespective of the profitability of the canals, they had transformed the 'cul de sac' of Bradfordale and had linked the town to a navigational system whose increased connections put Bradford in touch with the woollen towns of West Yorkshire and the expanding ports of Hull and Liverpool (viz Fig.11). Tonnage and increased traffic on the Leeds–Liverpool Canal were the real indices to the Bradford region's economic growth in the late eighteenth century.

Table XX indicates the central importance of the coal and limestone industries whose vast resources were, as a result of the canals, worked on a large scale and with considerable capital investment in and around Bradford after 1770. The two canals in the Bradford region had 'opened up the prospect of a coal-fired economy' and had afforded a transformed transport network for a small number of Bradford landowners eager to play to the full the role of industrial entrepreneur. In order to break from the strait-jacket of the traditional transport system such men involved themselves in the promotion of banks, turnpike trusts and, most important of all, in canals and in so doing they enhanced the development of the regional economy as a whole. Coal began Bradford's industrial revolution, not wool.

Table XX Toll Revenue on the Leeds–Liverpool Canal 1820–1835 (£)

Year	*Merchandise*	*Coals*	*Limestone*	*Lime/ Manure*	*Stone*	*Total*
1820	29,605	33,870	2,503	1,311	5,123	72,412
1821	32,421	32,909	2,486	1,169	5,825	74,812
1822	39,741	32,436	2,221	1,047	6,149	81,594
1823	43,011	35,235	2,979	1,073	7,190	88,489
1824	44,188	37,878	2,913	1,422	8,022	94,423
1825	47,036	42,191	3,453	1,643	9,004	103,327
1826	37,346	39,800	3,326	2,889	6,984	90,344
1827	47,804	39,824	3,200	1,596	7,640	100,064
1828	50,198	43,234	3,436	1,513	8,243	106,625
1829	50,210	46,687	3,371	1,547	8,858	110,673
1830	52,772	47,267	3,235	1,782	9,842	114,900
1831	49,542	1,377	3,840	2,172	9,405	116,336
1832	49,673	43,663	3,799	1,893	7,666	106,694
1833	52,098	37,584	3,565	1,742	7,618	102,606
1834	56,042	41,159	4,138	1,597	9,342	112,278
1835	59,667	45,711	3,916	1,560	9,084	119,978

Source: *P.R.O. Rail 846/124*

Within fourteen years of the completion of the Leeds–Liverpool canal a Bradford millowner commented upon the local canals in these terms. 'We have prepared no evidence against the canal as we are of the opinion that we prove sufficiently its inadequacy to the business of the town by showing the great and increased business of Turnpike Roads'.[60]

His statement came in support of a railway scheme between Leeds and Bradford in 1831. Railways had evolved as a refined and sophisticated form of colliery waggonways many of which had been spawned, somewhat ironically, by canal companies as feeders between colliery and wharf.

As early as 1780, Bradford had received its first railed road. It was a wooden construction on 'an inclined plain or waggonway...on which the coal waggons descend down the hill from Wibsey Slack to the town of Bradford...their velocity being regulated by convoys.[61] These primitive railroads connected the collieries of Low Moor and Horton and transferred the coal to the yard or staith in the centre of the town. The original idea was probably that of Edward Leedes, on whose property they were to be found and who, prior to his bankruptcy, worked extensively the minerals of his land. With the establishment of large-scale ironfounding after 1789, both the Low Moor and Bowling companies developed and extended these waggonways but neither firm showed sufficient initiative to run them by an engine (as the Brandlings had done at Middleton, Leeds).[62] Details of these 'Newcastle waggonways' are given elsewhere but several of the local ironworks and coal companies were linked to the head of the Bradford Canal by similar tramways. The towns 'amphitheatre' location made it ideally suited to this network of waggonways bringing coal into the heart of the town for export and after 1800, for use in Bradford's steam powered spinning mills.[63]

By 1802 the Low Moor Company was seeking to extend their system of waggonways into the Calder valley at Ravens Bridge. A survey was made by Israel Rhodes who proposed a double-lined road of seven and a half miles in length. The ground sloped slightly and the rail trucks were to be horse-drawn. Each carriage was on four wheels and was capable of carrying three and half tonnes. The whole scheme seemed justifiable in view of the prosperous country through which it passed and also in view of the 'intolerable condition of the common roads'. The coal from both Bowling and Low Moor was cheaply wrought, but transport costs drastically increased its final selling price. The railroad could carry coals at a much cheaper rate and, therefore, benefitted all parties. Rhodes' estimate of the cost was £24,000 of which almost £16,000 would be spent on cast iron rails which the Low Moor Company produced themselves. Consequently the scheme proved cheap and profitable and consequently, was undertaken.[64]

Bowling Ironworks also invested considerable capital into waggonways as each of their new collieries was opened after 1788. In the early years the trucks functioned on a system of winding gear which used the inclines of the area and horse power. Their trucks could hold as much as three tons of ironstone or coal and were made by the company. By 1831 there were three central lines to the network, of which two were linked by branch lines.[65] Perhaps the most important was the one running down into the centre of Bradford to the Company's coal staith alongside the canal. Its importance was stressed in 1814 when the tenants of Bierley Ironworks, Marshall & Leah, applied to Sir Francis Lindley Wood for a lease for a railroad. Sturges & Company of Bowling protested, 'we could not for a moment suppose you would grant facilities to any other person for bringing to market a much better article in Black Bed Coals than we have to offer, particularly when we have so much at stake'.[66] As a result Wood refused the lease. By midsummer 1815, however, there were 12,938 double yards of wagon roads in and around Bradford. This network had obvious effects on the speed and transportation of bulky raw materials, as well as upon the quickly changing landscape of Bowling. As the company spread in all directions, it also ensured that communication and effective industrial intercourse were maintained over the whole area.

Both companies, Low Moor and Bowling produced their own cast iron rails and flanged plates which made feasible the introduction of locomotives for horse drawn tramways. In 1812 Matthew Murray built steam locomotives for use at the Middleton Colliery near Leeds. These engines, which carried up to 110 tons at a speed of three and a half miles an hour, were the first commercially viable steam locomotives in operation in England.[67] With the success of the railways between Stockton and Darlington (1825) and Liverpool and Manchester (1830), other urban and industrial centres began to establish their own schemes. As early as 1802, mention had been made in the Leeds newspapers of a railway from Leeds to Selby. Not everyone approved of this scheme. Bradford's opposition to railways was led naturally by Samuel Hailstone, who was clerk to the Leeds–Liverpool Canal Company and a member of the Aire–Calder Navigation Company committee. Hailstone was representative of the old landed families and his reaction to railways demonstrates the direct economic clash of new industrial families with men of his own breed. Hailstone's prejudice however seems to have confused all judgement, 'With regard to Rail Roads I hope the public feeling is coming to a more healthy state and that the mania is subsiding. I believe it is the opinion of the most acute and emminent engineers that they never can be made to answer the public purpose or benefit the proprietor'.[68] Hailstone was staggered when Parliament approved 'the pariah of all mischief' the Liverpool–Manchester railway:

> 'Parliament will not suffer old established concerns which have served the country so well for so long a period and where there is such immense capital embarked to be ruined and destroyed by nothing less than a new set of speculators with a new fangled and untried scheme'.[69]

Within three years of this statement a 'new fangled' scheme was proposed for Bradford. By 1827 the Bradford Canal was obsolete and inadequate for a growing industrial town. The three mile journey from Shipley into the Canal Basin, often took vessels three to four days.

Several Leeds industrialists had, since 1824, wanted a Leeds–Selby railway and, when surveyed in 1830, an extension was added to Bradford via Holbeck and Pudsey. The line was to run from its depot in George Street (near Vicar Lane) to Laisterdyke, rising 220 feet in the first mile. It was 'intended to be adapted for the employment of horse as well as steam power; and it is presumed that its adoption will not materially affect or oppose the interests of its neighbouring Canals as it is a fact that more than two-thirds of the whole traffic between Leeds and Bradford is already upon the Turnpike Road'.[70]

It was true that over three hundred people travelled daily between the two towns and most of them were connected with the worsted trade. Consequently, it is little wonder that a large majority of the Bradford men behind the scheme were involved in worsted manufacture. They included the Horsfalls, Margerisons, Rands, Salts, Listers, Woods and Messrs. Riley and Leah of the iron trade. Paley's support is shown in this extract from a letter to Thomas Mason, 'We were all much gratified with the Railroad and I feel convinced that if conveyed with economy will equal if not succeed all canals and public roads....'[71] These men gave their backing to the line which ran through Pudsey, Holbeck and Hunslet and connected with the Selby line at Temple Newsam. By this route, Bradford was linked to the port of Hull. George Stephenson was to be responsible for the engines which ran along it. George Hudson gave the scheme his full support but a powerful opposition emerged, 'a more formidable opposition than we anticipated' wrote millowner Jeremiah Horsfall. This rival group included landowners of large estates like the Marchioness of Hertford and William Aldham of Frickly Hall, who strongly opposed the scheme in order to protect their canal interests. However, Aldham later invested large sums of money in railways and eventually became chairman of the Huddersfield and Manchester Railway. In addition to landowners, the opposition ranks also included Bradford bankers like Becket and Harris and the Bradford vitriol maker, George Leather. Bradford millowners were in favour of the scheme to a man. James Wade argued that foreign merchants, particularly from Hamburg, were frequently visiting the town. The railway would improve the bad communications and inadequate transport facilities that Bradford offered her overseas customers. Wool grown in the south of England 'has been changed to suit the Bradford market' and a speedier supply would have its benefits. James Fison of Thetford, later to move into the Bradford trade, believed that farmers and others in his part of the country were in favour of the railroad for it 'would afford them a cheaper and more expeditious mode of conveyance to Bradford for their produce, particularly wool'.[72] By February of 1831, the proposed bill had the support of county M.P.s Lord Morpeth and Mr. Strickland, but in July a parliamentary committee decided that the preamble of the bill had not been proved.

Bradford was not incorporated into the railway network until 1846 after fourteen unsuccessful attempts by the town's leading merchants and manufacturers to place it in the statute book. The Leeds–Bradford Company (which was absorbed by the Midland Railway in 1841) ran a line from

Bradford via Shipley and the Aire Valley to Wellington Street, Leeds. By that time the respectability of the railway engine was beyond dispute. It was no longer a 'new fangled scheme' and a lot of Bradford capital was poured into the great boom of the 1840s.

Landowners like Spencer-Stanhope, Plumbe-Tempest, Field and Ferrand each invested many thousands of pounds into various companies. The prospering industrialists found the railways a fruitful investment for their surplus capital. Millowners like the Rand brothers invested almost £320,000 in railway stock in the years 1845–6.[73] However, the great age of the railway lies beyond the boundaries of this book. By 1830 Bradfordians were cognisant of the potential of the railway system, its speed, accessibility and ability to relate to upland locations. Railways continued to stimulate industrial and economic growth and were an important agent of change in that period when Bradford became one of the great Victorian cities. The success of Bradford's ironworks at Low Moor and Bowling and the early development of some nascent textile firms stemmed originally from the individual activities of a small number of landowners anxious to play to the full the role of industrial entrepreneur.[74] In order to break out of the confines of the traditional transport network they involved themselves after 1740 in the promotion of turnpike trusts, banks and, most important of all, in the development of a regional canal system. Their efforts richly enhanced the efficiency of the regional economy as a whole, and of Bradford in particular. The West Riding of Yorkshire became one of the most important growth regions of industrial Britain in the nineteenth century. The economic activities of a small group of Bradford land and coal owners in the 1760s went some way in preparing the seedbed of that growth. In the following chapter we shall examine the important role of that small group of entrepreneurs and their influential activities in Bradford's mineral industries.

1. T.C. Barber and C.I. Savage, *An Economic History of Transport in Britain*, (1974) and R.A. Dodgshon and R.A. Butlin, *An Historical Geography of England and Wales*, (1978)
2. J. James, *History of Bradford*, p.1
3. C. Richardson, *Geography of Bradford*, p.47
4. J. Chartres, Road Carrying in England in the Seventeenth Century – Myth or Reality, *Economic History Review*, XXX No.1 (1977) pp.73–94
5. H.J. Dyos, & D.H. Aldcroft; *British Transport* (1974) pp.66–84
6. C. Richardson op. cit. pp.48–50
7. J. James, op. cit., p.87
8. W. Scruton, *Old Bradford* op. cit. p.175 and various trade and town directories
9. W.Y.C.R.O. Bradford–Colne Turnpike trust 1755–1822 Box 50
10. W. Cudworth, *Round About Bradford*, p.132
11. C.T. Barker, The Beginnings of the Canal Age in the British Isles, in L.S. Pressnell, (ed.) *Studies in the Industrial Revolution* (1960) pp.1–22
12. J. Priestley: *A Historical Account of the Navigable rivers, Canals etc.* (1831) rep. (1969) pp.385–97

13. G. Firth, Bradford Coal, Craven Limestone and the origins of the Leeds and Liverpool Canal 1765–1775 in *Journal of Transport History* 4/2 Sept. 1983
14. W. Cudworth, *Round about Bradford* (Bradford, 1886) pp.56–7 and A.L. Green, *Geology of the Yorkshire Coalfield* (1878) pp.658–76
15. B.G. Auty, 'Sir Richard Shireburn's Esholt Ironworks', *Bradford Antiquary*, new series, VIII (1960) 243–57
16. G. Firth, 'The Genesis of the Industrial Revolution in Bradford' unpublished Ph.D. thesis, University of Bradford, 1974, pp.237–67
17. York Minster Library (hereafter Y.M.L.), Hailstone Mss.BB 42.1
18. Y.M.L. Hailstone Mss. HH 5.31 and pp 5
19. H.M.L. Hailstone Mss. BB 42.3
20. W. Cudworth, undated note in Bradford Central Library (hereafter B.C.L.) Miscellaneous Mss. Indenture, 12 January 1775
21. A. Raistrick, *Old Yorkshire Dales* (1967) pp.67–81
22. W.E. Preston, 'Some notes on an old Bradford firm', *Bradford Antiquary*, new series V (1907–11), 312
23. T.C. Barker and C.I. Savage, *An Economic History of Transport in Britain* (1974) pp.20–3
24. Parliamentary Papers, Journal of the House of Commons, 1 February 1744
25. Richardson, op. cit., pp.48–51
26. J. Hustler, *A Summary View of the Proposed Canal from Leeds to Liverpool* (Leeds 1770) p.10
27. B.C.L. Scruton Collection, 16/1/14
28. *York Courant*, 7 August 1764
29. T.C. Barker, 'The Beginnings of the Canal age in the British Isles', in L.S. Pressnell (ed.) *Studies in the Industrial Revolution* (1960), pp.1–22
30. C. Hadfield and G. Biddle, *The Canals of North West England* (Newton Abbot, 1970)
31. R.G. Wilson, 'Three brothers: a Study of the fortunes of a landed family in the mid–eighteenth century', *Bradford Textile Society Journal* (1964–65), 111–22
32. B.C.L. Spencer-Stanhope Ms 2246/65, Walter Stanhope to John Stanhope, 2 July 1765
33. Ibid, 1170, undated letter, John Longbotham to John Stanhope
34. Ibid, 2246, various letters, John Tempest to John Stanhope
35. Public Record Office (hereafter P.R.O.) Minute Book of Leeds Liverpool Canal Company, 9 January 1769, Rail 846/2
36. Ibid, 14 July 1766
37. *Leeds Intelligencer*, 5 August 1766
38. C.T.G. Boucher, *James Brindley, Engineer, 1716–72* (1968) p.68
39. Harris, loc.cit. 161
40. J. Langton, *Geographical Change and Industrial Revolution*, (Cambridge 1979) pp.169–74
41. P.R.O. Leeds & Liverpool Canal, Letter Book, 19 December 1768, Rail 846/2
42. B.C.L., Spencer-Stanhope Ms 1170, John Hustler to John Stanhope, 24 December 1768
43. P.R.O. Leeds & Liverpool Canal Minutes, 24 July 1769, Rail 846/2
44. 10 Geo. III cap. 114: Hadfield and Biddle op. cit.., pp.70–1
45. P.R.O. Leeds & Liverpool Canal Minutes, 19 July and 31 August 1770, Rail 846/2

46. Langton, op. cit. p.170
47. Alphabetical List of the Proprietors of the Leeds–Liverpool canal, 1770, 1789, 1800, B.C.L., Misc. Ms. See also E.M. Sigsworth, 'Bradford on the eve of the Industrial Revolution', *Bradford Textile Society Journal* (1953–54), 61–4, A. Raistrick *Quakers in Science and Industry* (Newton Abbot, 1968) p.78
48. Langton, op. cit., p.224
49. P.R.O. Rail 846/124
50. C. Hadfield & G. Biddle, op. cit.
51. W. Robertshaw, *Historical Links between Bradford & Shipley* (Bradford 1850) and T.R. Roberts, Bradford Waterways, Rise & Fall, *Bradford Textile Society Journal* 1962–3, pp.147–155
52. P.R.O. Canal Co. Minute Book 19 July 1771
53. B.C.L. Ms 6/1 7 September 1774
54. B.C.L. Spencer-Stanhope mss. 1170
55. G. Firth, The Bradford Lime Kiln Company 1774–1800 *Bradford Antiquary* XLVII 1982, pp.129–134
56. J. Priestley op. cit. p.53
59. P.R.O. Rail 826/2
60. B.C.L. Bowling Ironworks Ms 1/11 2 March 1831
61. Rees *Cyclopaedia* (London 1783)
62. W.G. Rimmer, Middleton Colliery Leeds 1770–1830, *Yorkshire Bulletin of Economic and Social Research*, VIII No.1 (1955) pp.41–57 and M.J.T. Lewis, *Early Wooden Railways* (1970) pp.130–31
63. C. Richardson, op. cit. pp.55–7
64. B.C.L. Spencer-Stanhope Ms 2274
65. C. Dodsworth, Recent Uses of Horse Plateways in West Yorkshire, *Industrial Archaeology* 17 No.2, pp.139–140
66. B.C.L. Bowling Ironworks Ms uncatalogued
67. M.J.T. Lewis, op. cit. p.130
68. B.C.L. Spencer-Stanhope Ms 2168 17 April 1824
69. A.M. Stirling, Letter Bag of Lady Elisabeth Spencer-Stanhope, in *Annals of a Yorkshire House*
70. B.C.L. Proposed Bill for Leeds–Selby Railway 1830
71. B.C.L. Bowling Ironworks Ms 5/19 8 October 1830
72. B.C.L. Ms 46/3/1 Petitioners Minute Book 1830/31
73. J.T. Ward, West Riding Landowners and the Railways, *Journal of Transport History* 4, 1960, pp.243–51
74. G. Firth, op. cit. (1983) pp.59–60

5

The Mineral Industries of Bradford

The worsted textile trade upon which Bradford's commercial prosperity and economic reputation were established in the nineteenth century had its origins in the previous century. Yet the initial impetus to large-scale industrial capitalism, towards the end of the eighteenth century, came not from the enterprise of worsted manufacturers but from a small group of individuals eager to exploit the mineral resources and subterranean potential of the Bradford region. It was the proprietors of the lime kilns, ironworks and collieries who were the first to employ capital and labour on a scale hitherto unknown in this area.

It is the purpose of this chapter to examine the origins and development of large scale industrial capitalism in Bradford. The organisational and managerial problems of entrepreneurial activity on this scale will be considered. A management structure had to be evolved which could provide technical, marketing, personnel and accounting skills to meet and overcome such problems. By 1800 a handful of firms, primarily associated with the extraction and working of ores, had been organised on these lines and set relevant precedents for a worsted industry which was, as yet, under-capitalised and under-structured.[1]

The Bradford Lime-Kiln Company

This small business venture pioneered joint-stock industrial capitalism in late eighteenth-century Bradford. It was not a successful essay into that field but it provided long term lessons for several industrial enterprises which followed it. Until the company's formation in 1774, industrial undertakings in Bradford had been limited to the efforts of ambitious and adventurous individuals. It was perhaps the Leeds–Liverpool Canal project, promoted in the 1760s, which whetted the appetites of Bradford's entrepreneurs for joint-stock industrial schemes. The close association of the Bradford colliery owners with the canal scheme from its inception, has already been noted. The provision and beginnings of the local canals coincided with the opening of the Bradford Lime Kiln Company in March 1774.[2]

The use of calcinated limestone for building purposes had been known for many years. In the sixteenth century it was put to a wider use as a fertiliser. The mixing of marl or lime to a light and sandy soil became one of the general improvements of the 'agricultural revolution'. The practice was quickly taken up in local covenants between landowners and tenants. Much of the limestone in Airedale was located around Skipton and Bingley where it was burnt in the rectangular 'pye-kilns' close to the quarries.[3] It has been argued earlier in this book that the local coal and limestone trade was the motivating factor in local canal provision. The lime-kiln company grew out of the Bradford Navigation Company. There were ninety company shares of which sixty two were owned by John Preston, Abraham Balme, William Hardcastle and John Smith, all of whom were coal merchants. Eight hundred pounds was provided by the shareholders in the first year to cover the cost of erecting eight new kilns.[4]

The site of the works was several hundred yards from Broadstones going towards Spink Well Lock and on the western side of the canal (viz Fig.13). The eight kilns were brick-lined and fired by local coal, supplied by Balme, Hustler, Leedes and Leach. By 1777 Thomas Leach of Riddlesden had become the principal supplier of limestone (3,388 tons of the 7,696 tons burnt). In the first five years business was brisk and the limestone consumed increased, from 3,858 tons in 1774 to 11,217 tons in 1778.[5]

Figure 13 Spinkwell Lock, Bradford Canal. This surviving lock of the Bradford Canal can be found close to the junction of King's Road and Canal Road. This was one of ten locks on the six mile stretch of the canal which lifted it 86 feet from Shipley to the summit pound. Close to here was the site of the Bradford Lime Kiln Company. *Photo: Ian Beesley*

Local farmers were good customers as was the Leeds–Liverpool Canal Company and other building contractors. John Hustler noted in the *Leeds Intelligencer* of June 1774, the thriving state of the lime industry on the canal.

> 'On the Yorkshire side we found 18 boats of burthen already built, a number of which have been for some time fully employed between Skipton and Bingley in the lime and coal trade. There are forty lime kilns now erected and preparing between Skipton and Bradford and the business on the line in this article and in coal must be soon very large'.[6]

Burnt lime was sold by the company at ten pence per load and sales increased from 4,621 tons in 1774 to 57,442 tons in 1777 and 46,752 tons two years later.

After five years of profitable trading the company ran into difficulties.[7] The management structure of the company had not been clearly defined. There are no references in the company's records to specific personnel with responsibility. The proprietors made all the decisions relating to trade. As many of them were dealing as individual customers or suppliers to the company, a consistent and uniform policy was out of the question. Bad management may not have been wholly to blame for the company's poor showing after 1780. The building trade had prospered since 1762 (naturally, timber imports rose from £56 million in 1762 to £110 million in 1769) and canal projects had reinforced this trend locally. The colonial war and government loans at an attractive 5½% took capital away from the building sector. Farming too suffered in these years and between them agriculture and building accounted for ninety per cent of the lime industry's market. The Bradford company sold all the limestone that it burnt but the total fell annually after 1779.

Consumption and output fell after 1779 in accordance with national developments. The markets of the company were local and, in both agriculture and building, they were inactive after that date. The Kiln Company showed no enterprise in trading further afield and made no effort to stock for better times. In fact, their approach to trading remained very conservative and showed no element of daring entrepreneurial activity. The company, after only nine years of business, was ready to wind up its affairs by 1783. By July of that year, the coal company of Preston, Hird & Jarratt made it known that they were willing to lease the kilns and pay off some of the company's debts. 'They have also agreed to purchase the whole of the remaining Debts now owing to the Concern for lime, including the Boat "Recovery", for the sum of £80'.[8]

Within twelve months the company owed £509 which was paid off according to the shareholdings. From that time forth, Preston, Hird & Jarratt paid an annual rent of £33. As holders of one third of the shares, their actual rent was only £22. The records of the Bradford Limekiln Company cease at that point.

Preston, Hird & Jarratt like many early entrepreneurs spread their interests across the local economy and had pooled some of their capital and business acumen as early as May 1778 when all three men bound themselves for £1,900 to William Rookes for the purchase of premises in Bradford, which included offices, a warehouse and workshops.[9] Preston and Jarratt were both involved in the local woollen trade and were also investors in a number of coal mining schemes. In the year of their partnership they were supplying the Lime Kiln Company with limestone. All three were considerable shareholders in the Leeds–Liverpool and Bradford Canals.[10] They leased a number of mineral estates at Low Moor and Bankfoot and their take-over of the Lime Kiln Company in 1783 was an obvious development of their widening industrial activities. When the whole company was reorganised in July 1797 Preston, Hird and Jarratt received £640 for their shares.[11] The lime-burning concern eased them into the role of joint industrial entrepreneurs. Its early trading had highlighted problems of internalised supplies, ineffective management, poor distributive organisation and the general inability to maximise capital investment. When the mineral estates of Edward Leedes of Low Moor came onto the market for the third time in September 1789 Preston & Company were ideal candidates for ownership.

The Low Moor Ironworks

This examination of the establishment of the ironworks at Low Moor will be primarily concerned with a consideration of three crucial factors, relevant to the successful foundation of a large scale industrial enterprise. Firstly, the recruitment of skilled staff able to implement the rapidly developing technical and commercial skills of the time. Secondly the need to establish an internal structure of managerial efficiency and finally, the maintenance of financial stability through thoughtful investment and the utilisation of reliable credit facilities.

Hitherto, coal mining in Bradford had been conducted piecemeal and in a small way by individual landowners and their tenants. Outcrops of coal had been worked at Horton, Wibsey and Baildon before 1600, but in the eighteenth century shaft-mining was widespread across the Bradford parish. Local landowners encouraged collieries and occasionally worked their own pits but proved reluctant to invest large amounts of their capital.[12] This accounts for the spasmodic and irregular approach to the industry before 1780. Flooding, short leases, inadequate capital, poor transport facilities and fluctuating economic trends inhibited the enlightened business acumen of local landowners.

Low Moor was part of the ancient manor of Wibsey and of the wapentake of North Bierley. Before 1790, the area was a large expanse of open moorland, two miles north of Bradford, standing on the sloping land adjoining the main highway to Huddersfield. Below the surface of the soil was a three-feet seam of Black Bed Coal which supported a very thick and irregular stratum containing the district's invaluable ironstone. A hundred and twenty feet below, lay the second and most important coal seam, the Better Bed Coal (18–28 inches thick). A further 700 feet down lay the Halifax coal seams and immediately below them, the millstone grit formation.[13]

These were the mineral deposits at Low Moor, but it was not until the last quarter of the eighteenth century that their true value was realised. The coals had been worked for at least three centuries. In Jacobean times the manorial family, the Rookes, had leased mineral rights to colliers and to anyone willing to scratch at the surface for a few house coals. William Rookes was succeeded by his eldest son, Edward, who took the name of Leedes from his first marriage. Leedes' activities in the field of mineral extraction were ambitious.[14]

However, Leedes visualised wider markets, perhaps exports, and as we have already seen by a vigorous investment in several local transport schemes, he hoped to realise the true potential of his land.[16] In his attempts to raise capital he failed, money was scarce as a result of the American war and in August 1781, Edward Leedes was declared bankrupt. His 'plan' had failed. During his bankruptcy he continued to believe in the potential of his lands. He informed James Graham, his attorney in August 1784, 'there is the manor of 500 acres of Common, Ironstone etc. Reversion of the £1,000 p.a. Colliery at the 3rd year and which will bring in £10,000 a year and coal getting 200 years....[14]

His chance was gone; even though his claims were justified, his attorney did not believe them for he accused Leedes of over valuing his estate, 'you make the principal increase of value which you suppose will take place a few years hence upon speculation only'.

The amount of capital required was too great for Leedes alone, and others were to succeed where he failed. A valuation of the Royds Hall estate was made by Jonathan Sharpe who estimated the annual value to be £2,119 6s. 5d and the total capital value at £45,494. Mr. Nathan Jowett, a good friend and neighbour to Leedes who later acted as one of his executors, commented upon this valuation, 'I should suppose this to be a very moderate value put upon the estate and in my own opinion it is worth more, but what the creditors will allow the assignee to take I do not yet know....[15]

The estate 'in toto' was placed under auction in December, 1786 at the Sun Inn, Bradford. Bids failed to meet the required selling price and most men wanted the estate to be distributed in small lots. The sale was withdrawn but ten months after the first auction, the estate was brought under the hammer once more. Again, a reserved price was not met and the lot was withdrawn.[16]

On a journey to North Milford in August 1785, Leedes took his own life. There was some hurry to sell the estate and pay off creditors. Consequently, in the early days of September 1789, the estate was bought by a group of Bradford businessmen for the ridiculously low price of £33,200. The purchase was made by a private agreement and the original partners were John Preston, Richard Hird and John Jarratt. Although Preston was a partner, he died (15 June 1789) before the actual purchase was made. Certainly these three had leased parts of the Low Moor estate previous to the purchase, as well as collieries at Bankfoot. Preston and Jarratt, it has been argued, were experienced and commercially equipped to appropriate the Low Moor estate and develop it accordingly.

Within months of the purchase of Low Moor, the number of partners was increased to six. Buying the land had badly punctured the accumulated funds of Preston & Company. Extracting minerals on a scale large enough to be profitable meant the investment of even more capital into extending the works and equipment which Edward Leedes had used. Into the partnership were brought John Hardy, Reverend Joseph Dawson and the only outsider, John Lofthouse from Liverpool. Hardy was an attorney at law and one of his commissions was to act as land steward to Walter Spencer-Stanhope of Cannon Hall in South Yorkshire.[17] As such, he was also responsible for Stanhope's collieries at Thornton and Horsforth. Hardy himself had invested in the Silkstone coals in South Yorkshire, 'but the bad roads made him part with his purchase there'. He continued to supervise the working of the Silkstone bed and was learning all the time of colliery techniques and management.[18]

In 1784 Hardy played an important part in persuading Prime Minister Pitt not to introduce a duty on coal. He organised colliery owners into a county committee and with the assistance of William Wilberforce M.P. the petition to Pitt was successful.[19] It was such qualities, as well as his cash, which John Hardy brought to the Low Moor Company in 1789. His knowledge of the law and his ability to transform a justified cause into a coherent opposition at county or national level (and in accordance with the law) were qualities invaluable to any nascent firm and industry.

The Reverend Joseph Dawson brought a different kind of talent, that of science and technological skills. Of Nonconformist stock, he was born in 1740 and attended a Dissenting Academy at Daventry where he had met the celebrated Dr. Joseph Priestley of Birstall, and whose friendship he retained until his death. Dawson put in a short appearance at Glasgow University. He returned to his family in Idle, Bradford, where, at the age of twenty nine, he was ordained minister of the Upper Chapel. His salary of forty pounds per annum was obviously not enough for his needs, for, within a short time, he had opened a number of coal mines close to the chapel.[20] Dawson, in combination with others also quarried stone in Idle. The stone was of varying qualities and sizes and was sent along the Leeds–Liverpool Canal.[21] These small industrial beginnings were supported by an active farming of the lands which his living gave him. His spare time was spent in experimentation in general science and Joseph Priestley tutored him in this field.

For some years, Dawson's Arian preachings had antagonised many of Idle's dissenters. His congregation began to dwindle and criticism mounted. Consequently, in 1788, he resigned his ministry and devoted himself to what he liked most, science and business affairs. Although Dawson was not a brilliant scientist, he had a scientific and enquiring mind, for it was he who first spotted the advantages of Better Bed coal as counterpart to Black Bed ironstone. This was the very formula which brought prosperity and success to the company and the one on which a whole new industry in Bradford would be based.[22]

By December 1789, Lofthouse was acting as a sleeping partner within the partnership. John Preston's will carefully stressed the importance of his personal industrial investments:

> I have sunk a very considerable sum of money in certain collieries held by me together with my good friends Richard Hird and John Jarratt...none of the said collieries shall be sold or disposed of for any purpose of this my will because I have great hopes that by continuing the same, the money I have sunk therein will be returned to my estate and because I am confident that no sale could be made thereof without great loss.[23]

Preston's son had not yet reached his majority and the management of the investments may have caused trouble until such time as he came of age. Whatever the reason, Preston's executors went directly against the instructions of his will, by withdrawing his shares and cashing them in. It is perhaps significant that Richard Hird was one of the three executors. With Preston's death, and Jarratt as sleeping partner, the running of the company was left in the hands of Hird, Dawson and Hardy, whose families managed the firm through its difficult early life.

For the fifty years after 1790 the Low Moor Company became the most renowned of all Yorkshire ironworks. The iron industry had made significant progress throughout the eighteenth century. In spite of the successful experiments at Coalbrookdale with the carbonisation of coal into coke, charcoal continued to be the predominant fuel for ironmaking. Professor Ashton went into some detail to explain why this was so.[24] Whatever the reasons, the coking process was not popularised and charcoal remained the standard fuel at most ironworks. For this reason, ironmaking at Low Moor was not carried out on a large scale before 1789. The area was stripped of any forest land and without timber, the smelting process was impossible. By 1775, Watt's power-driven blowing cylinder in the blast furnace, removed that 'impossibility'. Steam was a new source of power for the industry and took it to areas with bountiful supplies of coal. Hence, Low Moor, with little water power, developed automatically as an ideal location for large scale iron production. It was this which Edward Leedes had visualised; this was his 'great plan'!

Following the American war, the iron industry passed through a recessionary period. High metal prices and a decline in demand caused a general depression throughout the trade. The war had boosted output but its sudden end caused an accumulation of products and a fall in the number of buyers. By 1789, when the Low Moor partners founded their company, the industry as a whole was recovering, by seeking new outlets for its products. At the same time, metal prices were slowly finding a more realistic post-war level. Richard Hird and his partners had joined the industry when its fortunes could have gone either way. As it turned out, it was the beginning of the industry's greatest period of growth.

The economic climate was unpredictable but the general condition of the industry augured well for the future. Technical improvements provided greater potential each year. The industry was now fuelled by coal, great supplies of which Bradford possessed. The transport revolution had been at work in the area for some years. When sufficient capital was raised, the partners commenced business.

There was no problem in the choice of their new industrial site. The Common at Low Moor was the most convenient and cheapest site.[25] It was upon the lower stretch of this wasteland that the new ironworks developed (viz Fig.14) When the board of the new company first convened, their major problems were threefold. Firstly, despite Dawson's scientific knowledge, it was necessary to employ a professional agent and engineer immediately. Through him the company could keep abreast of all technological changes. Secondly it was essential, whilst expanding the works, to maintain a very high standard of administrative and technical efficiency. Finally, as most of the partners had relinquished their previous trades and professions, it was imperative that they maintain the financial stability of the company. By analysing the methods which they used to overcome these three problems, we shall see the 'lift-off' period of the ironworks.

Figure 14 Survey of Low Moor Ironworks 1811

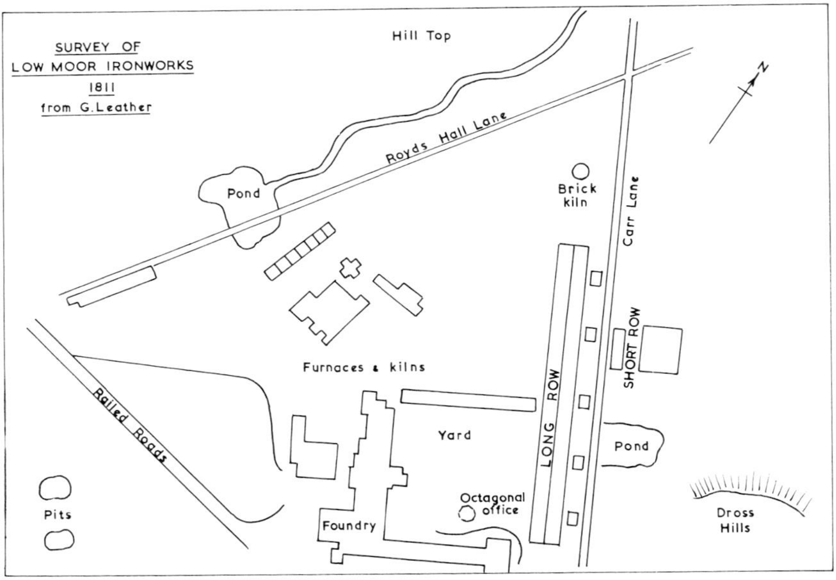

The engineer which the company hired to instal the plant was a Mr. Edward Smalley (at an annual salary of £150, plus house and coals). He was brought from Wigan where he had been employed by several notable industrialists in work on various colliery and engineering projects.[26] Smalley's ability and character we know little about, except for one solitary reference from the pen of

James Watt Jnr. in 1795, 'A very intelligent man and engineer...he is really a very excellent engineer in the old kind, and a very unreserved and honest man and above a mean action I have every reason to believe.'[27]

Watt's praise was confirmed by results, for within two years, Smalley had erected the blast engines and furnaces on an area of marshland, Black Syke, south of Wibsey Moor. The engine was designed by Smalley, but constructed on the Boulton and Watt principle. In fact, the atmospheric engine which Smalley installed had an open top cylinder of five feet diameter at one end and a single blowing cast-iron cylinder of 101 inches diameter at the other end. The stroke in each case being 114 inches. The blowing engine itself was built by a small local firm, Messrs. Emmetts of Birkenshaw.[28] The foundations of the furnaces were being dug whilst the blowing engine was being built. This work had begun at Christmas 1789 under Smalley's supervision. The construction of the furnaces was left to a specialist who was to be chosen by Smalley. Naturally, he chose a man with whose work he was familiar and at the beginning of 1790 brought Thomas Woodcock from Wigan. Woodcock was already engaged in building two similar furnaces at the Haigh Ironworks where the Earl of Balcarres and his brother Robert Lindsay had recently formed a company with James Corbett, a local iron-founder.[29] Fortunately for the Bradford firm Corbett's management of the Haigh Ironworks, 'had been conducted with great want of economy and that they had cost a much more considerable sum than they ought to have done'. Output ceased, workmen left and the works temporarily stopped. Doubtless, Woodcock was relieved to hear of an offer of fresh employment from his friend Edward Smalley.[30]

Woodcock was born at Chapeltown near Sheffield in 1755 and was reared within the Sheffield iron industry. He was a fully qualified engineer and a recognised specialist in his field. He probably had good cause to move across the Pennines for his father was employed as foreman moulder at the Birkenshaw works.[31] The two furnaces which he put up were stone built, square and fifty feet high. They were hand fed from the top. The ironstone was brought by baskets or wheeled corves to a platform, level with the furnace top. Woodcock's plan of the furnaces included a casting house and a row of stone kilns for calcining the ironstone. The foundry was probably first opened in 1791. Smalley ordered a modification of Woodcock's plan by installing a moving overhead crane which efficiently carried the heavy castings around the foundry.

Both Smalley and Woodcock were offered permanent contracts and remunerative salaries. Smalley was certainly still with the company in 1803 in the capacity of chief consulting engineer to the works.[32] Woodcock had been described as 'architect and general manager to the Company'. He retained that position (with special responsibility for the furnaces) until his death in 1833. On 13 August 1791, the two blast furnaces which Woodcock erected were blown by Smalley's engine and three days later the Low Moor Iron Company's first casting was made.

Between them, these two men had brought to the company the high degree of technical knowledge which such a new project required. They were responsible for the consolidation of strength which the company attained in its early years. By keeping up with new processes and equipment, they made sure the fixed capital, at Low Moor was refreshed and that the technological revolution did not pass the works by. The fixed capital assets were first recorded in the stock book in October 1795, as the following:

> By the Casting Houses, Bridge Loft, Boring Mill, Workshops in the Yard: on the Common, 2 Fire Engines, 4 Air Furnaces, Two Cupolas: 8 Cranes all used for carrying on the works in their present state.[33] £22,030

In subsequent years several important additions were made; a new engine, waterhouse and ironstone kilns were added in 1800 at a cost of £8,000. A further £3,000 was spent the next year on a steam engine and engine house for the new forge. Depreciation in 1802 was not taken into account as the Company suffered a bad fire. Nevertheless, another thousand pounds was invested in a steam engine for the blast furnace. By 1800 the advantages of wrought iron were great, owing to the introduction of Cort's puddling and rolling process. Smalley, using charcoal fires, had produced wrought iron and profited from it. However, by 1803, the partners had provided £6,000 for a new forge and rolling mill, to accommodate Cort's process. The refinery was fired in 1803 and produced the first puddled iron in that year. Refined pig iron was passed to the puddling furnace where it was reheated, stirred and sifted; then sent through rollers. Government armament contracts during the French Wars helped to create surplus capital for such new investments. Cannon and shot required special techniques and cannon production required a very accurate boring rod. Ordinary cast iron cutting tools which the company made themselves, were not hard or accurate enough for the job. Consequently, the partners decided to purchase cast steel from the Sheffield and Rotherham area. This worked perfectly!

Whilst dealing with the techniques involved in the processes of iron making, one must not forget the working of the raw materials involved. The company extended the pits of Edward Leedes and added a new one of their own, (value £1,000).[34] Leases were made and work began immediately in 1789, in the digging of both coal and ironstone. The partners negotiated contracts directly with individual colliers and tried to avoid group contracting or sub-contracting. These men worked the seams by 'Bord and Pillar' (which was often wasteful) or occasionally by the Longwall method. The secret of the top quality iron produced at Low Moor lay in the complementary qualities of the minerals which these men were working. The Better Bed Coal according to Mr. George in 1836 'makes an excellent coke which from the absence of sulphur and earthy matter is peculiarly suitable for making of iron'.[35] It was the exceptional purity of the coal which contributed to the quality of the finished product, for the iron ore was of only average quality. South Staffordshire had ores of similar richness and free from sulphur. Both veins of ironstone, White and Black, were worked.

Table XXI Analysis of Ironstone at Low Moor

	White %	*Black* %
Oxide of Iron	36.58	36.75
Oxide of Mencanese	0.94	1.38
Lime	2.22	2.05
Magnesia	0.80	0.52
Carbonic Acid	0.43	0.34
Iron Pyrite	1.85	1.77
Bituminous Matter	0.25	2.40

Source: E. George, *On the Yorkshire Coalfield* (1836) p.19

For a speedier transportation of these minerals from the pit heads (widespread across the moor), a system of railed roads was built. At first, this was a network of wooden rails along which trucks were horse-drawn. The partners made a necessary modification to this system by casting their own iron rails and at a later date by developing the network all the way to their coal staith alongside the wharves of the Bradford Canal in the centre of the town.[36] Technological progress also occurred in the mining process. At most of the company's collieries, the minerals were drawn up by a horse gin. By the end of 1796, the demand for coal and coke from local ironworks necessitated a complete restructuring of mining operations.

The second problem which faced Dawson, Hardy and Hird in pioneering a new industrial enterprise, was administrative and technical efficiency. This was largely the responsibility of the partners themselves. They could not buy it, as they could the skills of Edward Smalley. The initiative had to come entirely from themselves. We might look now at the lead given by two of them, John Hardy and Joseph Dawson. In September 1794, Richard Hird died and was succeeded in the business by his son-in-law, the Reverend Lamplugh-Wickham who became, for all intents and purposes, a sleeping partner. The active partners were Hardy and Dawson.[37] The former naturally handled the legal side of the business and by his involvement in national issues did much to promote the reputation of the firm. Part of William Pitt's economic reforms of 1797 was to propose a tax on iron. Meetings of the Ironfounders were held all over the country to defend themselves against this imposition.[38] In late October of that year, Joseph Dawson received a letter from James Watt,

> 'Dear Sir,
> We have lately seen a letter from a very respectable member of Parliament saying that he "is informed by good authority that Mr. Pitt proposes to lay a tax upon Pig Iron at the furnace and to accompany it with a proportionate addition to the duty upon foreign iron."

The bad consequences of such a tax are obvious as well as those to be proposed on coal. They ought to be opposed and we think that the opinions of those concerned will have more weight if given to Mr. Pitt before he brings the subject before the House, than they will have after. M.P.s should therefore be requested to wait upon Mr. Pitt to know his intention and to use arguments against these taxes'.[39]

The consequence was a meeting of the West Riding ironfounders at the White Hart Inn, Wakefield on 13 November 1797. Of the thirteen ironfounders present, five were from Bradford; Dawson and Hardy of Low Moor, Sturges of Bowling, Aydon of the Shelf Ironworks and Emmott from Birkenshaw. Several resolutions were passed.[40] Hardy and Joshua Walker of Rotherham were requested to go to London as deputies of the meeting. In fact, Dawson also went to the metropolis, although he did not attend the interview with the premier on 22 November 1797.[41]

No progress was made and, therefore, Hardy was once again summoned to London. He attended several ministerial meetings but finally Pitt refused the entreaties and Parliament passed the proposal. Hardy, by his contribution to the opposition movement had conveniently 'flown the flag', for the company. Dawson brought about a similar effect but in a different way.[42]

After 1790 Dawson had moved into Royds Hall, Low Moor, and, unlike Hardy, spent much of his time at the works. He was fully acquainted with the plant and how it functioned. He thought that the meeting of the ironfounders in 1797 had been beneficial to the trade, and, not wishing that the meetings should terminate, he was instrumental in the formation of the Friendly Association of Yorkshire Ironfounders at Sheffield in August 1799.[43] At the meeting which he chaired, Dawson suggested that mutual problems could be discussed along with new techniques and ideas for analysis and research. He did not overstate the technological revolution.

'Individuals have done much in the making and manufacturing of iron in the last sixty years and yet the subject is very far from being exhausted. Perhaps it may be said with truth that we have no complete knowledge of any one operation; and consequently in the whole we may be said in some measure to grope in the dark.'[44]

Dawson's proposals were enthusiastically approved. Future meetings were arranged and he was unanimously elected President. In June of the following year he gave the first lecture on the effects of air and moisture on blast furnaces.

The results of his initiative in the field of technology were as beneficial to the company as were Hardy's. He gained the respect and goodwill of his colleagues in the trade and created a reputation for the company as a forward-looking and progressive enterprise. Yet his ideas were not all on paper. Technical efficiency was not only given to the company by its salaried officers. Dawson carried out his own experiments at the works (often in consultation with Joseph Priestley). Dawson had noticed in 1792 that the furnaces, in the summer months, never worked as effectively as they should. Consequently, in the following year he began to experiment by cooling the air. He increased the air pressure to 2½lb. per inch and this meant that the rate of condensation was greater than the varification of air by the sun's heat, 'The engine worked well and for 5 or 6 days lifted up the valve. The furnaces ran faster but the metal was not at all improved.'[45]

He realised that, in summer, there was a lack of oxygen in the air, but this could be supplied by steam. Knowing that the water in the coke would lead to an immediate release of the steam via the furnace top, he added a boiler, hoping that some of it might remain and revive the air within the furnace. This trial was attended with some success.

In addition to his experiments on the scientific side of the business, Dawson was also responsible for the general day to day running of the firm. He had an octagonal office built in 1791 in the very centre of the works. There, he could be consulted by his departmental managers. He had a carefully planned work force, delegating responsibility to each man down to the foreman moulder or collier ganger. As early as 1795, James Watt jnr., on a visit to Low Moor, could say this of the works, 'He (Smalley) showed us through the whole works which are very extensive and systematic. Better forged work I never saw nor better castings.'[46] Systematic was indeed the right word and it had been achieved essentially by the partners, Dawson in particular.

The final problem which the partners faced in the early years of their enterprise, was sustaining the financial stability which was essential to any firm at this embryonic stage.[47] Having made the initial purchase of the Low Moor estate with its collieries, farms and manor hall, it was now necessary for the partners to supply cash for the construction of an ironworks with its furnaces, engines, workshops and cranes. In the first year of construction the partners advanced the following sums; Hird = £5,000; Jarratt = £4,632; Dawson = £3,355; Hardy = £3,770. During the next four years a further £42,049 was provided by these four for the general construction of the ironworks.[48] Although in operation since August 1791, the works continued to be improved by various specialist machinery. However, in the years 1795–6 little capital was advanced. A further £14,000 was added in 1797 but in the following year nothing was supplied. Almost £6,000 was advanced in 1801 and this was probably used to finance the new puddling and rolling department of the works. After that year no further capital was introduced by the partners into the business, although interest was collected by them on their original capital investments as late as 1804.[49]

Table XXII Interest on capital at Low Moor Ironworks 1790–1804

	£		£		£
1790/93	4,208	1797	5,267	1801	7,216
1794	2,586	1798	5,886	1802	8,106
1795	3,228	1799	7,687	1803	8,962
1796	5,256	1800	6,880	1804	9,899

Source: *B.C.L. Misc Mss C33*

With the re-investment of such large sums of money, the balance of the annual capital stock naturally soared. The first balance sheet taken at Low Moor on 24 October 1795, has been summarised below in contemporary terms.

Table XXIII General Account of Low Moor Iron Company 1794–1795

		£	£
Fixed Assets			
Casting House, Bridge Loft, Boring Mill Workshops, 2 fire engines, 4 air furnaces 2 cuppolas and 8 cranes			22,030
Repairs and additions since 11.8.94		2,305	
			24,335
Current Assets			
Stock in Trade			£20,891
Debtors		£25,586	
		46,477	
		70,822	
Less	Current Liabilities		
	Creditors		3,102
Net Assets			£67,720
Representing:			
Capital Employed			£
Mr. Jarratt, Mr. Dawson, Mr. Hardy			13,108
Mr. Hird			13,181
Mr. Jarratt			13,811
Mr. Dawson			13,810
Mr. Hardy			13,810
			£67,720

Source: *As in Table XXII*

The stock balance rose meteorically from £53,337 in 1797 to £162,846 in 1800.

These figures could not have been sustained without the company carrying on good trade. The markets and customers which they used will be examined shortly, but from the demand for all kinds of iron goods, came the accumulation of vast profits. Such a thriving state of affairs enabled the partners to withdraw capital from the company as early as 1798, in addition to the interest received on their original investments. The profits of the Low Moor Company, a nascent firm, compare favourably with those of a more established company like that of the Carron Ironworks in Scotland. From 1790 to 1793, £14,258 profit was made at Low Moor before interest on capital which was £4,208 for those three years. This represents a 27.3 per cent return on their capital employed at that time, i.e. annual average of 9.1 per cent. This compares with the Carron Company where their annual profit for 1793 was £25,915 or 9.6 per cent return on their assets.[50] Figures for subsequent years are tabulated below (Table XXIV).

Table XXIV Profit and Return of Low Moor Ironworks 1794–1800
(Carron Company figures in brackets)

Year ended	*Capital Employed (book value)* £	*Profit (before Interest on Capital)* £	£	*Return on Capital Employed* %	%
1794	48,114	11,805	(33,772)	17.3	(14.0)
1795	77,698	9,249	(25,199)	11.9	(9.5)
1796	93,138	15,440	(20,053)	16.6	(7.4)
1797	123,349	16,278	(20,905)	13.2	(8.4)
1798	133,796	15,458	(16,266)	11.5	(6.2)
1799	137,602	18,078	(14,913)	13.2	(5.5)
1800	142,431	15,828	(12,873)	11.2	(4.4)

Source: *B.C.L. Miscallaneous Ms C33 Account Books 1790–1804*

Thus, trade was flourishing on such a scale that capital assets could be renewed and increased from profits alone. There were no further capital advances after 1801 and in 1798, capital was already being withdrawn into private accounts. This was a trend which continued, for by 1800, a sum of £30,284 had been withdrawn. Such confidence bears testimony to the early consolidation of the company and to the prosperous state of its trading in the first decade.

One important matter contributed to this state of affairs, the Low Moor Company was fortunate that the international situation was in its favour at the time of the company's inception. To most trades, peace was a prerequisite of prosperity. For the iron industry, war was the greatest stimulant to output and production. With the blast furnace at Low Moor in operation only eighteen months, the wars with France broke out and continued for almost a quarter of a century. The Navy created a consistent demand for armaments and the Low Moor Company were fortunate enough to have captured such a government contract by 1795. Two boring rods were installed for cannon and the furnaces were working continuously. James Watt observed in September 1795, 'I saw no bored guns except cannon of which they make great quantities for governments. They have two furnaces making about 60 tons of pig per week'.[51] This busy state of affairs continued and was consolidated by the rising price of foreign iron. Britain's clash with Russia caused high import duties on Russian iron-stone. For those ironfounders without their own supplies, this raised their costs substantially (1795 = £13–15 per ton, 1801 = £23–26 per ton).[52] This forced up iron prices on the domestic market, for supply fell short of the growing consumption of iron goods. Business was more than brisk at Low Moor. From the output figures one can presume that Dawson and his partners obtained new contracts and clients and found fresh markets. The order books were full and output was at a maximum by 1797.

Bowling Ironworks were experiencing a similar prosperity although their output tended to be lower. Their combined expansion caused one Bradford

Table XXV Tonnage Output of Pig Iron at Low Moor 1792–1797

	Tons
Metals made in 1792	1,764.5
Metals made in 1793	2,196.5
Metals made in 1794	2,152.5
Metals made in 1795	2,537.75
Metals made in 1796	2,177.5
	(+200)
Metals made in 1797	2,658.75
Total	13,487.5
Annual average = 2,248 tons	

Source: *Y.M.L. Hailstone Ms Box 5.16*

worthy to remark in June 1797, 'that Messrs. Sturges, Dawson & Co. have at this time, near £30,000 due to them from government'.[53] With revenue on this scale there can be little reason to doubt the tremendous increase in the profits made by the firm, they leapt from £9,249 in 1795 to £26,408 six years later, when almost £6,000 was added to the fixed capital employed in the business.

Much of the work came from government armament contracts but the domestic demand remained high. By 1799, Low Moor produced a greater diversity of goods than ever before. High on the list were cylinders of several sizes and various other requisites for steam engines.[54] The construction of such parts brought the company unwittingly to an infringement of Boulton & Watt's patent rights. In 1795 George Hawks of Gateshead placed a rush order with the firm for a cylinder and air pump. They promised to complete the order, for they were already making one for Matthew Murray of Leeds, who, they understood, had the rights. James Watt jnr. heard of this violation and interviewed Smalley about the matter. The latter's plea of ignorance convinced Watt that the company was not intentionally breaking the patent (as was the case at Bowling Ironworks). He left the works on good terms but not before Smalley had tried to get more business from him![55]

In addition to steam engine parts the company introduced a new line of metal goods for the newly industrialised textile trade. A popular item on the company's price list was the rail for iron waggon roads which cost 74/- per cwt. This list reflects the growth and expansion of the Company in its first decade. Another indication of the company's expansion was the erection of an automatic ironstone feeder. Previously the minerals had been fed into the furnace by hand. If output was to be kept at maximum, operations of this kind had to be automated in order to save time. A water wheel was built which drove a chain pulley. This hauled the tubs of ironstone to the top of the furnace where they were tilted and a disconnected clutch system reverted them. The truck returned to the bottom to be filled again. Consequently the Low Moor Ironworks had consolidated its position as one of the principal iron producing centres in the North in its first decade. One must not overestimate the achievement of the company nor forget the existence of others. A comparative table taken from an enquiry of 1796 may keep a proper perspective.

Table XXVI Output of Selected Ironworks 1796

Firm	*No. Furnaces*	*Excise (tons)*	*Supposed (tons)*	*Exact (tons)*
Coalbrookdale	3	7,175	4,162	2,659.5
Cyfartha	3	6,000	6,000	7,204
Carron	4	5,200	5,206	5,616
Low Moor	2	2,000	2,000	2,500

Source: *Y.M.L. Hailstone Mss. Box 6.12*

Nevertheless, the company had taken full advantage of the expansion in the iron trade, resulting from the war. In so doing, the proprietors were able to successfully circumvent the early difficulties which faced the nascent firm. The skill of its employees, the efficacy of its owners and a wise financial policy, all laid the foundations for the stimulus to growth which the French wars brought.

By 1810 there had been considerable accretion of land to the original purchase of the Royds Hall estate. A map surveyed by George Leather in 1811 demonstrates the acquisition of land around Rooley Hall, adjoining the Bowling estates.[56] To the south of this lay Odsal Moor, also in the company's possession. The works were located at the apex of two roads, Carr Lane and Royds Hall Lane (viz Fig.14). The rectangular layout of the plant faced south. The eastern boundary of the works ran parallel to Carr Lane and there were two rows of terraced cottages, Long Row and Short Row, for the workforce. Long Row flanked a large rectangular yard in which stood the octagonal office of Joseph Dawson. Running into this yard was a railed road which came from the west side of the works. On that western side were the four furnaces and coke kilns fed by looped railed-roads which came from Wibsey Slack or from the staith in the centre of Bradford.[57] The kilns or 'beehive ovens' for converting coal to coke were conical shaped and usually lined with firebricks. Between the cottages and the furnaces were the forge buildings and casting house. Finally, on the west side of Royds Hall Lane was a large reservoir lined with flagstones and mortared with cement.

The expansion of the works in its first quarter of a century obviously had repercussions on the development of the surrounding area. The terraced cottages of Long Row and Short Row were some of the earliest houses to be erected for the new ironworkers.[58] These houses, costing £4320, adjoined the works and meant a punctual and reliable work force. As the company expanded so did its labour force and cottages sprang up throughout North Bierley. They were usually small single-storey dwellings with long tall chimney stacks which burnt the coal given to the workers by the firm. The once deserted moorland yielded its rural charm to the housing of an industrial work force. Local landowners sold their lands to builders who erected upon each plot as many houses as they could, 'huddled into line or shouldered each other into corners with a delightful contempt of regularity.[59] Whole estates disappeared in this way, including Hill Top and Fiddler Hill Farm in order to meet the needs of an expanding industrial enterprise (viz Table XXVII).

Table XXVII Inhabitants of North Bierley and their Occupational Status 1801–1831

	Houses	*People*	*In Farming*	*In Trade*
1801	743	3820	70	390
1811	769	4766	40*	106*
1821	1156	6070	110*	1054*
1831	1393	7254	81*	1458*

*In families

Source: *W.Y.C.R.O. Census Enumeration Extracts 1801–31*

Many of these people came from other neighbourhoods but some came from as far away as Cornwall. Life, for this early industrial community, was hard. There were few occasions like Carr Lane Tide which celebrated annually the first casting of 16 August 1791. There were many accidents and conditions were shameful.

> 'Lads were drafted off to the pits at such tender years that it was no uncommon sight to see mothers (who also worked at the pit bank) carrying young lads of 6 or 7 years old on their back to work. The hours were then from 7 to 6 o'clock, with an hour's stoppage for dinner, and for this long stretch, day after day, a hurrier received 1/6 or 2/- a week and a man's wages for getting coal were only 15/- for a full week'.[60]

In the mines, there was little thought or capital given to ventilation, drainage or lighting. Nor were there any wheeled corves. In spite of these shortcomings, Dawson did concern himself with the welfare of his workers and in 1794, a boarding house was opened for young collier lads from Hunslet and Leeds. There, they received food, clothing and a simple education, all at the company's expense. By 1814 these educational facilities were inadequate for the large working-class community at Low Moor. In that year, the Hardy family subsidised a new school, designed to accommodate over a hundred children and costing £762.[61] Although it was extended in Victorian times, this school still stands today. Social investment of this kind was important to the well-being of the firm. Equally, reinvestment into the fixed capital of the company and up-dating of the plant were essential if the firm was to meet the demands of a vital and quickly changing industry. Consequently the early capital investment was consolidated in the new century. In 1801 a forge costing £3,000 was opened in order to make wrought iron, and a slitting mill for nail rods was added alongside. By 1805 large hammers had been installed in the forge, driven alternately by a low-pressure reversing condensing engine. In the same year as the Wibsey estate of George Leather was purchased for £3,900, the company laid out capital for three new limestone kilns and twenty four ironstone kilns with adjoining gangways to the stacks. The waterwheels and pumps for each of the four furnaces were in constant need of repair.[62]

Not all of their reinvestments and capital outlay proved successful. The increasing demand for coal compelled the company to acquire numerous sources of supply, including the Silkstone coals in South Yorkshire from Walter Spencer-Stanhope. By 1805 the company had invested almost £46,000 in the Silkstone Colliery and in spite of several concessions by the owner they were unable to profit from it. By November of that year Dawson was ready to surrender his interest in the colliery.[63] He and Jarratt visited Spencer-Stanhope (John Hardy had died several months earlier) to insist on 'greater indulgences' and more favourable transport rates on the Barnsley Canal. Matters did not improve, and in March 1807 Dawson decided to stop work in the lower seam at Silkstone,

> 'We have been settling our stock account at the Silkstone Colliery and I am sorry to tell you that without reckoning one farthing for the interest of our large capital employed in it, we have actually lost by the last year's trade not less than £3659 18s...[64]

The company were reluctant to run the colliery through an agent and consequently were forced to rescind the agreement in July 1807. By September the engine had been stripped and the railroad network taken up. Silkstone Colliery had proved an expensive and worthless investment.[65]

In spite of this particular setback the company's capital investment programme was impressive and during the war years the total stock balance expanded from £167,649 in 1802 to £288,312 in 1815.[66]

The company built on these substantial foundations in the early decades of the nineteenth century, aided by armament contracts for wars overseas and colonial growth.

The figures in Table XXVIII are taken from the company's accounts and adequately illustrate the prosperity experienced by the partners in the second and third decades. With the exception of 1808 healthy profits were obtained in return for the company's investment. With regard to profits the company policy seems to have resembled that of other ironworks whereby the partners received a fixed interest of five per cent on their capital which was credited to their private accounts, and the surplus was divided into four shares.[67] By allowing profits to accumulate in the firm the capital was enlarged automatically.

These successful accounts occurred as a result of the favourable trading climate and in particular, the continuation of the European wars. The company continued to fulfil its government contracts for armaments. Yorkshire ironmasters were working twenty two of their twenty six furnaces in 1806, producing an average of 1,275 tons of pig iron per year. At Low Moor all four furnaces were in operation and produced 5,143 tons in that year.[68] By 1814 the works had increased the output of pig iron to 6,868 tons, an increasing proportion of which was exported. However, the countries to which Britain

Table XXVIII Profit and Loss Account of Low Moor Ironworks Company 1801–1816

Year	*Capital Employed (Book Value) £*	*Capital Withdrawn £*	*Profit before Interest £*	*Return on Capital Employed %*
1801	173,604	1046*	26408	15.2
1802	185,456	8495	20347	11.0
1803	195,658	1109	11311	5.8
1804	210,917	–	14650	6.9
1805	210,568	11122+	10568	5.1
1806	218,236	10568	18236	8.4
1807	211,860	18236	11860	6.0
1808	205,552	11860	5552	2.7
1809	215,655	9552	19655	9.1
1810	222,290	11655	18290	8.2
1811	224,430	18290	17430	7.8
1812	222,000	17430	18000	8.2
1813	220,200	18000	16200	7.4
1814	227,200	16200	23200	10.2
1815	239,200	11200	23200	9.7
1816	243,200	11200	16000	6.6

*£5811 introduced as capital; + £205 introduced as capital

Sources: *B.C.L. Misc Mss C33*

was supplying her iron goods were beginning to manufacture ironware for themselves and also to compete in international markets.

> 'The making of iron and iron wares is rapidly increasing in the U.S.A. and has been doubled within the last ten years. There are furnaces, forges and foundries, established in many of the different states which are carried on with great encouragement and success. Iron ore is found in the greatest plenty and American bar iron is much stouter than English, being made from charcoal pig iron'.[69]

Even more important, countries like France, Germany and Russia were able to compete at lower prices because of cheaper costs. They paid for their labour at half the British wage rate and had plentiful supplies of charcoal. For these reasons Dawson and Hardy strongly opposed the proposal to impose export duties on British iron goods which would have increased the cost of British iron at the very time when it needed to be at its most competitive. Dawson argued, through the Iron Masters' Association, that the government stood to gain a quarter of a million pounds from the tax but would lose for the British iron trade a large slice of the three million pounds of exports. The ironmasters won the day and exports continued to grow. However, it is important to emphasise that the principal market for the English iron industry at this time was England and her own domestic needs. Collectively the production of ordnance and of iron for structural purposes at home and abroad carried the iron industry along a continued path of prosperity in these years.

The resumption of peace in 1815 marked a new age for English ironmakers,

> 'War conditions resulted in a rapidity of development that was far from healthy.... Just as the war of 1793–1815 had been most effective in energising the ironmakers so it resulted in poverty and disorganisation more intense that that which had followed the earlier struggles and more lasting than that which fell upon other British industries in the post-war years'.[70]

Prices slumped in spite of attempts by the Ironmasters' Association to fix them and this had a catastrophic effect on several of the smaller works. At Low Moor the company was not affected until 1819 when iron prices plummeted by thirty shillings per ton in all grades. Profits at Low Moor fell from £34,500 in 1819 to a £2,440 deficit in 1823 (viz Table XXIX). This first major set back for the company was handled by a new set of partners. Dawson, who had died in 1813, was succeeded by his son Christopher who remained at the works until his death in 1865. John Hardy had passed on his interest to his son of the same name. This gentleman achieved fame in several fields, one of them as Bradford's first Member of Parliament. Never a manager himself, his son Charles was to play an active part in the management of the firm.[71] Richard Hird's daughter had married Reverend Lamplugh-Wickham and their son, Henry, took up his father's responsibilities at the works. In 1814 John Jarratt had also left the company.[72] In addition, Mr. Hardaker replaced Edward Smalley who had probably formed his own business in Bolton as early as 1805.

As smaller firms went under, Low Moor continued to blast in all four furnaces and in 1823 produced 6,200 tons of pig iron. Of the 27,311 tons of pig iron made in Yorkshire in that year, twenty three per cent was produced at Low Moor. There was a temporary recovery in the trade in 1824–5 but the company was unable to cash in immediately on the sudden improved state of trade, as they had run down their stock to only one hundred pigs of iron. Consequently, their own four furnaces were in blast continuously and were producing 180 tons of pig iron each week in 1825. Thomas Butler of Kirkstall Forge confirmed the sudden surge of activity at Low Moor in that year, 'The furnaces of Low Moor and Shelf worked in conjunction. They have a large contract for shot for the East India Company. 4 Air Furnaces going daily are making a quantity of 20 tons per day of 18 and 24 pounds and are as busy as bees in a hive....'[73]

However, only four puddling furnaces were in use and consequently their bar iron trade and stock was negligible. The casting shop was also underworked, but the steam engine department was kept busy meeting the demands of the local textile mills, as well as meeting a Caribbean demand for engines for sugar mills. The engines produced at Low Moor were of different sizes and powers, 'but of the most approved construction and of the best material'.

The year 1825 brought the company its best ever profit of £42,493 and transformed the stock balance from £289,922 to £355,122. Another healthy profit margin followed in 1826 but subsequent years were indifferent.

Table XXIX Profit and Loss Account of Low Moor Ironworks Company 1817–1835

Year Ended	*Capital Employed (book value)* (£)	*Capital Withdrawn* (£)	*Profit before Interest* (£)	*Return on Capital Employed* (%)	*Stock Balance* (£)
1817	243,000	16,000	14,000	5.8	293,169
1818	241,200	14,000	22,800	9.5	299,357
1819/20	250,000	22,800	34,500	13.8	287,394
1821	261,700	34,500	6,480	2.5	283,484
1822	233,676	6,480	4,828	2.0	272,150
1823	232,024	4,828	-2,440	-1.0	279,154
1824	224,760	–	9,176	4.1	289,922
1825	233,932	9,176	42,492	18.1	355,121
1826	267,252	42,492	25,152	9.4	334,553
1827	249,912	25,152	-4,832	-1.9	321,325
1828	219,924	–	-11,320	-5.1	315,858
1829	208,600	–	9,228	4.4	315,407
1830	217,832	9,228	10,672	4.9	305,426
1831	219,276	10,672	17,272	7.9	309,509
1832	225,876	17,272	18,068	8.0	304,968
1833	226,672	18,068	25,120	11.0	310,698
1834	233,724	25,120	23,600	10.0	333,971
1835	232,204	16,000	32,335	13.9	352,483

– = deficit

Source: *As in Table XXVIII*

After an earlier amalgamation the company finally bought out the Shelf Ironworks in 1827 for £4,452. They promptly lost their last munition contract to the Bowling Ironworks which was considered 'a great injury...and disappointment' to the firm. Throughout that year iron prices slumped and business continued slack. There were internal management conflicts in 1827 which hindered progress, 'several unpleasant occurrences have taken place as regarding our partnership...which have had a tendency to disturb our engagements....'[74]

The stock in hand had reached an enormous 5,500 tons and all four blast furnaces were still in operation. By 1828 Hardy attended a meeting of the Ironmasters, 'crammed and stuffed on the occasion, prepared with calculations to show that the price of pigs was at its lowest ebb and that the making of bar iron was more work than which to push, on account of the consumption of coal'.[75]

His calculations and reasoning persuaded his colleagues to lower the trade price of bar iron by two pounds per ton. Unfortunately it failed to increase the sales of the product at Low Moor. In consequence, two of the furnaces were allowed to go out in the following year and the company would 'not put them in again until some change takes place for the better in trade'.[76]

For the furnaces to be put out, the situation had to be grave. And so it was, for in the years 1827–28, the company made respective annual losses of £4,835 and £11,320. The slump affected all sides of their trade, 'Owing to the great reduction in the value of iron, the stock of Goods and Implements has been taken this year at a lower rate than last. The difference amounts to £9504/18/8'.[77]

There was some recovery of trade in 1829–30 as the company developed its production of iron rails for new railway companies. As early as 1824 the following advertisement appeared in the *Bradford Courier*, from the Liverpool–Manchester Railway Company:

> 'for tenders on 400 waggon wheels and 200 axles. This may be noticed as the 1st commencement of a demand for iron in a new mode of transit on the late general introduction and future extent of which it is impossible to calculate...'[78]

The company had already provided the iron rails for its own intricate railway system, and in 1826 the Prussian engineers Von Deynhausen and Von Decken visited Low Moor and noted with approval the rails made there.[79] The acquisition of early railway contracts was directly attributable to the company's recovery in those years which are beyond the bounds of this book. By 1832 the fluctuations of the 1820s were forgotten as the company continued to develop its capital investment and production improvements, 'The premises... are now being enlarged both as to new buildings, engines, furnaces in a proportion not less than as two to three',[80] so that by 1835 the fixed capital assets at Low Moor had increased thus,

Table XXX Fixed Capital Assets of Low Moor Ironworks Company 1795–1835

	Estates £	*Fixed Capital £ (buildings)*	*Stock & Utensils*
1795	23,086	22,030	20,890
1800	28,405	30,300	35,290
1805	39,578	46,700	66,972
1810	65,975	42,000	67,511
1815	64,789	38,000	91,072
1820	80,837	32,500	55,507
1825	84,774	29,000	132,184
1830	100,965	23,000	104,520
1835	108,464	47,173	138,770

Source: *As in Table XXIV*

The Low Moor Ironworks, in 1835 were ready for a new era in iron production as they prepared the ground at New Biggin for what was to become the New Works. By 1836 there were two new blast-furnaces and a casting-hearth, making a total of six new furnaces (including three at Shelf). The company was gearing itself, financially and technologically, for another great age of civil engineering just as it had done a half century before when it helped pioneer Bradford's launch into large-scale industrial capitalism.

Already in this book we have seen how the subterranean wealth of the Bowling estate south east of Bradford township had attracted Abraham Balme during his office as land steward to Thomas Pigot, Lord of the Manor at Bowling, between 1753 and 1766.[81] On Pigot's death in 1770 the manorial estate passed to his cousin Charles Wood, a captain in the Royal Navy. During Wood's long absences at sea, management of the estate was left to his wife Caroline and the Bradford attorney John Eagles.[82] Consequently, Wood did not concern himself directly with the collieries, leasing many of them to a small number of colliery tenants, including John Greenwood and Preston, Hird & Jarratt. Both companies were kept on a tight rein. In 1779 Greenwood was allowed to work only one mine until such time as the price of coals reached four pence per load. Wood insisted, 'I will have no more pitts sunk until that happens or they are on the last pitt, and no extra work carried on more than what is absolutely necessary. That with a good set of colliers in one pit, I hear in winter and summer they will get more than will be sold'[83]

Wood urged his wife to ignore Greenwood's protests, who because of his methodism, 'would serve the poor before he would serve his master'. The manor lord treated Preston, Hird & Jarratt in the same way. They were allowed to dig for coals only when stock was low, usually in winter, and 'when I would have my own price'. He assured his wife 'Don't fear Hird & Co. It's not worth their while to play tricks with me'.[84]

Wood's cautious approach to the minerals on his estate contrasts with the ambitious approach of Edward Leedes at Low Moor at about the same time. The pits were often closed for many months and given inadequate investment. As a result they brought Wood little real financial gain and remained an under-utilised resource.

Charles Wood lost his life in naval action off Madras in 1782 and as his son was a minor, the care of the estate passed to his brother Francis Wood, sometime merchant in the East India Company. Francis Wood had little respect for the Bowling minerals, 'As to your coal pits I should trouble myself no more with them than to make up my house expenses and to find employment for such men as you wish'.[85] At Christmas in 1783 he proposed selling the main colliery. Edward Leedes, already bankrupt, urged Wood not to do so,

> 'By no means part with the coals, they are a treasure unknown and will soon be doubled in value. Their goodness and situation must increase their value'.[86]

The advice went unheeded and Francis Wood continued to lease the collieries. However, in 1792 his young nephew, Francis Lindley Wood came of age and he introduced a more positive approach to the management of the mines, by appointing a mineral agent, Mr. Isaac Wells. During the first year of Francis Lindley Wood's possession, several borings were made on the estates. Wells drew up plans of mineral locations and then delegated the mining to a number of contractors. Francis Lindley Wood also concerned himself directly with the mining of his coals and invested capital on some scale, unlike any of

Figure 15 Charles Wood. Originally from Barnsley, he became a captain in the navy. He inherited Bolling Hall and the manor of Bowling from his uncle Thomas Pigot in 1770. Wood married Caroline Lacon Barber of Otley in that year. He died of wounds aged 51 and was buried with military honours at Madras.

his predecessors. The public and commercial demand for coal brought him larger profits but his costs increased in the summer of 1792, when some of the colliers insisted on a wage increase. After some opposition he yielded to their demands but joined in a local agreement not to take the workmen of other employers. Some months later a dozen of his colliers were offered an increase of several shillings per man by a neighbouring mine-owner. They threatened to leave work if he did not raise their wages. Wood regretted the fact that there were 'in our neighbourhood three or four little landowners who are

Figure 16 Caroline Wood

determined to get out their coal at any price'. Wood's only alternative was to close the mines but this he could not afford to do, so important was the income from the minerals, 'The produce of the coal is a good deal greater than that of the estates...the perpetual discontents of these subterranean gentlemen are somewhat tormenting and give grounds to wish that the surface of the land was much more fertile'.[87]

In spite of some disenchantment with coal mining Wood continued to work his collieries under the management of Isaac Wells and a number of other mineral stewards who received weekly wages of fifteen shillings each, irrespective of output. Each collier with his hurrier received three shillings per tub for getting the coal and bringing it to the surface. In addition, he was paid four pence per yard for working the shaft, or 'straitwork' as it was called. He worked by candlelight and two pound of candles were given to each collier per week. At the beginning of each year, in return for his contract, he took two guineas as hiring money. On the surface, the banksman received one shilling per tub for raising the coals to the surface and delivering them for sale.[88] The banksman's job at New Haigh had been made easier in 1793 when Francis Lindley Wood laid out capital for a machine to raise the coals, which was 'employed from the beginning of the year to the end almost without intermission'. By 1796 New Haigh Pit at Bowling was producing twenty tons of coal per week.

The capital which Wood provided must have been minimal, for the machine proved to be no more than a simple variation of the common gin. Indeed, 'the expense of erecting the machine was trifling and inconsiderable, not much more than that of a Common Horse Engine'. Wood's capital did not stretch to a steam engine. His industrial intentions were apparently not to compete with the large-scale enterprises like Low Moor that were beginning to appear in the area. In fact, this particular colliery brought Wood an average annual profit of £1,365 in the period 1795–1800. However, his timber bill came to £40; repairs to tools and covers £60; carriage of materials to Pit Road and general labour £50 and finally £15 taxes, all of which gave a more realistic profit of £1,200 p.a. from this colliery.

This profit rate was consistent between 1795 and 1800. The two most remunerative Bowling mines were those at Spout Ing and New Haigh. They were worked continuously throughout this period and provided regular employment at reasonable wage rates. 'Our coals go off pretty well. We have sold all the coals we had stacked up'.[89] In spite of Wells' optimistic reports Francis Lindley Wood began to concede to his more progressive neighbours. The mineral estate at Bowling was worked up to 1805 by both Wood and a sub-contractor, John Sturges. After that year Wood's interest declined and the Sturges Company stepped in to complete the extraction alone in the name of the Bowling Ironworks Company. Like Edward Leedes at Low Moor, Wood's capital as anindividual landowner was insufficient to develop the Bowling mineral estates as a large scale industrial enterprise. It was left to the collective resources of a joint-stock partnership to effect large scale iron making at Bowling.

Professor Ashton maintained that many of the pioneers who came into the iron trade at this time, entered mainly from secondary metal trades (with some exceptions).[90] The founders of the Low Moor Company were a good example of the exception to this rule. The original partners of the Bowling Ironworks however, confirmed Ashton's general theory. Prior to 1790, John Sturges, John Elwell and Richard Paley were partners in a cast iron foundry at Fall Ings, near Wakefield. There is some doubt about Paley's involvement but certainly Sturges and Elwell had been running the foundry there for smithy work since 1784.[91] In December 1787 they and John Sturges Jnr., subscribed money to the value of £2,800. The younger Sturges contributed £1,050; his father and Paley £700 each, and Elwell £350. Nine months later William Sturges supplied a further £700.[92] By 1788, the partners had negotiated with Benjamin Rawson for the Birks and Dyehouse Close, land adjoining Bowling manor. Their second purchase of fifty eight acres was for minerals at £140 per acre (total cost £8,128). This new Bradford enterprise was, at its inception, to be nothing more than a subsidiary to the concern at Fall Ings. Pig Iron made at Bradford was to be converted to wrought iron at Wakefield and then returned as household irons, boilers, tongs and a general variety of small ironware.[93] In October 1789 the subscribers signed the articles of partnership 'and agreed to carry on the iron trade at Bowling and Wakefield for the term of 40 years'. It barely lasted four years for in February 1793 Elwell broke from the Bowling interest, 'The rest of the partners conveyed their interest in the works at Wakefield to Elwell and since that time the two works have remained unconnected'.[94]

Before this break, John Sturges, Snr. had divided his shares amongst his children and soon after was afflicted with some paralytic illness. This rendered him incapable of transacting business, although the firm continued to trade under the name of John Sturges and Company until 1849.

However, work had already begun on the construction of the new plant. It was situated in a U-shaped valley north east of Bowling township (viz Fig.17). The first buildings, the blast furnaces and blowing engine, were built in the valley bottom. Henry Leah constructed two blast furnaces adding special core ovens, and the first blast took place, 13 August 1791. As early as 1793, the slitting mill engine was ready for use but was ineffective as the completion of the forge took several years.[95] A bar mill and plate mill were also installed by 1790. Mines were opened some distance away and 1790 has been given as the date of the first narrow gauge railway built by the company. A complex network of lines developed as the firm expanded. Sturges was largely responsible for the erection of the works, although it was decided that a qualified engineer should be permanently employed. The choice fell upon a Mr. Barnet described as 'a Soho or Bradley man' and it was he who helped to install and modify the first steam engine which powered the two furnaces.[96]

In 1793 Sturges and Paley who had become the principal partners, negotiated a further lease from Rawson, Lord of the manor of Bradford, for coals at £160 per acre at a total cost of £8,185. In 1793 they also contracted with Francis Lindley Wood when minerals in Bowling (Low Lane) were leased from him for £528. They found Wood more amenable in the following year when ninety acres of ironstone in Hall Lane, Bowling were obtained at £63 per acre at a total cost of £5,664.[97] Meanwhile the war against France had the same salutary effect on trade at Bowling as it had at Low Moor. Munition demands for guns, shot and shell consolidated an already flourishing business in boiler-making, domestic ovens and various kitchenware. However, a new line of goods brought the company into a legal wrangle in 1796. After the successful construction of their own atmospheric engines, the firm went on to build one for Wilkinson, Holdsworth & Co., corn millers, and another for cotton manufacturer Richard Paley, both of Leeds.

An indecisive result of a suit brought against Boulton and Watt of Birmingham in May 1794, suggested that there were reasonable grounds for questioning the validity of Watt's patent.[98] The outcome was that a number of manufacturers simply waived the patent and began constructing steam engines. The Bowling firm was one of the companies involved. Unfortunately several of the Leeds textile manufacturers, including Benjamin Gott, had conformed with the patent rights and had paid for the use of them. Paley's evasion caused a stir and an agent from the Birmingham firm arrived at Bradford on 25 September 1795. Southern, the agent, had already seen Paley

Figure 17 Plan of the Bowling Ironworks

who denied a knowledge of mechanics and referred him to Sturges at the works. Sturges refused permission for the agent to see the engines at the works. Southern wrote to his employers thus, 'that it appears absolutely necessary to defend in some way or other your several patents both original and for parallel motions which are infringed in this neighbourhood without modesty'.[99]

James Watt Jnr. informed Sturges of this communication and the Bradford ironfounder replied that some months before one of Watt's agents named Harris had passed the modifications. By November 1795, Watt had built up a substantial case against Sturges and his partners. He demanded a public apology and full payment of the premium, on threat of legal action. Chancery proceedings were taken and Sturges was informed of this in December.[100] He insisted however, that the engines were not covered by patent rights and in January was willing to go into arbitration. Watt tried a different approach in February and persuaded Richard Paley to pay the premium, thus confirming the illegality of the engines.[101] By the end of the month, Watt could write, in a lighthearted manner, to his partner Boulton, 'Inclosed you have a copy of the treaty of peace, not amity concluded at Leeds on Saturday last between me Minister Plenipotentiary to your highnesses on the one part and the Bowling pirates on the other part'.[102]

Paley sent the Birmingham firm details of his engines as did Sturges who pleaded a new line of ignorance, 'we were led into error by our engineers without either knowing ourselves what we did'. Having supplied particulars of the engines and excused himself, he had the effrontery to request, 'As we understand you are going on with some Patent engines in this neighbourhood we shall be glad to serve you with castings and wrought ironwork for ye same'.[103] An enclosed price list completed the insult! The result of this clash with the celebrated Soho firm was a licence to erect steam engines on the Watt principle but at the cost of a full premium. The final cost to Sturges & Co. of the conflict with Boulton and Watt was perhaps £2,000 including all the legal costs.

The amount of business the company was doing by that time and the profits it was making, made these costs derisory. Edward Baldwyn's remark about £30,000 being owed by the government to the companies at Low Moor and Bowling hints at the firm's expansion. An enquiry into the state of the trade in 1796 revealed that Bowling Ironworks was operating two furnaces from which they annually produced 2,000 tons of pig iron.[104] Several more pits were opened in 1799 but not all were successful. Those that were, Sturges immediately linked to the railroad network. The capital of the Company was increased by £35,000 in 1804 when Thomas Mason, a lawyer from Horton and Reverend J. Simons from Kent, were brought into the partnership. The former became an invaluable asset to the company over the next decade. With his legal knowledge, he was able to handle the great extensions in the estate holdings of the company. The majority of these were negotiated with Sir Francis Lindley Wood (he had succeeded to his uncle's baronetcy in 1795). The first of these was completed in 1803 when a large expanse of land in the area of Bierley Hall was leased and later purchased for £34,000. Another enormous sale was made in October 1806 for land and minerals in the Parks for £36,593. This included the lease of coals, two great railed roads, Fish Pond and Spring Wood. The Wood family muniments reveal the piecemeal disposal of their Bowling estate in the first fifteen years of the new century. Geographical expansion was complemented by an overall increase in productivity, employment, mineral consumption and net profits. A modest 2,500 tons of pig iron were made that year, in only two of the company's furnaces. The reason for this, might be explained by the acute labour shortage experienced at that time. Mason in a letter to Sam Buck regrets, 'There is still a great many improvements and alterations to make about the works here but we cannot find workmen for the purpose'.[105]

As the firm expanded, its goods and trade became more varied and its processes were more complex. In addition, its management personnel was enlarged accordingly. Richard Paley's cousin, John George Paley, came to the firm in 1798, and living in the works yard, he was resident manager for forty years. Barnet, the chief engineer was replaced by Michael Billingsley from the Birkenshaw Ironworks in 1803. His salary of £150 per annum was substantiated by house and coals. His immediate task was to design some new pumping engines for the badly drained land. He was assisted by two deputy engineers, Edward Billingsley and Eli Stott who were probably the respective heads of the furnace and forge departments. The post of senior sales manager and traveller fell to John High who accepted a salary of £100 and £10 expenses. Senior accountant and cashier was John Cole who was appointed in 1798 and was an employee for half a century. The position of chief clerk went to Henry Leah at £150 per year but he soon became an ironmaster in his own right at Bierley.[106] Although there are few surviving records of the numbers of the general workforce, the evidence of the annual wage bill gives us more than a suggestion of growth, This increased from £195 in 1795 to £346 a decade later and by 1810 had reached £440. Thereafter it rose continuously until 1816 when it reached £510. The company wage bill slumped badly in 1817–18 but recovered in 1819.[107]

There is a single reference to the labour force at Bowling for July 1814 when 459 persons worked for the company. The largest category was young boys of whom there were 225 (50%). Women and girls numbered forty eight or ten per cent. The physical size of women and children made them ideally suited to the thin Bradford seams and narrow galleries. The miners of Low Moor and Bowling in 1819 testified that they were receiving wages which varied between 2/4 and 2/8 each day. Their working day was of ten or eleven hours duration, in conditions which have been graphically described in other publications. Certainly the working of the minerals at both Bowling and Low Moor was not achieved without several accidents. A large number of these can be found in the Quarter Sessions records. A typical one occurred on 21 October 1817 in Bradford, when five people were burned to death. The explosion of carburetted hydrogen was caused by a faulty Davy Lamp.[108]

However, it was on the issue of the low wages, not conditions, that the local miners took action in 1819. Combining through their various Friendly Societies, the miners of the West Riding demanded a wage increase from November of that year. They asked for 5/- per day for the hewer and 1/- to 2/6 for the young hurrier lads according to their age. An eight hour shift was also demanded for the younger boys. Their requests were rejected by the owners and 400 Bowling miners came out on strike.[109] For some years a steady flow of

Cornish tin miners had found work in this area. During the strike, black-leg labour was brought in from Cornwall by the mine owners. As in most of the early strikes, eviction and starvation were the only victors and the miners were back at work by Christmas. How far Bradford miners went in their demands for increased wages, it is difficult to say. Certainly, they made a separate statement from their Yorkshire comrades but little else is known.

In May 1815 the company and Sir Francis Lindley Wood met to discuss the outright purchase of the remainder of his mineral estate and the whole of his property at Bowling. Through Isaac Wells, Wood had continued to work his single colliery which, by 1814, brought him a yearly income of £539-6-0. Although the turnover had been severely reduced, he also received over £2,000 per annum from mineral rents. In 1803, Wood had purchased the fine East Riding estate at Garrowby, which was an early 'stage in the family's long escape from industrialisation'.[110] The sale of Bowling was an equally important stage in that flight. In addition to the fine manor house of Bolling Hall and eighty acres of minerals, there was little to attract Wood to the defaced manor lands with their towering slag heaps. Wood was more than willing to part with the estate. The company were naturally keen to buy, in spite of the termination of the French wars and the subsequent depression in the iron trade. Raising large amounts of capital at that time was both difficult and inconvenient,

> 'Yet in consequence of the very great capital we have embarked on the works and from the great anxiety we have, no smelting coal within reasonable distance of us should be sold to the country, we should be induced to strain every nerve to accomplish the purchase'.[111]

Negotiations commenced and an estate value of £20,000 was quickly agreed upon. The first dispute came with the credit arrangements. Wood suggested £2,500 a year in order to keep some hold on the property (in case of bankruptcy), and to benefit completely from minerals if they had been underestimated. Mason, representing the company, wanted to clear the whole transaction with £22,500.[112]

The company completed a thorough survey of the estates involved and was in close consultation with Isaac Wells,

> 'The Company are very active looking over the ground and making every possible enquiry about the estate. I have been twice with them talking about it, they desired me to give them a copy of our borings in 1792 – which I have done and they can find nothing unfavourable in them. They seem to be very well satisfied with the proposed agreement and say the only thing they could wish to be satisfied in, is the quantity of minerals. I told them they had not much to fear on that head'.[113]

Wood proved intransigent on a number of issues. He was apprehensive of the company falling into debt and was anxious to insure himself against such a misfortune. It is important to remember that negotiations were being conducted at a time of recession for the iron trade. He was well aware of the recent closure of the ironworks at Birkenshaw but underestimated the resources of the Bowling company. Wood's obstructionist tactics discouraged the partners who threatened to withdraw from the negotiations. Wood hurriedly conceded on certain issues and by July the articles of agreement were drawn up and completed in February 1816.[114] Interest was to be paid on the £20,000 purchase money, in addition to Wood's annual income of £2,500 from previous leases. By 1821 the manor of Bowling belonged to John Sturges & Company, including all the mineral rights which were purchased out right for £24,500.

The main proprietors of Bowling Ironworks in 1816 therefore were John Sturges, John Green Paley and Thomas Mason. Other principal shareholders were Henry Symons and George Paley. By June 1821, the purchase of the Bowling manor was completed and the three partners decided to divide the estate into three lots. All minerals went to the company but the estate was divided and a lottery held. Thomas Mason was fortunate enough to draw the lot of Bolling Hall and its surrounds. He moved into the house during that year whilst John Green Paley remained in residence at the works. It was Paley who asserted full authority and took complete control of the management of the works in the post-war years, particularly after Sturges' death in 1823.[115] In fact, Sturges had officially retired from the management of the company in June 1821 and Mason had played no managerial part after 1816, when the contract with Sir Francis Lindley Wood was assured.

The European peace of 1815 meant a decline in the company's munitions trade. Large contracts had been made with the government since 1804, for 'ordnance stores and for castings for incombustible buildings'. In order to maintain influence in London, it was decided to appoint a full time agent. Within a year, Henry Symons had come of age and had taken the job at a salary of £100 a year. Symons was also responsible for extending the market in Ireland where several engines were imported from Bowling. Mr. Thomas Deane of Cork had purchased one such engine and additional ironwork in 1817. Symons, who was in Cork, promised to help erect the engine but feared, 'he could not induce any of the Yorkshire folk to come over to this land of Wild Men....'[116]

In spite of the temporary loss of armament contracts, the business continued to thrive. There was certainly no deterioration in the consumption of raw materials. The mineral acquisitions of 1816 were immediately put to use and there was a steady rate of consumption of both coal and ironstone, thus:

Table XXXI Ironstone and Coal mined by John Sturges & Company 1811–1819

	Coal (tons)	*Ironstone (tons)*		*Coal (tons)*	*Ironstone (tons)*
1811	29,707	–	1816	35,373	16,428
1812	32,329	16,451	1817	34,408	13,668
1813	35,177	18,863	1818	–	14,416
1814	33,222	16,508	1819	–	16,496
1815	36,576	17,259			

Source: *B.C.L. Bowling Ironworks Mss Unclassified*

The financial records of the Bowling Ironworks do not match those of Low Moor in their detail or completeness. However, from a number of fragmentary sources it is possible to discern how the company fared in the years after the French wars. Consumption of both iron and coal slipped after 1815 but not significantly so. The three furnaces continued to produce pig iron, output increasing in these years in spite of falling prices.

Table XXXII Pig Iron Output 1817–1823

Year	*Bowling Ironworks Output (tons)*
1817	3,696
1818	4,076
1819	4,527
1822	4,287
1823	5,368

When the upturn in trade came in 1825 the company's depleted stocks prevented them from obtaining the abnormal profits which some firms made. By maintaining production and taking orders throughout the period of stagnation, the company suffered when prices began to creep up again in the early months of 1824 (viz Table XXXIII).

Table XXXIII Prices of Quality Pig Iron 1824–1825 (Grades 1–3)

Year	*Month*	*Grade 1*	*Grade 2*	*Grade 3*
1824	January	150/-	140/-	130/-
	July	160/-	150/-	140/-
	October	190/-	180/-	170/-
1825	January	230/-	220/-	210/-
	February	240/-	230/-	220/-
	April	250/-	230/-	220/-

Source: *S.R.L. Jackson Collection No 1297*

The works had concentrated for some years on the production of 1 and 2 Pig Iron and Symons boasted that he 'was making the best common iron in England'. The furnaces had been in full blast throughout the slump, averaging 130 tons of pig iron per week. Unlike other firms, Sturges & Co. had been able to capture contracts in that time, but these were negotiated at low prices. By April 1825, several of these contracts had not been completed and the company was unable to take full advantage of the enormous price increases. Their stock was so small (sixty tons of pig iron) that they literally had none for sale and clients were turned away.[117]

Other sidelines continued to thrive, a great number of castings were made, as well as, 'engine work, boilermaking and heavy work for the government'. It was pig iron however which monopolised their activities and only Paley was to blame for the company being unprepared for the price rise of 1825.

Nevertheless, he continued to work the firm at its maximum output. The average output of each furnace was about forty five tons each week. This was stepped up in response to the inflationary prices of 1824–5. In those years the total output rose to 5,700 tons and 5,829 tons respectively. This consistency of production can also be traced in the records of the company's mineral consumption.

Table XXXIV Iron and Coal mined by John Sturges & Company 1823–1827

	Acreage	*Tons*	*Value*
Coal			
1823	12-3-28	35,803	£1751
1824	11-1-18	38,296	£1534
1825	13-2-04	38,742	£1787
1826	12-2-25	38,276	£1723
1827	10-1-06	37,042	£1370
Iron			
1823	8-2-13	n.d.	£1030
1824	10-3-00	–	£1294
1825	12-2-27	–	£1583
1826	15-2-22	–	£1914
1827	15-2-21	–	£1925

Source: *B.C.L. Bowling Ironworks Mss – Unclassified*

A very large percentage of both coal and iron came from the newly acquired Bowling Hall estate. Woodhouse Hill provided much smaller amounts and the Parks estate supplied the rest. The brisk trading of 1825 was consolidated in the following year by the capture of an East India Company ordnance contract from Low Moor. That year the iron trade slumped dramatically.

At Bowling all three furnaces were kept going in order to build up a stock of No.1 and No.2 iron.[118]

Table XXXV Stocks of No.1 and No.2 Iron 1825–1830

Year	*Tons*
1825	5,829
1826	5,382
1827	5,270
1830	5,117

Doubtless, Paley was not to be caught out a second time. Also the colliers were kept busy throughout 1827 on the Black Bed coals in spite of the massive stock piling which occurred. There was, however, little business in either coals or iron and Paley contemplated a shorter working day and enforced redundancies. The company wage bill fell, in response to a further cut in prices, from £690 in 1827 to £488 in 1832.[119] In June 1827 Paley described the trade as 'at the lowest ebb I can remember it' and by December, 'the dearth of orders continues and without any good prospect, the only consolation that I know of is that others must feel it as well as ourselves'.[120] The recession took its toll on the shareholders' dividends which fell sharply from £128 per Share in 1824 to £70 in 1830.

The economic difficulties posed by the British iron and coal industries were further complicated by an internal managerial crisis within the company which seriously threatened the direction and survival of Bowling Ironworks. The enormity of this board-room squabble threatened the complete ruin of the firm at a time when trade demanded prompt decisions and effective management. Officially the death of John Sturges Jnr in 1823 had put an end to the partnership with Mason and Paley. However, they had continued as managers of the company without accepting any replacement for Sturges. In fact, the latter's daughter had married Joshua Pollard, a local stonemason of Coppy Delf and Spink Well.[121] By 1828, Pollard felt that it was his responsibility to his wife and family to represent their financial interest more directly by acting as a co-manager. Paley and Mason who had married the two daughters of George Barber, attorney of Clockhouse, Manningham, were very much opposed to such a move. The original deeds of partnership of 1804 gave the representatives of John Sturges, the lion's share of the company.[122] However by 1828, Paley and Mason between them had obtained effective control of the company provided that they remained in close alliance. The Sturges faction possessed fifty six of the total share issue whilst the remaining forty four belonged to Paley, Mason and J. Symons.[123]

For several years, Paley had had full control of the administration of the business. If anyone was to be brought into the management of the firm, it was to be his son, John. Mason handed over company business to Paley after 1815 and the latter had come to regard it as his right. In view of this, Pollard's decision to enter the company annoyed Paley, whose first reaction was to attack Pollard's business acumen. Pollard had, in a previous enterprise, fallen into debt. Mason, however, was equally adamant that Pollard's promotion would cause irreparable harm to the company as a whole. 'If we cannot in the end agree, I shall prefer parting with my interest in the works rather than having to run the chance of the evening of my days being disturbed by repeated disputes'.[124] Paley was also quite willing to withdraw if Pollard ever became a company manager.

On January 16 1828 Paley heard for the first time of Pollard's definite intentions. Paley talked of a 'plot' in which, 'Joshua Pollard has had a hankering to come here and during his stay in London there have been several meetings to adjust that object'. Mason tried to compromise by offering Pollard managerial status without an effective say in matters. A salary of £200 was promised (£300 after three years), but Pollard refused such terms. He insisted on full directorial responsibility and authority, equal to that of J.G. Paley.[125]

The controversy went on for some years but Paley and Mason held fast to their views of the company's management. Paley preferred an agency to run the firm rather than Pollard and by 1833 was prepared to bring this about. The internal wrangles of those five years occurred at a time of unease and inactivity for the iron trade. Their effect can have been nothing but detrimental to the progress and welfare of the firm, 'the affairs of the company cannot be well or satisfactorily conducted unless the managers are on a good understanding with one another'. So antagonistic were Paley and Pollard that this harmony could never have been achieved. A valuation of the total capital was taken in 1833 which totalled £238,937.[126] The partnership ended on Christmas Eve of that year and from that time a new age dawned in the history of the Bowling ironworks, one beyond the scope of this book.

Figure 18 Bowling Ironworks. Part of the extensive premises of the Bowling Ironworks about 1850.

Other Local Ironworks

Birkenshaw

The ironworks at Birkenshaw was the earliest of all the local foundries. It was established by a group of Halifax merchants in 1782, principal among whom were the brothers John and William Emmott. Within four months of its foundation, Thomas Holden withdrew his capital of £700 from the partnership and three years later in July 1785, William Bolland took out £500 and left the company.[127] The brothers never really overcame the setback. Nevertheless, pig iron was made from the rich iron deposits below Birkenshaw and from coal which was carried along a narrow canal from the Blue Hills to the works. The barges were horsedrawn along this Navigation Bank, as it was called. In February, 1796, the firm's single furnace was in blast for forty seven weeks and produced only 847 tons of pig iron during that time.[128] The firm apparently used the local canal network for the distribution of their goods,[129] but not to the same effect as their neighbours at Low Moor and Bowling.

The Emmotts were unable to increase their capital and improve the works sufficiently to compete with their expanding neighbours. The wars against France failed to stimulate production at Birkenshaw, for only 612 tons of pig iron were made in 1806 when the naval requirements were great. The firm continued in this very small way until 1815 when rock-bottom prices brought business to an end and their stock of 4,000 tons of ironstone was purchased jointly by the companies at Low Moor and Bowling, at six shillings per ton. The weakest of the three smaller ironworks, Birkenshaw was the first to be absorbed into the larger establishments.

Bierley

This iron foundry was originally founded by Nathaniel Aked who obtained a lease on the mineral estate of Miss Frances Richardson Currer about the year 1810.[130] Unfortunately the business did not long remain in his possession. James Marshall, an ironmonger of Bradford, and Henry Leah, cashier at the Bowling ironworks, purchased the concern. Later Marshall's son joined the firm, along with Mr. T.G. Clayton. In time, Leah became the principal shareholder and general manager of the works and by his keen business acumen took the firm from strength to strength. In 1823 the single furnace produced 2,450 tons of pig iron. Throughout the post-Napoleonic War period, Leah insisted that the firm confine itself to the pig iron trade, particularly No.1 and No.2 qualities. This policy proved successful, for by 1825, they had completed all former contracts and accepted business only at the high prices of that year. Consequently, by April a second furnace was in blast and the total weekly output of pigs was 150 tons.[131] Had it not been for the small steam-powered engine, a greater output could have been achieved. In spite of this handicap and other 'immense difficulties...which at one time nearly upset them', the company took the best advantage of all the ironworks in this area of the advanced metal prices in that year of 1825. In the opinion of Thomas Butler, 'the Bierley works are realising more profits than any other works, according to the capital employed'.[132] Doubtless the depressed prices of 1826 affected the company, as they did with all the other firms in the area. The Bierley Ironworks maintained a high rate of production and by 1830 produced

4,590 tons from two furnaces. This apparently was not their full potential for a local historian of the last century stated that even, 'up to about 1830 when the works had become fairly established, iron was only made six months in the year'.[133] The Bierley Ironworks used the same mineral fields as those of their neighbours at Low Moor, consequently, both were connected by the interlocking network of narrow gauge railroads. In 1854 their affiliation became more definite when Low Moor bought out the Bierley partnership.

Shelf

John Elwell, an original partner of Bowling ironworks and pioneer of the foundry at Fall Ings, Wakefield, was also a contractor of coals from Richard Lumley Savile's lands at Shelf. Partnered by John Crawshaw and John Stocks they eventually obtained the mineral rights of that estate in 1793. In March of the following year, Crawshaw and Stocks withdrew from the concern. Elwell was already highly mortgaged to Samuel Aydon of Flanshaw who consequently came into the works as a partner. In 1795 these two bought minerals at Hedge End Farm in North Bierley for £2,800.[134] Further mineral purchases were made in the Wibsey area and the firm began to concentrate on the production of pig iron. From 10 March 1795, (which one can assume as the first blast) to 10 February 1798 they made 3,442 tons (annual average 1147 tons), 'in which time we have been 12 weeks out of blast. The average quantity for the above time will be about 22 tons 12 cwt'. A government enquiry of 1796 confirmed this average by stating that Shelf produced 1140 tons of 'pigs' from their single furnace.[135] During the next decade, Aydon and Elwell built up their capital with a further two furnaces. By 1806, their annual output of pig iron was 2,716 tons using only two furnaces. It may be noted here that their output was 300 tons greater than that of John Sturges & Company in that year. Like other local concerns, the firm reaped the advantages of wartime armament contracts. In addition, the company began to specialise in iron bridges and was responsible for that at Newlay over the River Aire and for the iron bridge at Scarborough. Both proprietors built themselves fine gentleman's residences; Elwell at Shelf House and Aydon at Carr House. In 1816 the proprietors financed the Carr House School from the healthy trading situation. However, in the difficult post-war years, Aydon sold out (some of his shares going to the Low Moor Company). The ironworks at Shelf came under the management and control of John Field who played an important role in the Ironmasters' Association.

By 1825, prices were high and, 'if the price of pig iron continues as now for one year I think they will clear as much money as they gave for the works'.[136] Unfortunately, like both Low Moor and Bowling, Shelf was not prepared for such a sudden increase. Their stock in hand was only twenty tons (half a week's output). Nevertheless, they worked as contractors for their neighbours at Low Moor and took a large contract for shot from the East India Company. This provided round-the-clock employment for several weeks, 'they had 7 air furnaces melting 4 heats per day; 49 tons per day. But week after week they melted 250 tons to 270 tons into shot and shells'.[137]

Whilst Low Moor concentrated on grape shot and carronade, Shelf produced the heavy eighteen and twenty four pound shells. This trade association with Low Moor was not new, for a government enquiry of 1823 gave their combined output of pig iron as 6,200 tons. By 1830 Shelf shared in the very healthy combined production of 7480 tons of pig iron. By that time, the proprietors at Shelf had sold out, as the Bierley works were subsequently to do, to the larger firm of the Low Moor Iron Company for £4,452.[138]

This chapter on the Bradford mineral industries has examined the contribution made by the local ironworks, principally at Low Moor and Bowling, to the early industrialisation of the Bradford region. It has been argued that these businesses made significant changes in the size of economic organisation and pioneered large scale capital investment and equivalent management structures long before manufacturers of worsted cloth were able to conceive of operations on such a scale. The development of mining and metal manufacture at this level has been linked directly to improvements in transportation, in particular to the opening of the Leeds–Liverpool and Bradford Canals in the 1770s. In the case of the Low Moor Ironworks this connection with the canal companies has been made explicit by tracing the industrial activities of Preston, Hird & Company between 1778 and 1788. The subsequent success of the Bradford worsted trade has tended to deflect attention from the size and success of the region's coal and metal production in that period known to historians as the Industrial Revolution. As early as 1796 the Bradford ironworks produced 4,390 tons of Yorkshire's 21,984 tons of pig iron (twenty per cent). At the peak of Bradford's coal output in 1866 the town's forty six collieries produced 1,875,000 tons of coal or twenty per cent of the total Yorkshire output of 9,714,000 tons.[139] Thus, the economic development of these important and interdependent mineral resources, linked with the advance of cheap water transport, provided Bradford with new concepts of economic organisation and with a broad commercial and financial base upon which to build a completely new industrial economy of textile production in the years after 1800.

1. A. Birch, *The Economic History of the British Iron and Steel Industry, 1784–1879* (1967); M.W. Flinn, Revisions in Economic History; The Growth of the English Iron Industry 1660–1760, *Economic History Review*, 2nd Series SV (1958–9) pp.144–153 *Bradford Lime Kiln Company*
2. G. Firth, The Genesis of the Industrial Revolution in Bradford 1760–1830, unpub. Ph.D. thesis University of Bradford (1974) pp.237–267
3. A. Raistrick, *Old Yorkshire Dales* (1967), pp.67–81; R.C. David, *A Hundred Years of Portland Cement 1824–1924*, (1924), pp.13–23
4. B.C.L. Bradford Lime Kiln Company Mss. DB2/C1 & 2
5. Ibid Ledger 1777–82

6. *Leeds Intelligencer*, 28 June 1774
7. Ibid Ledger 1774–1777
8. Ibid. Minute Book 30 July 1783
9. Y.M.L. Hailstone Mss. PP73, 1 May 1778
10. W.E. Preston, 'Some Notes on an Old Bradford Partnership', *Bradford Antiquary* N.S.111 pp.312–25
11. B.C.L. Lime Kiln Minute Book 31 July 1797
12. G. Firth, *Genesis of Industrial Bradford*, pp.237–260
13. A.H. Green, *Geology of the Yorkshire Coalfield*, (1836) p.659
14. Y.M.L. Hailstone Mss PP5
15. Ibid HH 5.31
16. J. Parker, *Illustrated Rambles from Hipperholme to Tong* (Bradford 1904) pp.36–7
17. J. Parker, *Historical Sketches of Wibsey, Low Moor etc.* (Bradford 1900) pp.31–2
18. B.C.L. Spencer-Stanhope Ms 2168, 2 February 1801.
19. Y.M.L. Hailstone Mss. Box 5.16
20. A. & S. Henry, *Fortunes Made in Business* (1887), Vol.1 pp.93–128
21. *Leeds Intelligencer* 15 September 1789 and S.C.L. Spencer-Stanhope Ms 60579 17 November 1803
22. A. & S. Henry, op. cit. pp.93–95
23. Y.M.L. Hailstone Ms. PP70
24. T.S. Ashton, *Iron and Steel in the Industrial Revolution*, 2nd ed. (M.U.P.1951) pp.23–37, and more recently, G. Hammersley, The Charcoal Iron Industry and its Fuel 1540–1750, *Economic History Review* 2nd Series XXVI (1973) pp.593–613
25. W. Cudworth, *Round About Bradford*, p.48
26. A. Birch, The Haigh Ironworks 1789–1856, *Journal of John Rylands Library*
27. Birmingham Reference Library (hereafter B.R.L.) Boulton & Watt Ms Box 19, B10 25 September 1795.
28. *Souvenir Record of Progress of Low Moor Ironworks 1791–1906* (Bradford 1906), pp.23–25
29. J. Parker, op. cit. note 20, pp.31–32
30. John Rylands Library Manchester, (hereafter J.R.L.M.) Haigh Mss. Dissolution of Contract, 1791
31. J.W. Banks, Progress of Engineering in Bradford, *Journal of the Bradford Engineering Society*, 1925/6 pp.4–7
32. Smalley was an original subscriber to J. Fairbank's 'The Power of Machines' (1803). See also J. Parker op. cit. in notes 19, pp.37–38
33. B.C.L. Misc. Ms C/33 Company Stock Book 1795–1835, 24 October 1795
34. Ibid C/33 Stock Book, October 1795
35. E. George, *On the Yorkshire Coalfield* (1836)
36. I.C. Dodsworth, Recent Uses of Horse Plateways in West Yorkshire, *Industrial Archaeology* 7, (1970) pp.139–140
37. W. Cudworth op. cit. pp.57–58
38. T.S. Ashton, op. cit. p.175
39. Y.M.L. Hailstone Ms. Box 5–16
40. Ibid. Minutes of Meeting 13 November 1797
41. Ibid.

42. P. Riden, The Output of the British Iron Industry before 1870, *Economic History Review* 2nd Series, XXX No.3 (1977) p.449
43. Sheffield Central Library (hereafter S.C.L.) Jackson Collection, Ms 1297. Friendly Association of Ironmasters, Minute Book 1799–1828
44. Y.M.L. Hailstone Ms. G3 11 August 1799 at Sheffield
45. Ibid. 11 June 1800 at Bradford
46. B.R.L. Boulton & Watt Ms. Box 19 B10 25 September 1795
47. F. Crouzet, *Capital Formation in the Industrial Revolution* (1972)
48. B.C.L. Misc. Ms C/33 Ledgers 1790–1804
49. Ibid. Stock Book 1790–1815
50. R.H. Campbell, *Carron Company* (Edinburgh 1961) pp.329–333
51. B.R.L. Boulton & Watt Mss Box 19 B10
52. T.S. Ashton, op. cit. p.144–147
53. Y.M.L. Hailstone Ms G3
54. Cusworth Hall, (hereafter C.H.M.) Barnsley Coal Company Mss. Draft minutes including price list of goods produced at Low Moor, November 1799
55. H.W. Dickinson and R. Jenkins, *James Watt and the Steam Engine* (1927), pp.320–321
56. B.C.L. Maps & Plans Property of Low Moor Company. G. Leather, 1811
57. B.C.L. Maps & Plans. Staith of Low Moor Co. BRA 1835 PEA
58. B.C.L. Misc. Ms C/33 Stock Book December 1796
59. Ibid. December 1801 and W. Cudworth, op. cit. pp.49–50
60. Ibid.
61. J. Parker, *Illustrated Rambles*, p.16
62. B.C.L. Misc. Ms C/33 Stock Book 1811
63. S.C.L. Spencer–Stanhope Mss 60579 17 November 1803
64. Ibid. 20 January 1807
65. Ibid 28 July 1807
66. B.C.L. C/33 Stock Book 1802–1815
67. T.S. Ashton op. cit. p.158 Referring to Coalbrookdale and Thorncliffe, Professor Ashton wrote 'the partners received a fixed interest rate of 5 per cent on their capital and the surplus was then divided into shares...'
68. Y.M.L. Hailstone Ms. 6.12 and P. Riden op. cit. p.450
69. Ibid. Hailstone 6.12
70. T.S. Ashton, op. cit. p.153
71. W. Cudworth, op. cit. pp.64–65
72. W. Cudworth, *History of Bolton & Bowling* (Bradford 1891) p.313
73. Kirkstall Forge Mss (hereafter K.F.M.) T. Butler, A Tour Amongst the Derbyshire and Yorkshire Ironworks, April 1825 and R. Butler, History of Kirkstall Forge Through Seven Centuries (unpublished paper) p.130
74. S.C.L. Jackson Collection, Uncatalogued Letterbook T. Field
75. B.C.L. Bowling Ironworks Mss. Box 12 13 June 1828
76. S.C.L. T. Field Letterbook 23 May 1829
77. B.C.L. C/33 Stock Book 1827
78. *Bradford Courier* 25 January 1826
79. Deynhausen & Decker, Report on Railways in England 1826/7 in *Transactions of the*

Newcomen Society II (1953–5)

80. B.C.L. C/33 Stock Book 1830
81. W. Cudworth, *Bolton & Bowling*, p.287
82. J. Wilkinson, *Worthies, Families Celebrities of Barnsley & District* (Sheffield 1883), pp.17–19
83. Paper & Muniments of Lord Halifax of Garrowby (hereafter G.M. Hickleton Papers) A2/6.22 January 1780
84. Ibid 30 October 1780
85. G.M. Hickleton Papers A2.6/3 23 July 1782
86. Ibid. A2 1/5 5 February 1784
87. Ibid. A2 2/4 12 December 1792
88. Ibid. B2.6 1799
89. W. Cudworth, op. cit. p.229
90. T.S. Ashton, op. cit. p.209
91. C.H.M., Fall Ings Mss Indenture June 1792
92. B.C.L. Bowling Ironworks Ms 5/19 Articles of Partnership December 1787
93. W. Cudworth *Bolton & Bowling*, op. cit. p.205
94. B.C.L. Bowling Ironworks Ms 5/19 8 February 1793
95. H. Long, Bowling Ironworks, *Industrial Archaeology* Vol.5 No.2 (1968) pp.171–178, I.C. Dodsworth, Further Observations on Bowling Ironworks, *Industrial Archaeology* 1969, Vol.6 No.2 (1969)
96. B.R.L. Boulton & Watt Mss. B10 Box 19 Letterbook 25 September 1795
97. W. Cudworth, *Bolton & Bowling*, pp.207–211
98. Dickinson & Jenkins, op. cit. p.325
99. B.R.L. Boutlon & Watt, op. cit. 3 August 1795
100. Ibid. November 1795
101. Ibid. 2 January 1796 and 9 and 19 February 1796
102. S. Smiles, *The Lives of Boulton & Watt*, (1904) p.418
103. B.R.L. Boulton & Watt op. cit. 9 May 1796
104. Y.M.L. Hailstone Ms. 5.16
105. G.M. Hickleton Ms B1/3 23 December 1805
106. W. Cudworth op. cit. p.239
107. B.C.L. Bowling Ironworks Mss. 5.14
108. Northern Star, 1817
109. F. Machin, *The Yorkshire Miners*, (Barnsley 1958), pp.31–32; *Leeds Mercury* 20 November 1819 and 4 December 1819
110. J.T. Ward, East Yorkshire Landed Estates in the Nineteenth Century, *East Yorkshire Local History Series*, No.23 (1961) p.48
111. G.M. Hickleton Ms B 1–3 22 May 1815
112. Ibid. 15 July 1815
113. Ibid. 10 June 1815
114. Ibid. 4 July 1815
115. B.C.L. Bowling Ironwork Ms 4/3 9 June 1821
116. Ibid. Unclassified Ms 22 June 1817
117. T. Butler, Tour 1825, op. cit. 29 April 1825

118. B.C.L. Bowling Ironworks Ms Unclassified
119. Ibid. Ms 5/19
120. Ibid. Ms 12. 13 June 1827 and 12 December 1827
121. W. Cudworth, op. cit. p.220
122. Y.M.L. Hailstone Ms G1
123. B.C.L. Bowling Ironworks Ms. 12 January 1828
124. Ibid 16 January 1828
125. Ibid Unclassified Ms.
126. S.C.L. Wharncliffe Muniment, Sheffield M.D. 2441/4 Deeds, 28 June 1782
127. J. Parker, *Illustrated History*, pp.290–96
128. Y.M.L. Hailstone Ms 5.16
129. W. Cudworth, op. cit. p.230
130. T. Butler, op. cit. 29 April 1825
131. Ibid
132. W. Cudworth, op. cit. p.231
133. J. Parker, *Historical Sketches*, p.264
134. Y.M.L. Hailstone Ms. 5.16
135. T. Butler, op. cit. April 1825
136. Ibid
137. B.C.L. Misc. Ms. C/33 Stockbook 1827
138. P.P. Report of the Select Committee on Coal in the U.K. Vol.III (1871) p.89 & Appendix 27 p.21
139. Ibid

6

Bradford and the Rise of the English Worsted Trade 1760–1830

During the second half of the eighteenth century the West Riding of Yorkshire superseded Norwich as the main centre of worsted cloth production in this country. Since 1700 worsted cloth exports had played a prominent part in Britain's overseas textile trade. It is difficult, however, to estimate Yorkshire's share of this growing sector. Dr. R.G. Wilson has attempted an analysis and measurement of the Yorkshire textile industries which he valued at £1 million in 1700 i.e. a fifth of the national output.[1] Certainly by 1772 the West Yorkshire contribution to woollen and worsted output had increased dramatically. Thomas Wolrich's reliable estimate for that year calculated that West Riding merchants exported more than seventy per cent of the total national output which Wolrich valued at £3,273,000. Productivity accelerated after 1781 when output more than doubled. Wilson concluded,

> 'output of the wool textile industries in Yorkshire increased some eight times from around £1 million to over £8 million in the course of the century'.[2]

Norwich and East Anglian manufacturers continued to prosper until the last quarter of the century but the greater volume of business being done in the Eastern Pennines was noticeable as early as 1752 when David Stansfield of Leeds noted,

> 'Those out of the East of England who look with a jealous eye on the rising manufacture of Yorkshire'.[3]

Why then did the wool textile business of West Yorkshire thrive and expand after 1780 at the expense of the traditional regions of production like East Anglia and the West Country?

In 1910 Sir John Clapham dismissed Victorian misconceptions about West Yorkshire's rich factor endowments of wool, water, coal and ironstone. They brought only the kiss of death to an East Anglian worsted industry already in an advanced state of terminal decline. Clapham argued that social and personal considerations had played a more important part,

> 'It is the ordinary case of a pushing, hard working locality, with certain slight advantages, attacking the lower grades of an expanding industry'.[4]

Regional comparisons of entrepreneurial initiative in the late eighteenth century are almost impossible to evaluate. Moreover, Dr. J.K. Edwards has suggested that East Anglian enterprise in the worsted trade continued well into the nineteenth century bringing with it 'a new access of vitality' which lasted until the 1860s.[5] If positive entrepreneurial attitudes continued to benefit the East Anglian trade, West Yorkshire supremacy can only be explained by its distinct organisational structure and, in particular, by its different sales procedures.

Dr. R.G. Wilson has argued that Norwich and the West Country depended wholly upon the merchant houses and trading companies of the metropolis which:

> 'took a good profit, but since they were often involved in a complex import trade and frequently exported other ranges of goods they were not experts in handling cloth'.[6]

Whereas in the West Riding of Yorkshire, merchants were local and fully cognisant of the manufacturing side of the trade, eager to convert their cloth sales 'into a flow of good bills so that they could speedily go into the cloth market again'. It was in the 1730s that West Riding merchants turned from their traditional north European markets to enter Iberian and Italian ports with their cheaper priced items and a quick turnover for cash. This kind of successful competition with East Anglian stuffs recurred in the 1770s when North America and the West Indies were also opened by enterprising West Riding merchants. London merchant houses, acting on behalf of East Anglian manufacturers, failed to follow this lucrative precedent and continued to persevere with the traditional European outlets, as well as the domestic market. Thus, cheaper goods and a knowledgeable merchanting community, eager to break into new markets, caused the West Riding woollen and worsted traders to capture a much greater volume of business than ever before and to surpass the productivity of East Anglia and the West Country. Those who were responsible for this shift of manufacture away from East Anglia were the independent clothiers of West Yorkshire, thousands of small men who bought their raw materials and relied upon their own labour and skill assisted by their wives and families and occasionally apprentices and journeymen to work up the wool into clothpieces for sale at the markets and Cloth Halls. These clothiers worked their own cloth on their own looms in their own homes – the domestic system.

> When calculated in terms of goods the wealth of clothiers varied considerably from individual to individual, some men possessing goods valued at more than £100 whilst others were scarcely worth more than £1.

Those individuals who owned property, working the land, alongside their activities as cloth manufacturers were known as yeomen-clothiers, so distinguishing them from the lower social category of clothiers. We turn now to look at the activities of two such clothiers from the Bradford area in the pre-industrial era of the eighteenth century.

In order to understand how this domestic system of the worsted industry influenced the development of Bradford in the latter half of the eighteenth century, it will be helpful to examine the activities of two individual master manufacturers. John Hustler was a prominent and distinguished figure who made important institutional and structural changes to the West Riding worsted trade in these years. Robert Heaton was relatively insignificant, one of hundreds of smaller manufacturers but whose operations within the trade are representative and moreover, well documented in a detailed collection of business papers.

John Hustler was the son of William Hustler who had married Jane Jowett, from Bolton, near Bradford in 1714. Both were Quakers and brought up their son (born in 1715) in that faith. John also followed his father in farming the lands at Apple Tree Farm, Low Fold in Bolton. William, and his brother John at Yeadon, had also undertaken business as wool merchants. The younger John succeeded them on terminating his apprenticeship as both a sorter and stapler of wool.[7] In the late 1740s, this side of the family business flourished. Like many others, Hustler concentrated his efforts on the purchase of wool and the distribution of cloths. Some indication of his growing status can be traced in the part which he played in the marked-wool controversy of 1752. Woollen merchants all over the country clamoured for legislation to control the brandings and false windings practised by farmers. This came to a head in 1751 when meetings were arranged with a view to petitioning parliament. Staplers and manufacturers of the West Riding met on 20th November and resolved on a system of certificates for wool winders and forfeits on all frauds. John Hustler was elected to the committee. Another Bradfordian, Samuel Lister of Horton, was given charge of the committee's finances.[8] They were to attend the House of Commons and procure, if possible, a preventitive bill. Hustler was given the responsibility of organising a petition for the gentlemen of the Wolds and Holderness. His Quaker connections with the Gurneys and Peckovers in Norwich made him an ideal link between Yorkshire and East Anglia. Shortly after Christmas 1751, Hustler travelled to London,[9] where he was called before a parliamentary committee testifying that the practice of false wool winding had been common since 1740, around the time when he commenced his journeys into Lincolnshire and the Wolds. Hustler believed the advance in the price of wool in 1740 had accounted for this fraud of mixing 'various other sorts of wool of inferior qualities and winding them within their good fleeces, which makes fewer fleeces go to a tod, by which means he has frequently been imposed upon; and is very injurious to him by subjecting him to buy wool not fit for his purpose and a great deal that he cannot comb at all'.[10] The demand for wool from the West Riding manufacturers forced the staplers, like Hustler, to purchase from growers who had previously cheated them. The positive recommendations of the committee were not passed into law and Hustler returned to Bradford a disappointed man. Nevertheless in the subsequent twenty years Hustler's career exemplified the increasing prosperity of the West Riding textile trade as a whole. The importance of an independent and effective retail and distribution system to West Yorkshire textiles has already been noted. It was Hustler's initiative which institutionalised the sale of worsted cloth in Bradford with the foundation of the Bradford Piece Halls.

By 1770, Bradford's small market was hopelessly inadequate and its manufacturers used the facilities of the other major West Riding towns. Wakefield had benefitted from the opening of the Aire–Calder Navigation in 1702 and had been established as the central wool market of the region. Leeds was the traditional textile capital of the area and, in addition was the recognised finishing centre of the trade. Halifax emerged as the main worsted market although it also continued as an important exchange for woollen cloth.[11] Throughout the 1770s, the enterprise of Bradford men did much to redress this imbalance. Hustler's efforts in this direction have already been discussed with his promotion of the local canal system. He made a more direct contribution to the progress of the textile trade in Bradford by contributing to the founding of the town's Piece Hall.

Previously, the worsted trade had functioned largely through private negotiation rather than through the open market. However, most manufacturers of the district leased their own piece rooms whilst others made use of a number of stalls in a large room near the White Lion Hotel in Kirkgate.[12] The expansion of trade and the increased overseas opportunities confirmed the need of a central exchange. In 1773, John Hustler, William Hardcastle and George Kellett, representing the local merchants, leased land at the lower end of Kirkgate, (viz Fig 19) from John Woolmer. A subscription was opened for the erection of a Piece Hall containing one hundred stands, which cost £1,555. The inadequacy of the first building was all too apparent and a second hall was soon erected.[13] Although the early records of the Piece Hall Trustees have not survived, the original deeds show John Hustler to have been a leading signatory in the foundation of the Halls.[14]

The Worsted Committee

Hustler was even more instrumental in the founding of the manufacturers union, the Worsted Committee, in 1777. The domestic system proved an adequate means of production but was open to wide abuse from the operatives. With the expansion of the labour force, and the rising price of good English wool, the manufacturers were faced with an ever-increasing number of embezzlements and thefts. Combers would extract wool for their own use. Spinners reeled short hanks and there were direct thefts of cloth pieces. Detecting frauds of this nature proved difficult and bringing them before law proved expensive. Consequently, by 1775 northern worsted merchants and manufacturers demanded a confirmation of the laws and an efficient body to enforce them. There had been some form of manufacturer's union before that

Figure 19 Kirkgate. One of the ancient thoroughfares of Bradford. Kirkgate is seen here leading towards the junction with Westgate and Ivegate. In the distance on the right hand side of the road can be seen the gateway of the Manor House. Opposite is the Talbot Hotel and set back from the road to the left of the illustration is the Piece Hall (1773). On the right are the premises of the Bradford Banking Company.

time, but its effect was minimal.[15] The Worsted Acts of 1777 were the result of several petitions and appeals from the northern worsted manufacturers. These acts prohibited malpractices, which had hitherto gone unpunished, by the founding of the Worsted Committee. At a meeting at the Talbot Inn, Halifax, 9th June 1777, the new system of inspection and supervision was launched. A Yorkshire committee, consisting of seventeen worsted merchants from the main towns, Halifax (6) and Bradford (4), elected John Hustler as its chairman. Lancashire and Cheshire also had their own committees. These area committees were responsible for the execution of the provisions of the acts. There was to be a team of seven area inspectors whose full time job it was to investigate and bring to court any transgressors of the statutes. At the third meeting of the Yorkshire Branch of the Worsted Committee at the Crown and Cushion, Bradford, William Haley of Horton was appointed Superintendent of the inspectorate. John Hustler's industry and enterprise were acknowledged in January 1778 when the committee officially thanked him for his services.[16]

The Worsted Committee certainly proved an effective remedy against fraudulent practices. Thomas Hardcastle was active in prosecuting the embezzling woolcombers of Bradford and Horton. On several occasions the Committee's policing functions were obstructed and undermined by uncooperative magistrates like Henry Wickham and John Busfeild of Bingley who discharged Betty Anderson (and several others like her) of embezzlement in September 1784. The Committee hoped that the magistrates 'would see the necessity of supporting the inspection in the execution of their duty, otherwise the good purposes of the Worsted Act would be entirely defeated'.[17] However, this was not the only function of the committee for it encouraged new techniques, suppressed combinations and encouraged the trade generally. In

September 1792 a sub-committee was elected to observe the activities of several benefit societies.

> 'The Committee being of the opinion that the Associated Benefit Societies may have a prejudicial tendency by enabling the members thereof to form illegal Combinations'.[18]

And in January 1774, the Worsted Committee had subsidised a Mr. Mordaunt for his new idea of spinning wool. The Committee, therefore, brought benefits to many different sectors of the West Riding worsted trade.

Another major crisis to affect the Yorkshire worsted and woollen trades occurred in the early 1780s. Hustler and the Worsted Committee were once again at the very centre of the new controversy. The agricultural improvements in sheep breeding and increased enclosure for pastures and the like, all produced a temporarily overstocked domestic market for wool after 1780. The woolgrowers of Lincolnshire and Kent were prevented by law from seeking higher prices abroad but in the latter months of 1781, they sought to repeal such prohibitive statutes. The northern Worsted Committee reacted immediately by appointing Messrs. Hustler, Currer and Hebdin to attend a meeting at Lincoln and give their point of view and prevent the exportation of wool. A parliamentary commission (before which Hustler testified) turned down the request of the woolgrowers in January 1782. Nevertheless, in East Anglia and along the South Coast illegal exportation of wool occurred on a very large scale. Hustler was able to offer a solution for he 'had the satisfaction of being the planner... and being Chairman and Treasurer from 1764 to 1776, he had the principal hand in conducting a committee at the small expense of less than £600'.[19] Apparently, before the creation of the Worsted Committee, Hustler had led and operated a combination of manufacturers. Part of their function, had been the prevention of exporting worsted yarn. This was effected through the appointment of ten mounted officers (at £250 per annum) who would visit places along the coastline and make known the laws and penalties regarding smuggling. Hustler estimated for the parliamentary committee that the annual English wool product was 600,000 packs of which 11,000 found their way out of the country.[20] The outcome, as previously stated, was that the growers were refused permission to export their wool. As a result smuggling reached new heights in the subsequent years. Finally, in 1787, the situation was so bad that the Worsted Committee petitioned parliament for more stringent control of illegal exportation. The result was a new act in 1788 confirming the illegality of exporting English wool.

Thus, the Worsted Committee had centralised the interests of the northern worsted manufacturers whose theatre of operations covered a very large area. The committee had protected their rights and welfare as a commercial group. At a time when central-government influence in the provinces was weak, the committee acted of its own accord, financed by a drawback of the soap duty allowed to each manufacturer. It was a central and representative body of an otherwise disorganised mass of manufacturers and merchants, functioning under the shapeless and scattered system of domestic production. Hustler had played a large part in its foundation and its subsequent workings, as he had in the establishment of Bradford's retail centre, the Piece Hall. Hustler in the period 1766 to 1782 had provided, for the Bradford manufacturer and merchant, an institutional framework within which the progress of the worsted trade was developed and coordinated by its numerous entrepreneurs.

Such an entrepreneur was Robert Heaton of Stanbury and Haworth, townships which were part of the Bradford parish and which looked to its market for exchange and distribution. Robert Heaton was born in 1726, the son of a substantial yeoman-farmer at Stanbury. He was typical of the many stuff makers in and around Bradford in the last quarter of the eighteenth century. His three marriages brought additions to the original family estate at Ponden Hall, as well as three sons and a daughter. After 1750, the hall had fallen into disrepair and Robert Heaton moved to Bridge House, in Haworth.[21] His estates, including Ponden, were mostly leased out, for Heaton made his living by the wool trade and had done so since the age of twenty three. An account of his operations as a manufacturer has been given elsewhere by Professor Sigsworth.[22] It will be necessary here to re-examine and develop that study.

Heaton worked on the putting out system, employing two agents, John Irwen (up to 1760) and his successor, Joseph Shackleton, who carried wool and yarns to the outworkers. In the 1760s Heaton purchased some of his wool from the well known staplers of Bradford like William Hardcastle and John Hustler.[23] He did not venture to the markets and fairs of Lincolnshire himself. Professor Sigsworth has estimated, that Heaton was employing over forty spinners in the 1760s, some living in the Haworth area, others farther afield. The agent often travelled well into Lancashire to Whalley, Bispham and Thornton Cleveleys.[24] After 1761 Heaton began to work the yarn into shalloons employing his weavers from the immediate vicinity. His account books show that the weavers were usually the small tenant farmers, leasing Heaton's lands. These men Heaton took into his employ and paid by redeeming them of their rents. In 1775 for example John Sugden was, 'paid in Spinning and weaving and money – in all, this is for Whitsunday Rents for the year 1774. I received £10'.[25]

In this way Heaton obviated the use of cash which was often in short supply. Also, by employing his own tenants he lessened the risk of embezzlement and theft. Heaton was, in effect a forerunner of the factory owner, employing large numbers of workers, purchasing large amounts of raw material and whose output was considerably greater than the independent clothier who dominated the regional woollen trade.

Heaton, like other West Riding manufacturers, sold his finished goods through the Cloth and Piece Halls to a 'pushing group of merchants some of whom had been clothiers themselves...who specialised totally in the sale of cloth'. John Taylor and James Cousen, both merchants of Bradford, purchased Heaton's three classes of shalloons throughout the 1760s.[26] As already mentioned, West Riding merchants showed considerable enterprise in this period in their search for new overseas markets. By 1772 North America and the West Indies purchased thirty per cent of England's total woollen exports. This lucrative market accounted for the steady trade done by Heaton after 1760 and also for the increased range and quality of russels, plainbacks and lastings to be found in his daybooks. The revolt of the American colonies seriously damaged exports of woollen and worsted goods until 1782. It is significant that Heaton, between 1777 and 1783, directed the majority of his finished pieces to the London merchants Jones, Harvard and Jones who had continued to persevere with European markets largely on behalf of the East Anglian manufacturers.

The Haworth manufacturer seems to have weathered the colonial storm according to the output figures calculated by Sigsworth from Heaton's account books throughout this period.

TABLE XXXVI Annual Worsted Cloth Output of Robert Heaton 1762–1783

Year	*Value (£.s.d)*	*No. Pieces*	*Year*	*Value) (£.s.d)*	*No. Pieces*
1762	352 12 0	207	1773	1065 9 9	605
1763	740 7 0	421	1774	1162 15 0	746
1764	893 15 0	524	1775	1172 18 6	648
1765	897 12 9	512	1776	1290 18 6	686
1766	741 17 3	497	1777	1230 18 6	664
1767	1006 3 0	562	1778	1371 1 3	93
1768	839 9 0	610	1779	1253 15 6	653
1769	839 9 0	526	1780	1391 18 7	846
1770	987 2 6	681	1781	1347 2 3	796
1771	960 13 0	614	1782	1094 10 0	703
1772	748 18 3	427	1783	1226 10 9	597

Source: *B.C.L. Heaton Mss B146–8*

The financial crisis of 1781 had shaken the whole commercial system and it took some time for confidence to return. Money remained tight and credit was restricted. Both these factors affected Heaton's trading, in spite of the peaceful international situation which encouraged good trade. Heaton relied heavily on finance – credit trading which hinged on the system of promissary notes and bills of exchange. By 1789 his creditors, principal among them being Hustler and Peckover, were calling for their money (£800). He, in turn, was owed £1,509 of which £1,000 was debited to the merchants Messrs. Bramley who had always been poor payers.[28] In addition, the cotton industry was proving a troublesome competitor to worsteds throughout the 1780s and after 1785, Heaton's output slipped badly (viz Table XXXVII).

At the same time his son, Robert Heaton Jnr. experienced similar difficulties. In 1781, he had married Elizabeth Murgatroyd, daughter of John Murgatroyd of Royd House, Oxenhope. There, in partnership with his father-in-law, he had carried on the trade of clothier. Like his father, he had put out

Table XXXVII Annual Worsted Cloth Output of Robert Heaton 1786–1791

Year	*Value (£.s.d)*	*No. .Pieces*	*Year*	*Value (£.s.d)*	*No. Pieces*
1786	840 16 5	295	1789	778 9 0	342
1787	1483 17 9	586	1790	847 13 0	386
1788	863 8 0	361	1791	872 12 0	351

wool and yarn in the locality. He dealt mainly in russels and sold them at the Piece Hall, Halifax. In February, 1790, Robert Heaton Jnr. took stock and found a favourable balance of £125, and by the summer both he and his father were ready to make fresh starts.

At that time the expanding Lancashire cotton trade overflowed into the Eastern Pennines particularly in the Haworth–Keighley region, where a number of master-clothiers were converted to the new trade and its recent mechanisation in the form of water-frames, mules and jennies. Initial fixed-capital expenditure need not be great and credit facilities were available as were public fulling and scribbling mills.[29] Old mill properties were easily acquired and cheaply leased. Consequently, openings in centralised production (both domestic and factory) were there for those with the drive, industry, and initiative, like the Heatons, father and son.

> 'It was their vision, their capacity for hard work, their ability to save which lifted the Yorkshire textile industry out of the rut of domestic manufacture and on to the rails of nineteenth century factory production'.[30]

The Heaton family was typical of the small Bradford manufacturer in their transition to factory spinning, but unusually they simultaneously moved into the manufacture of cotton goods and temporarily turned their backs on worsted production. Robert Heaton Jnr. built a water-powered spinning mill close to his home at Royd House, Oxenhope.

The beginning of the March of 1791 saw a sudden and long expenditure in the younger Heaton's accounts. Stone, spades, axes were purchased and local masons were required to commence work on the foundations of the mill. Throughout most of the spring and summer of that year, Heaton Jnr was busy hiring contractors for the ironwork and machinery. Sturges & Company of Bowling were paid £14 for ironwork. Other local craftsmen were given the tasks of constructing roving frames. Tempest, the manager, was responsible for acquiring two cotton frames, three pairs of cards and two spinning frames, all with calculated specifications. By June Royd mill was almost complete and, in September, John Brigg agreed 'to act as engineer for the cotton mill erected there for one year upon this condition that he is to have his meat, drink and lodging at Roydhouse and also £40 as wage'.[31]

Over the hill at Ponden, Robert Heaton Snr. converted an old water mill at Pitcher Clough. His will later describes it as 'new in part erected' so it was probably an extended and altered corn mill. Labour was recruited from the area to construct the wheel race and dressed stone was brought in from nearby quarries. He also employed Haworth joiners to build his frames, e.g. William Smith who made two carding frames. Ponden Mill was also ready by June 1791 and the old man set to recruiting his work force. James Baldwin was hired at 9/- per week plus lodgings as the spinning master or overseer. Later, in October 1792, Heaton took John Midgeley (one of his former domestic workers) into his service as card master at 10/6 per week. A large part of Heaton's general workers were children who were hired at 3/- per week. Within two years of the Ponden Mill getting under way, Heaton died and left the concern to his sons, Robert and William. These two were hit by a further tragedy on the ominous Friday, 13th March 1795 when the mill was extensively damaged by fire. Their father had taken the precaution of insuring his mill with the Royal Exchange Assurance who paid out £493. The younger Robert Heaton laid out only £285 of this on the total reconstruction of the mill. It might be worth remembering the low proportion of fixed capital to fluctuating capital in these early days of factory production by stating that, in October of that year, Heaton purchased 6,200 lbs of raw cotton for £650, cash![32]

Having overcome this early crisis the brothers went on to build up their trade gradually. They had now turned to the West and did most of their trade in Lancashire. William travelled from market to market buying raw cotton from commission agents like R. Dobson & Company in Liverpool and Myers & Fielding in Blackburn. On his outward journey he took the cotton twist made by the spinners at Ponden Mill and Royd House. Since the reconstruction of Ponden mill, between July and October 1796, almost 17,000lbs of cotton were bought and 10,810lbs of twist were sold. The volume of their trade was slowly growing but Robert Heaton Jnr. received a further setback in January 1799. William had become well acquainted with the trade by his frequent visits to Lancashire and determined it would be more beneficial to him to set up as a broker. This he did, in Liverpool in 1799, taking with him £370 of the Ponden Mill capital.[33]

Robert decided to run both concerns at Ponden and Oxenhope and bought out his brother. During the period of transition, cost reductions were necessary and Heaton got rid of the old commissioners and sold the cotton twist directly to buyers which he reduced to two. By 1800, business prospered and Heaton resumed the commission system with Joseph Ainsworth of Blackburn.

Another sign of his prosperity was the move back to the family seat at Ponden Hall (viz Fig.20). In 1801 the whole of the upper storey was taken down and rebuilt. An extension was added at the west end and the house was given a new entrance hall and staircase. There followed eight years of flourishing trade with increased overseas and domestic demands.[35]

In 1806, Robert Heaton brought into the business his oldest son, John, aged 23. However he betrayed his father's trust, for as manager 'he embezzled and spent of my property more than the sum of £500'. In 1807 Napoleon's Berlin Decrees closed European markets, particularly Spain and Portugal. A year later, both Russia and America laid damaging embargoes on British

Table XXXVIII Cotton Twist sold by Robert Heaton 1794–1811[34]

Year	*No. of Packs*	*Year*	*No. of Packs*	*Year*	*No. of Packs*
1794	12 packs	1801	66 packs	1803	121 packs*
1795	16 packs	1802	124 packs	1809	88 packs
1796	71 packs	1803	116 packs	(March–December)	
1797	82 packs	1804	115 packs	1810	117 packs
1798	45 packs	1805	108 packs	1811	77 packs
1799	81 packs	1806	118 packs	(January–August)	
1800	96 packs	1807	95 packs*		

*packs sent off, not sold.

Source: *B.C.L. Heaton Mss 156 et al.*

imports, and as a result the cotton trade slumped. Between 1806 and 1809 Heaton suffered a loss of almost £350.[36]

The wolves were only kept from the door by a mortgage on lands at Kildwick. In order to improve his business, he tried in 1808 to weave calicoes but had little success with them. The depression worsened with the American war and cotton manufacturers in the West Riding were being drawn back to worsteds. Heaton carried on, but was operating at a loss and by 1813 had lost £569 over three years trading. This led to further mortgages on his estates but death relieved him from further burdens in 1817.

Figure 20 Ponden Hall. The home of the Heaton family from 1634. It was rebuilt by Robert Heaton in 1801 following his prosperous business in the textile trade. It is thought by some to have been the model for Thrushcross Garage in Emily Brontë's *Wuthering Heights*. The Brontë family often called here on their moorland walks. *Photo: Ian Beesley*

It has been necessary to follow the Heaton story through to the cotton and mechanised stage of manufacture. The adaptation of some West Riding clothiers to cotton manufacturing is an essential part of the metamorphosis of the Yorkshire worsted trade. It introduced new techniques and machinery as well as providing healthy competition. Cotton had been an important source of income and means of employment on the eastern scarps of the Pennines, as it was for those on the west. It was worked extensively around Bradford and Keighley in the period 1780 to 1820.[37] Robert Heaton was no exception when he transferred his small remote property over to cotton spinning. The activities of the Heatons have highlighted the nature and development of worsted production experienced by the numerous small master manufacturers who proliferated in the Pennine communities of the West Riding in the latter half of the eighteenth century. The evolution of the industry and its progression towards mechanised factory production have been traced through the ledgers, daybooks and accounts of Robert Heaton and his son. Their transition to the factory system was an exceptional one, for the typical worsted entrepreneur in 1790 remained largely an organiser of domestic textile production as the Heatons had been before that year.

By 1790, the inventions of Hargreaves, Arkwright and Crompton were geared to water power in Lancashire cotton mills. The growing demand for cloth, both at home and abroad, necessitated a more efficient and speedier means of production than the domestic system. In spite of the advanced techniques of men like Hargreaves, there was still a shortage of yarn, whether it was woollen, cotton or worsted. Thomas Crosley, a Bradford worsted manufacturer, described the local situation,

> 'We had spinning done in Lancashire, as far as Ormskirk, in Craven, and at Kirby Lonsdale. In Wensleydale, Swaledale and other parts of North Yorkshire. Much difficulty was experienced with the yarn; we had to sort it and from the same top there would be yarn as thick as sixteens and as small as twenty-fours'.[38]

Increased demand and poor supply no doubt convinced worsted men of the need of new machines and of the need to centalise the processes of production. However, it was some years before Bradford township took its first step in that direction.

Early Worsted Factories in and around Bradford

The first influential worsted mill in the Bradford area was erected at Addingham on land purchased by Messrs. Cunliffe and Cockshott. An account book of Blakey, Greenwood Company, cotton spinners of Keighley, refers to Messrs. Cockshott & Lister in the early part of 1786.[39] A recent article states that their mill at Addingham was built in 1787 for the purpose of cotton spinning.[40] According to the evidence above, the two men were in business before that year, probably operating under the 'putting-out' system. Using water power from a weir in the River Wharfe, they quickly transferred to the production of worsted yarn and, within seven years, operated thirty frames of one kind or another. Having built cottages for their work-people, it is surprising to find that within two years they had broken their partnership. Although the Low Mill at Addingham proved a successful venture, it failed to satisfy the ambition of John Cockshott. In 1790, he moved into partnership with Reverend Thomas Halliday who, since 1778, had shared the mill at Tong Park, Baildon. The mill stood alongside Gill Beck between the villages of Baildon and Esholt. The power was drawn from two water wheels, but these proved inadequate in times of drought.[41] Cockshott brought to Tong Park, fresh capital and several of his Addingham workmen. A quarrel with John Cunliffe Lister brought about a complete termination of his Addingham interests and the mill there was put up for sale. Henceforth Cockshott concentrated his interest and capital on the Tong Park Mills and in 1795, he and Halliday contracted for a steam engine with the celebrated Boulton and Watt Company of Birmingham.[42]

This enabled the mill to operate at all times in spite of water scarcity. The engine was to be 600lbs and 10 feet high, providing twelve horse power. Portfolio 130 in the Boulton & Watt collection contains twenty two plans which possibly relate to this particular engine with its rotating shafts and condenser cysterns. Cockshott & Halliday were to pay £507-14-6 in a series of thirty nine instalments, 'first payment..12 months after delivery...in the payment of which you will find us very punctual. The engine works exceedingly well and fully equal to our expectation'.[43]

The engine was installed at the mill in the early spring of 1796 and consequently, it became the first steam-powered worsted mill in the West Riding. A recent student has noticed,

> 'Before 1790 the mechanised worsted spinning industry (in the North of England) was undeveloped, only Baildon could compare with the Midland firms...'[44]

Another of the early worsted mills in the Bradford region was that erected at Hewenden, in Wilsden in 1792. The lands at Hewenden, including the water corn mill, were owned by Miss Mary Hodgson, whose lands had been in trust to Abraham Balme. In 1791, Miss Hodgson leased the lands at the mill to William Nichols of Farsley and John Barker who entered into partnership as worsted spinners. These two gentlemen constructed a small worsted mill alongside the old corn mill, both of which were driven by the water of Harden Beck, (10 h.p.).[45] William Nichols, after spinning worsted for nine years, died in May 1800 leaving a wife and eight children. His five-sixths share in Hewenden Mill (worth £966) was inherited by his second son, Richard, who was twenty three years old and two years out of his apprenticeship with Samuel Wate, a weaver at Calverley. In 1803, Richard Nichols purchased Hallas Farm, not far from Hewenden, and all the family moved there. He was now running both the farm and the worsted mill, but, on the death of his chief woolsorter, brought into the works his seventeen-year old brother John at 14 shillings per week.

Figure 21 Hewenden. Originally the site of an ancient corn mill in the deep valley between Cullingworth and Wilsden. After 1792, it was one of the earliest water-powered spinning mills in the Bradford region. It was converted to steam power in 1837. In the background looms the impressive 17 arched Hewenden viaduct (1884) of the Great Northern Railway between Keighley and Thornton.

In 1813 Richard Nichols saw the advantage of a London agency and, accordingly moved there, 'in order to extend the trade and open new channels for manufacturing'. He immediately awarded himself a yearly salary of £200 and delegated responsibilities at Wilsden. John was to be in charge of the mill and warehouses and to attend the markets, in return for a salary of £80 a year. His older brother, Abraham, looked after the farm and young Samuel was personnel manager at the works (£60 p.a.). The move was certainly a profitable one, for 1814 brought net gains of £3,000 most of which (along with some of their salary) was ploughed back into the firm's fixed capital.[46] In 1816, Richard purchased premises in Maida Vale, London on his own account and immediately precipitated a long family feud and an expensive legal wrangle which ultimately left Richard Nichols and his brother William as co-partners of the mill.

Hewenden Mill and the one at Tong Park, one water driven, the other steam powered, were isolated experiments for almost a decade. Worsted mills of this kind were numerous amongst the watery cloughs of the Halifax district, with their abundant supplies of fast running water. They did not mushroom on the weak watercourses of Bradfordale although there were such mills on the becks at Harden and Morton. Bradford manufacturers expressed their opinions of such innovations in 1793, when one Buckley attempted to build a cotton mill in the centre of the town. A strongly-worded petition from local gentry scared off the would-be entrepreneur. It is strange that the assignees of this petition included Joshua Lupton, John Rand and Nathaniel Aked, all future pioneers of the factory system in Bradford.[47]

As yet, however, the inconvenience of water powered machinery was greater than the inadequacies of the domestic system. The worsted manufacturers of Bradford were prepared to tolerate the slower production, the risk of theft, and the inability to accommodate a sudden demand for goods. An additional factor was the quality of machine spun yarn. It had a tendency to break whilst in the weft. It was coarse and gave a rough effect to the woven piece. The 'spring shuttle', used by ninety per cent of the weavers, made no difference to the goods. It altered neither the quality, the price nor the wage.[48]

Perhaps the most important point which deterred Bradford manufacturers from factory production was the poor supply of water which ran through Bradford. The beck had never been famed for a powerful flow and there had been occasions when the soke mill even stopped for the lack of running water. Finally, the 1790s were not good years for the worsted trade. Until the factory was driven by a more reliable and speedier source of power, the Bradford manufacturers were content with the established system. Walter Spencer-Stanhope believed that the two systems could compete healthily.

> 'I feel no apprehension that the factory system will very rapidly increase or have the effect of destroying the domestic system'.[49]

This was quite valid until the time came when the machines of the factories could be worked at a greater speed than the volume of production in the domestic system.

Having identified the early peripheral growth of the factory system in the Bradford region it would be appropriate to trace the transition to factory production within the town itself. In 1798 Robert Ramsbottom occupied premises in the centre of Bradford (now Bank Street) where he spun worsted yarn. In that year, he installed a horse gin to turn the new spinning machines which he had recently purchased.[50] Four years earlier James Garnett had first introduced spinning frames to Bradford in his premises at the Paper Hall. This was not the answer, and the factory system still held no advantage over domestic production. The issue was resolved two years later, when the patent rights of James Watt's rotary motion steam engine expired. It had been as recent as 1796 that John Sturges and Company at Bowling had clashed with Boulton & Watt over those patent rights. The businessmen of Bradford were well aware of the issues involved and the expense, should they themselves have risked installing steam engines. They also knew of the expiry date and when that day came there would be no premiums to pay. With two large ironworks in the area, a moderate price might be paid for an engine. With this clearly in mind, the worsted manufacturers of Bradford were content to wait.

The first step was taken by Robert Ramsbotham in partnership with Nathaniel Murgatroyd and a member of the Swaine family. The mill was built in 1800 in the Holme and was installed with a fifteen horse-power engine for the purpose of spinning worsted yarn. As Ramsbotham and Swaine were the bankers for Messrs. Aydon and Elwell at Shelf Ironworks, it is possible that the latter may have constructed the steam engine for them. This mill in the Holme claims the honour of being Bradford's first steam driven mill. Its life proved short for it was gutted by fire five years later. More important, it set a precedent for others to follow. It opened a new century and a new age. It transformed the staple trade irrevocably and put a further nail into the coffin of the East Anglian worsted trade.

The year 1800 marks a watershed in the textile history of Bradford. In 1760, it had been a small rural town concentrating on the production of worsted cloth. Although international conflicts had caused some setbacks in its development, the world wide demand for cloth brought the town prosperity and growth. Its isolated position had been partially changed by an improved transport system and the erection of a Piece Hall had made it the centre of a widespread rural industry. After 1760, Bradford was mildly affected by the infectious cotton boom from the west but gained much from it. The town remained a centre of worsted production but yarn shortage and tardy production turned it slowly to the improved mechanisation of the cotton trade. After 1800, the availability of the steam engine took the industrial units of spinning production in the domestic system and slotted them easily into the new factories. The growth of the worsted trade in Bradford up to 1800 had been an internal one. The coming of the factory system altered physically the external appearance of the trade and subsequently of the town. The year 1800 was truly a watershed between the old semi-rural parochial Bradford and what became a new, expanding city of the industrial age.

The example of mechanised and centralised spinning production which had occurred on the periphery of Bradford parish at Wilsden, Oxenhope and Baildon in the 1790s was, after 1800, followed by a number of initiatives in the centre of the town. One of the earliest factory owners in Bradford township was Matthew Thompson, who was apprenticed to his uncle, Benjamin Piele, a dyer in Thornton Road. Matthew and his younger brother Benjamin had learned the trade under Richard Fawcett. In 1800, their uncle Benjamin Piele, purchased land between Silsbridge Land and the Mill Goit, and there, a mill and outbuildings were erected at his expense (viz Fig.22). This mill was managed by the two brothers who ultimately acquired the complete ownership.[52] By 1832 the brothers had also obtained a reeling room and an old dyehouse. They employed, in the mill at Silsbridge Lane, more than one hundred worsted spinners but they also employed twenty outworkers on piece rate, (an indication of the coexistence of the domestic system alongside factory production).

In the same year that the Thompsons had begun to spin by power, Richard Fawcett erected the Union Street spinning mill. Fawcett, born in Hunt Yard in 1778, had been apprenticed as a woolcomber but became a worsted manufacturer under the putting-out system. In 1804, a fire at Ramsbotham's mill in the Holme gave Fawcett the opportunity to increase his productivity. He moved into the partnership with fresh capital and soon Ramsbotham left him to go it alone.[53] A new fifteen horse-power steam engine was installed in the Holme Mill and

Figure 22 Thompsons Mill and Buildings 1840

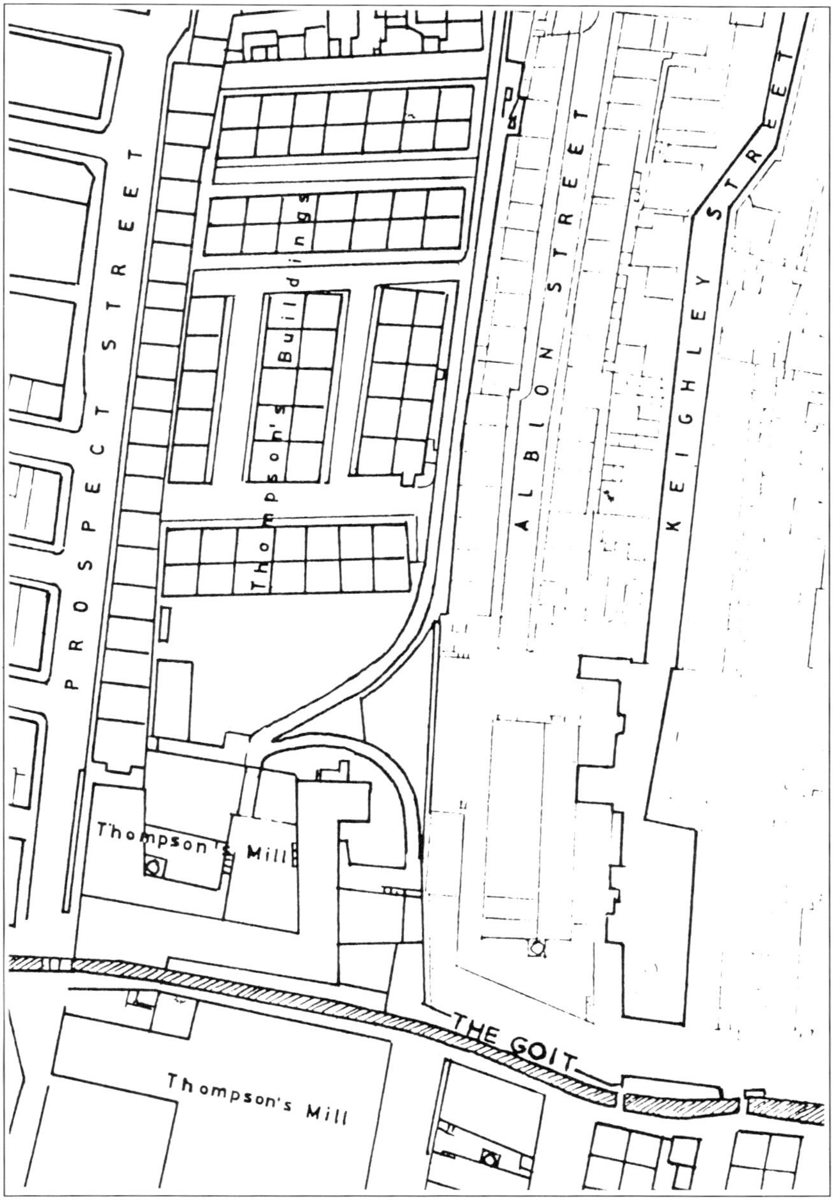

the machinery was all newly designed and recently purchased. By 1807 Holme Mill consisted of: '18 spinning frames (1044 spindles), 2 twisting frames (60 spindles each), winding frames, reels etc...also cotton machinery consisting of carding engines, drawing and roving frames, stretching frames, throstles etc'.[54] In 1807, Fawcett further increased his production potential, when he built a new mill which had two steam engines of fifty horse power and employed well over two hundred spinners. Fawcett's mills were later sold to Illingworth & Murgatroyd in 1830. However, Fawcett's main centre of production remained Union Street Mill which had opened in 1800.

Fawcett's fortune of £100,000 disappeared in a frenzy of property purchases. The source of his income was badly hit by the depressed state of certain markets and by 1832 'King Richard', as he was known amongst the labouring classes, was no more.

Another notable contributor to Bradford's early factory growth was John Rand whose family had come from Norwich in 1760. He had married the daughter of Samuel Swaine, of Legrams in 1785. In partnership with Swaine, he put out both cotton and worsted tops. The latter had priority, for Rand did a good trade in supplying Norwich with fine worsted yarn. In 1803, Rand erected, in Horton Lane, a worsted spinning mill, driven ultimately by two steam engines of a combined fifty-four horse-power.[55] By 1830, the mill was one of the largest concerns in Bradford, employing two hundred and fifty persons.

These men were the pre-eminent pioneers of factory spinning in Bradford township. There were others in the out-townships, but Bradford itself possessed, by 1810, only five mills with an aggregate of one hundred and twenty horse-power. A very large part of the spinning was still worked under the domestic system, as was all the weaving at this time and wool combing remaind a domestic occupation until the 1840s. The normal system of worsted production remained that of the manufacturer putting out his tops and yarn. Such a man was James Hargreaves of Shipley. He had taken a small farm at Delph Hill, Bolton. James Garnett, the worsted spinner of Paper Hall, sold Hargreaves his first warp which he converted into pieces. Hargreaves increased his trade in the 1770s and began to give out tops. In 1779 he moved to the Old Castle, Frizinghall, and gave out both weaving and spinning from there. He brought his sons, William and Joseph, into the trade and they later made their names in the new factory system. Hargreaves and his kind were the very life of the worsted trade at this time. The factories had made a sound start but their contribution could not match that of the many stuff manufacturers in the trade. One or two clothiers operated in a 'bigger way' employing unusually large numbers of spinners and journeymen weavers to work up the cloth for them in centralised loomshops like that of John Cockshott at Addingham which accommodated sixty two handlooms.

> 'With the exception of spinning, the typical worsted entrepreneur at the end of the Napoleonic Wars had been much the same as ever, an organiser of domestic textile production taking place in the scattered cottages and small workshops of the West Riding Pennines'.[56]

Both methods of production had helped the trade to withstand the vicissitudes of the international situation throughout the first decade of the nineteenth century. Both had contributed to the growth of the town of Bradford and to its emerging supremacy in the West Riding worsted trade.

Figure 23 Handcombers. This is a detail, in bronze, from the Samuel Cunliffe Lister monument in Lister Park, Bradford. It shows the traditional skill of combing wool by hand and the equipment involved. *Photo: Ian Beesley*

Bradford's Supremacy of the Worsted Trade

James, the first historian of the trade, used the figures for the drawback on soap to demonstrate this trend. Manufacturers were given a rebate on soap consumed in the cleaning of wool. Over the years, the drawback varied from a halfpenny to twopence per pound of wool. Consequently, the figures have been used as a guide for the estimated growth of the industry.

The figures certainly illustrate the leadership being established by the town of Bradford over Halifax. Why should this be so? Professor Sigsworth has suggested that the two towns were equal in most respects. Both were the religious and commercial centres for their areas. Neither had a real transport problem, and both were at the centre of an expanding industry. Halifax, however, had a better supply of water and had linked itself quickly to the new

Table XXXIX Drawback on Soap 1810–1830

	1810 (£)	*1820* (£)	*1830* (£)
Bradford	851	2,411	5,289
Leeds	353	254	289
Halifax	256	724	1,905
Keighley	199	848	1,866
Wakefield	111	144	725

water-driven spinning machinery. In the 1790s Bradford's water supply was inadequate for such mills and thus the town fell behind, only to surge ahead with the adoption of the steam engine. After 1800, Sigsworth argues, the Halifax manufacturers had laid out too much capital to start again and adapt to the more powerful and consistent power source of steam.[57] Recent research on capital investment in early factory production has demonstrated the small amounts of fixed capital required to initiate mill production. Robert Heaton, an early mill owner from Haworth, had the misfortune to have his mill burnt to the ground on Friday 13 March 1795. The Royal Exchange paid out £493 for the whole manufactory. Heaton rebuilt the whole mill for £285, yet he spent £1,700 on raw materials during that year.[58] Insurance records of local mills of this period bear out this low proportion of fixed capital. With the coming of steam power and purpose-built mills, the situation changed as specialisation demanded a considerable increase of fixed-capital investment. Nevertheless, in the early years, investment in plant was small. In many cases, early mills were simply converted corn mills and many manufacturers only rented the premises which they used. It is difficult, therefore, to sustain the view that Halifax manufacturers were irrevocably committed to water power, Their original capital outlays were not so great as to prevent them from changing to steam-powered production.

This factor may have contributed in some way to the relative supremacy of Bradford. A more important reason, however, for the secondary position of Halifax, might be the diversity of the textile business done there. Unlike Bradford, Halifax continued to produce, and market, both woollen and worsted goods. Its manufacturers were also concerned with the finishing trade. Bradford concentrated its resources on the manufacture of plain white worsted cloth and established a reputation for that alone. Halifax manufacturers spread their enterprise and resources over too wide a range, to be able to compete in one specific cloth. Halifax manufacturers continued to produce both cloths and stuffs and consequently failed to keep up with Bradford's concentrated worsted production. This reason alone does not adequately explain Bradford's emergent primacy of the worsted trade. It was probably the cumulative effect of several factors. Whatever the cause, the effect cannot be denied. Bradford in the second decade of the nineteenth century asserted its superiority as the centre of the English worsted trade.

With the European peace in 1815 and the continued demand for worsted cloth from the South American colonies, Bradford manufacturers stepped up their production. Both manufacturer and merchant were optimistic of resuming trade in former markets after the war. However, by 1816, the merchants were overstocked with goods and refused further supplies. The countries of Europe, after years of expensive warfare, could no longer afford the fine-quality English stuffs. They relied on the lower class of goods made by their own clothiers. This caused a marked recession in the local worsted trade which was only slightly relieved by the reopening of the American market with its restrictive 15% import tariff. This slump affected the woollen export trade more than the worsted, although the latter was not immune, as this statement from the Worsted Committee, in 1817, confirms,

> 'It appears to this committee from the very low state of their fund and from the very great depreciation of the worsted manufacturers, it is highly expedient to advance the allowance from the drawback'.[59]

However, the trade shrugged off such hindrances and continued to progress in both quantity and value. Even in ruinous years like 1816, the manufacturer continued to work at maximum output, accumulating a large stock but confident of its purchase at some future date. The year 1818 proved him right. Money became less tight; English wool prices tumbled and the import of foreign wool doubled; foreign markets, particularly the Americas, demanded large amounts of cloth. Consequently, a good trade was done in that year when worsted exports rose by over a quarter of a million pieces to 937,944 pieces. Bradford and Halifax continued to contribute to that expansion but in different ways. It was about this time that Halifax manufacturers introduced the better quality goods like crapes and bombazines. This type of cloth had traditionally been the staple of Norwich but henceforth, Halifax became the centre of the fancy stuffs trade and prospered from it. Without doubt, Bradford was, by 1820, the country's principal centre of plain worsted production.

Bradford and the Wool Supply

One serious problem, recurring throughout the nineteenth century, which confronted Bradford's manufacturing interest was the supply and price of English long wools. Although worsted cloth used mostly domestic wool from Leicestershire, Lincoln, Kent and the Cotswolds, the tax on imported foreign wool kept the price of such domestic clips at high levels. In 1819 the manufacturers of both cloth and stuffs joined forces to petition against the tax. The Bradford interest was led by Richard Fawcett and Matthew Thompson, the principal manufacturers of the town. They had little success but several supplications followed in subsequent years. Finally, they were faced with a compromise of abolishing the import duty, on condition that English wool could be exported. Such a move would have ruined the worsted manufacturers, or so they thought. Good English wool was already hard to come by (and at high prices), without shipping it off to other countries. Many manufacturers found it difficult to get enough wool to meet their demands without paying more exorbitant prices for it. Compromised in this way, Bradford's worsted manufacturers clamoured to prevent the legal exportation of English wool. A meeting held at Bradford 2 June 1823 resolved, 'that a free export of British wool would be destructive to the trade of Bradford and the neighbourhood'. The efforts of Richard Fawcett and Stuart Wortley M.P. were to no avail. In May 1824, the exportation of English wool was legalised for the first time in almost two hundred years. Fawcett was disappointed and adamant that the permission to export wool or yarn with a low duty must eventually produce mischief to this country; that every pound of wool or yarn taken from it, either in a raw or partially manufactured state must be to that extent injurious to the artisan and manufacturer...the policy is bad and no good can eventually come from it.'[60]

In spite of this setback, the expansion of the Bradford trade between 1820 and 1825 has been estimated at sixty six per cent. During those years, the number of spinning mills in the town alone, had increased to twenty six, whilst the drawback reached the unprecedented total of £3,804 for the township (£5,033 for the Bradford District). The wool consumption of the town had risen from 1,633,920lbs. in 1810 to 4,629,120lbs. in 1820 and then soared to 6,382,081lbs. in 1825. Export tables for this period do not distinguish between woollen and worsted, but it was obvious that Germany had become the industry's main buyer. A more credible sign of this trend was the increasing number of foreign agents employed by German merchants, who settled in the area. Merchants began to move from Leeds and reside in Bradford, while the Bradford Piece Hall was becoming the central exchange of plain worsteds for Keighley, Colne, and even Halifax manufacturers.

The fears of the manufacturers regarding the exportation and short supply of wool were not confirmed. This problem was partially resolved by the increased imports of Australian long wool:

Table XL Imports of Australian Long Wool 1816–1828

Year	*Amount (lbs)*	*Year*	*Amount (lbs)*
1816	13,611	1820	99,915
1818	86,525	1821	175,433
1819	74,284	1828	1,574,186

However, it must be noted that it was not until after 1825 that West Riding worsted manufacturers began to use this wool. Until that time, it was employed largely by the West of England manufacturers. By February 1825 the septennial festivities of the Bishop Blaize festival were being celebrated with extraordinary confidence and assured expectation by all concerned in the Bradford trade. However, by June, masters and men were locked in a determined and bitter conflict which led to the inevitable defeat of the workforce after twenty three weeks. Furthermore the strike of 1825 convinced the masters of the value of mechanised weaving, 'there is a powerful competition between hand and power weaving progressively increasing in Bradford and the neighbouring towns, and it may be confidently asserted that goods woven by power are superior in every respect'.[61] The aftermath of the strike saw Bradford mill owners gradually take up power looms and harness them to the increasing number of steam engines within their factories. In 1836, the seventy three worsted mills in the parish of Bradford used 1,647 horse power of which 1,455 horse power was produced by steam. By that time, J.G. Horsfall operated 378 power looms at North Wing, and others like Milnes and Dewhurst, and James Wade were beginning to combine power-driven spinning with weaving. There were only 2,768 power looms in the West Riding in 1836. However, weaving worsteds on power looms increased considerably in the 1830s, although as late as 1851 there were said to be 1,117 handloom weavers still operating in the Bradford district.[62] In the out-townships of the Bradford parish, handloom weaving prevailed, although the evidence given before the enquiry into the condition of the domestic weavers in 1838 shows clearly, that the majority of manufacturers were operating a dual system, replacing manual labour by power looms as capital became available. The introduction of the Jacquard loom in the 1830s made possible more intricate weaves and designs. The new incumbent of Bradford, the Reverend William Scoresby, noted in 1840,

> 'The Jacquard loom is an apparatus of standard employment... and by its singularly ready application, the Bradford manufacturers are enabled to produce an endless variety of patterns in damasks and fancy goods. Few of the products of mechanical science interested me personally more than this very admirable machine and the apparatus by which its functions are guided, drawing first of all a pattern no matter how complicated it may be'.[63]

Also by this time Bradford had attracted two very new important departments of the worsted trade. The period up to 1820 had been spent consolidating the town's position as the centre of worsted cloth manufacture in this country. However, in that year, Bradford manufacturers still relied upon the wool fairs of Wakefield for their supplies of raw materials and the merchants of Leeds and Halifax for the retail and distribution of their finished goods. Secondly, woven plainbacks were usually taken to Leeds or Halifax to be dyed and finished. These two sections, merchanting and finishing, became part of the Bradford worsted trade in the third decade. An increasing number of foreign merchants, particularly German, came to reside in the town after 1830. Although this trend was not accentuated until later years, certainly large numbers of worsted merchants had moved into Bradford to establish it as an independent centre (viz Table XLI).

Table XLI Number of Worsted Merchants in West Yorkshire Townships 1822–1842

	Leeds	*Bradford*	*Halifax*	*Wakefield*[64]
1822	14	5	6	2
1830·	42	24	12	1
1842	51	54	21	0

The Bradford Piece Halls also made alterations to accommodate this change. Although the worsted trade functioned by private order rather than the open market, the Piece Halls had provided facilities for the smaller manufacturers. The bi-annual reports for 1829/35 show an increase in the number of stands held, at the Piece Hall (60 in 1830, 78 in 1834 and 89 by November 1835).

Larger rooms were available for the bigger manufacturers living outside the town, like Moses Bottomley from Shelf.[65] However, by that time, few of the Bradford manufacturers used the Halls as most of them had personal show rooms or warehouses. Although these figures demonstrate the response of the Piece Hall Trustees to Bradford's new role as merchanting centre, the actual part played by the Halls in the distribution sector of the trade was declining by 1830.[66]

A similar trend can be identified in the number of Bradford staplers. Wakefield, long the centre of Yorkshire wool sales, gradually yielded its position to Bradford throughout the nineteenth century. The number of wool staplers for the respective towns are as follows:

Table XLII Number of Wool Staplers in Bradford and Wakefield 1822–1847

	Bradford	*Wakefield*
1822	39	51
1829	46	36
1837	74	19
1847	126	11

Source: *Various Directories 1822–1847*

In 1818, there were only three small dyehouses in and around the town. Rawson had one near his vitriol works, alongside the canal. Another was owned by a Mr. Walton at Dyers Field in Bowling. Four years later, Walton was partnered by George Ripley who had learned the trade at Washer Lane dyeworks in Halifax. Walton soon withdrew and George Ripley was joined by his son, Edward. Together they built up the firm over the next ten years so that, in 1821, they employed twenty one dyers. Business was carried out in a small room at the bottom of Talbot Yard in Hustlergate and goods were sent from there to the works.[67] With the aid of James Murgatroyd, the company discovered the means of black dyeing. By 1830, the works specialised in dyeing full pieces of cloth in addition to the old trade of dyeing individual shawls, suit lengths and stocking yarn. After the death of George Ripley in 1834, the firm monopolised the dyeing industry of the town.

These two new sectors of Bradford's trade were well established by 1830 and confirmed the town as the true centre of the English worsted industry. They helped to consolidate the steady progress which the trade had made in the post-war years. The manufacturers of Bradford had begun to transfer the trade from its domestic/rural environment to the mills and factories of the town. This was particularly true of the spinning process, for in 1830, of thirty three mills in the town, twenty five were spinning only. With their steam engines of almost 1,200 horse power, these mills transformed the face of Bradford,

> 'Never in my life did I see a more smoky place than Bradford. The great long chimneys are doubled I think in number within these two or three years'.[68]

and, in so doing, altered the whole way of life for many of its inhabitants. For the multiplicity of chimneys and the ever present pall of coal smoke was indicative not only of the expansion and wealth of the worsted industry but equally of the dirt, despondency and squalor of the future Victorian industrial city. In the 1820s and 1830s, Bradfordians from all walks of life were well aware of the change that had come to their lives. Change was to be the watch word for at least another two decades. Bradford and its worsted trade stood at yet another exciting threshold in 1830. Later generations would reap the harvest of the earlier enterprise, vision and determination, when Bradford became the international centre of the worsted trade. By 1851, its predominance as Britain's leading worsted producer was universally acknowledged,

> 'No single portion of the English provinces can boast of a greater prosperity during the last half century, than Bradford which from a comparatively insignificant market town, has during the period referred to risen by the energy of its inhabitants, the material resources for manufacturing purposes it possesses as its geographical position to be – beyond all challenge – the Capital of the worsted trade'.[69]

The new industrial city had already arrived by 1830. The days of the comber/weaver aristocracy and the domestic system were passing, if not gone. In February 1832 a handful of artisans determined to bury the 'remains' of the patron saint of hand combers Bishop Blaise in a final public ceremony. As the funeral procession left the Piece Hall gates and wound slowly down Kirkgate, an epoch in the industrial and social history of Bradford came to an end.[70]

1. R.G. Wilson 'The Supremacy of the Yorkshire Cloth Industry in the Eighteenth Century' in N.B. Harte & K.G. Ponting (eds) *Textile History and Economic History: Essays in Honour of Miss J. de Lacy Mann* (Manchester 1973) pp.225–246 and P. Deane The Output of the British Woollen Industry in the Eighteenth Century. *Journal of Economic History* XVII (1967) pp.207–23
2. R.G. Wilson op. cit. p.226

3. Y.M.L. Hailstone Ms 5.29 15 February 1752
4. J.H. Clapham, 'The Transference of the Worsted Industry from Norfolk to the West Riding' *Economic Journal* XX, (1910) pp.195–210
5. J.K. Edwards, Decline of the Norwich Textile Industry, *Yorkshire Bulletin of Economic and Social Research* Vol. 16, (1964) pp.310–12
6. R.G. Wilson op. cit. p.227
7. J. Mappey, On Some of the Decayed Families of Bradford, *Bradford Antiquary* Vol. 1 (1888) p.28
8. Y.M.L. Hailstone Mss. 5.29 20 November 1751
9. Y.M.L. Hailstone Ms 5.29 9 January 1752: and W. Hustwick, An Eighteenth Century Wool Stapler, *Bradford Textile Society Journal* (1956–7)
10. P.P. Report of the Committee into the False Winding of Wool 1752
11. H. Heaton *The Yorkshire Woollen and Worsted Industries* (Oxford 1920) p.271
12. J. James, *A History of the Worsted Manufacture in England* (1842 new ed. 1968) p.289
13. J.W. Turner, Bradford Piece Halls, *Bradford Antiquary* Vol. 1 (1884) and B.C.L. Ms 31/30, 18/7
14. Piece Hall Papers in possession of Messrs. Vint, Hill and Killick, Solicitors Bradford, Unclassified
15. H. Heaton, op. cit. p.380
16. J.B. Priestley Library, University of Bradford (hereafter J.B.P.L.) Minute Book 1 1777–1786
17. Ibid 27 September 1784
18. J.B.P.L. Worsted Committee Mss. Minute Book II 1786–1805 26 September 1792
19. Y.M.L. Hailstone Ms G.3 10 May 1787
20. Ibid.
21. B.C.L. Heaton Ms B.164
22. E.M. Sigsworth, William Greenwood and Robert Heaton, *Bradford Textile Society Journal* (1951–52), pp.61–72
23. B.C.L. Heaton Ms B.149 (1770)
24. Ibid B.146/7 (1794–1811)
25. Ibid B.148 2 June 1775
26. Ibid B.146 & B.151
27. E.M. Sigsworth op. cit. p.72
28. B.C.L. Heaton Mss. B.152 30 May 1789
29. D.T. Jenkins, *The West Riding Wool Textile Industry 1770–1835 A Study in Fixed Capital Formation* (Pasold 1975) and K.V. Pankhurst, Investment in the West Riding Woollen Textile Industry, *Yorkshire Bulletin of Social and Economic Research*, Vol. 7 (1966) pp.93–116
30. R.G. Wilson, *Gentleman Merchants*, (Manchester 1971) p.97
31. B.C.L. Heaton Ms B.154 (1791)
32. Ibid.
33. B.C.L. Heaton Mss B.156 (1794–6) and A.569 (1799)
34. Figures calculated from several account books in the period.
35. B.C.L. Heaton Mss B.164
36. B.C.L. Heaton Mss A.520 (1806–09)

37. W. Cudworth, *Rambles Round Horton*, (Bradford 1886), pp.29–31
38. J. James, op. cit. p.324
39. B.L.U.L. Marriner Ms.199
40. S.D. Chapman, The Pioneers of Worsted Spinning by Power, *Business History* Vol.7 (1965), pp.97–116
41. J. La Page, *The Story of Baildon* (Baildon 1951), pp.69–71
42. B.C.L. Boulton & Watt Mss. Engine Book, 9 December 1795
43. Ibid Letterbook (Ingoing) 5 May 1797 and Portfolio 130
44. S.D. Chapman op. cit. p.116
45. B.C.L. Miscellaneous Mss. A.385
46. Ibid A.352 and A.285
47. J. James, op. cit. pp.591–2
48. E.M. Sigsworth, *Black Dyke Mills*, (Liverpool 1958) p.3
49. P.P. Report of the Select Committee to Consider the State of the Woollen Manufacture in England 1806
50. W. Cudworth, op. cit. pp.42–3
51. J. James, op. cit. p.367
52. W. Cudworth, *Round About Bradford*, (Bradford 1876) p.424 and B.C.L. Claridge Collection 24/17
53. W.R. Millmore 'Richard Fawcett' *Wool Record* Vol. 79 (1951) pp.1773–4 and W. Scruton *The Fawcett Family*, (Bradford 1907). pp.1–11
54. *Leeds Mercury*, 19 September 1807
55. W. Cudworth, *Rambles Round Horton*, op. cit. pp.40–41
56. E.M. Sigsworth, 'The Woollen Textile Industry', in *The Dynamics of Victorian Business* edited by R. Church (London 1980) pp.181–198
57. E.M. Sigsworth '*Black Dyke Mills*' pp.21–24
58. B.C.L. Heaton Ms B.154
59. B.C.L. Worsted Committee Mss. Minute Book 17 June 1816
60. J. James, op. cit. pp.393–9
61. B.C.L. Master Manufacturers' Minute Book 38/3/6 September 1825
62. B.C.L. Empsall Collection Ms 24/17/5
63. Scoresby Mss. Whitby Literary & Philosophical Society, Ms 6/5
64. E.M. Sigsworth, Bradford and Its Worsted Industry Under Victoria 1837–1901, *Bradford Textile Society Journal* (1952–53) p.64
65. Piece Hall Papers, Ledger 1829–36
66. J.S. Roberts, *Little Germany*, (Bradford 1977) p.7
67. W. Cudworth, *A History of Bolton & Bowling* (Bradford 1891)
68. From the Diary and Journal of Miss A. Lister, 25 June 1831 quoted in T.W. Hanson, *Old Halifax*, (Halifax 1920) reprint edition 1968. pp.239–240
69. Collinson, Burton & Company, *West Riding Worsted Directory* (1852) pp.97–8
70. W. Scruton, Notes and Queries, B.C.L. Ms. 5.40 Vol. II p.21

7

The Urban Development of Bradford to 1840

'When I was young the town consisted of Westgate, Kirkgate and Ivegate. The main of the houses stood in Westgate...the back of Kirkgate on both sides consisted of meadows...there was a great rookery between Kirkgate and Bowling Green Square.... A good deal of cockfighting and bull-baiting prevailed in the neighbourhood when I was young.... There was not a house between Townend (where the roads from Little and Great Horton meet Manchester Road) to the Red Gin public house....'[1]

'The general state of the surface of the streets of Bradford is respectable but in most of the inferior and cross streets chiefly inhabited by the working classes the condition is quite otherwise. Few of these are paved at all...pools of slop water and filth are visible all over the surface. The dung heaps are found in several places in the street and open privies are seen in many directions.... Taking the general condition of Bradford, I am obliged to pronounce it to be the most filthy town I visited....' (1844)[2]

These two quotations, much beloved of students of local history, demonstrate the dramatic change in Bradford's urban profile which occurred between 1780 and 1840. This section of the book will examine the detailed developments of urban growth in those years. The pace of growth created social and administrative problems which will be discussed elsewhere. Of Saxon origin, the town was situated at the confluence of four small streams or becks. These flow down from the surrounding hillsides, (800–1,000 feet), the principal beck having its source at Bell Dean in Allerton. This runs into Thornton and picks up the spring head at Shay whence it passes Crossley Hall and flows into Horton Beck.[3] By this time, the stream is of some considerable force and deserves the appelation of the Bradford Beck. Once within the boundary of the town, the beck bends sharply. At this juncture the valley links with two small dells which give the appearance that the town lies in a geographical 'bowl'. Thenceforth, the stream and valley follow a level course for three miles where they then unite, with the main Aire Valley at Shipley. This stretch from the spring head at Thornton to the junction with the River Aire, was formerly known as Bradfordale.

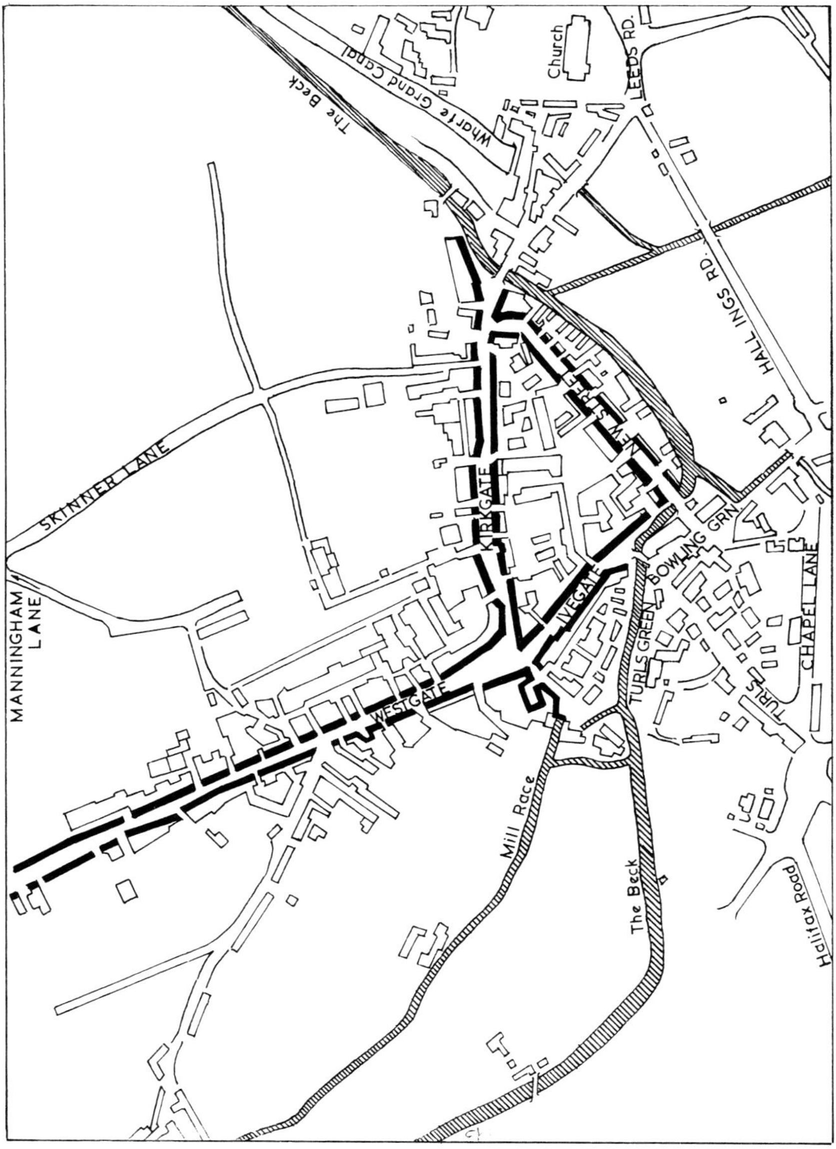

Figure 24 Bradford in 1802

By 1800 the township had changed little from its compact medieval origins and was dominated by the junction of three primary highways, Ivegate, Westgate and Kirkgate (viz Fig.24). These three highways joined within the bend of the main Bradford Beck and were the main focus of the town for many centuries.[4] In 1760, each of these thoroughfares had a distinct character of its own. Westgate, as part of the Roman road from Pontefract, is though to be older than the town itself. Until the last decade of the eighteenth century, the street functioned as the commercial centre of the town. At the bottom of Westgate, a twice weekly market was held, where stalls skirted the highway as far as the junction with Silsbridge Lane.

'There was an old cross at the bottom of Westgate, around which the market was held. Stalls for butchers and others were placed on both sides of Westgate and extended along way up the street....'

Westgate also housed some of the town's principal inns (of which there were fifty in 1787). The King's Arms, Bull's Head, Boy and Barrel and the Packhorse were all centres for the retailing of finished cloth. For two generations, worsted manufacturers and merchants known as the 'Bradford Club', met regularly at the Bull's Head to discuss the vagaries of trade.[5] The street also provided the town with its only supply of water, for here was the central tank of the Waterworks Company. As well as being a commercial highway, it was the town's most respectable residential area, and incurred the highest subscription under the 'watch' system after 1803.

Figure 25 Sun Inn, Ivegate. One of Bradford's leading hotels and coaching inns, the Sun Inn was noted for its dancing assemblies and social occasions. It hosted the start of numerous commercial and industrial schemes like the Leeds–Liverpool and Bradford Canals, the Piece Halls and the Worsted Committee, all began their life here.

An extension of Westgate drops sharply down to the beck, this is Ivegate. In 1760, the administration of the town's affairs was carried on from here. It was very much the town's 'official' street, where the offices of the Crown and the manor lord were to be found. At the top of the road was the Hall of Pleas, the Court House and the dungeon (viz Figs.26 and 27). Located at the lower end of Ivegate, close to the beck, was the Sun Inn, a meeting place for many institutions and groups (viz Fig.25). This tavern saw the birth of numerous public schemes like the Leeds–Liverpool and Bradford Canals, the Piece Halls, and the Worsted Committee. Kirkgate was essentially a residential quarter until thenew century. The manor house and park of the Rawsons were to be found on the site of the present Arndale Centre (formerly Kirkgate Market).[6] The street led down to the beck which it crossed at Church Bridge and ultimately on to the Parish Church. The simplicity and compactness of this urban geography is confirmed by an extract of a surveyor's map of 1722, (viz Fig.28). The Haycliffe Sough of the Waterworks Company was not opened until 1744 which casts some doubts as to this map's reliability. For all its weaknesses, the map does at least give an impression of the town in the early eighteenth century.

There was no significant addition to this street plan until 1787. The daily coach between Leeds and Halifax stopped at the Sun Inn via Barkerend Road and High Street, passing up the gentle slope of Kirkgate and down the steep hill of Ivegate. For the passengers, 'A more dangerous passage could hardly be found amongst the Swiss Alps' and by 1780 it was clear that a link road between Kirkgate and the bottom of Ivegate was necessary. The ubiquitous

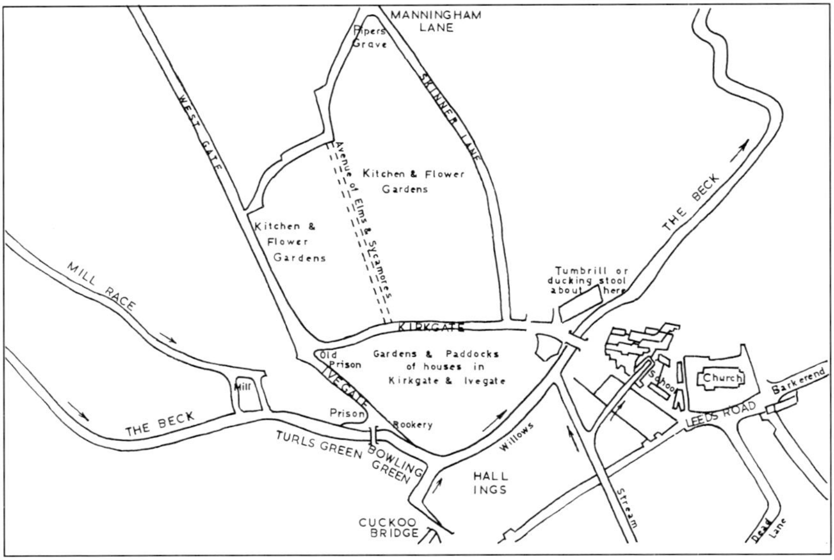

Figure 26 Conjectural Map of Bradford c.1650

Figure 27 Hall of Pleas. This ancient court of justice was situated at the junction of Kirkgate and Ivegate. Here also was the town's dungeon (in Ivegate) where the early Methodist preacher John Nelson was imprisoned in 1744, the same year that John Wesley made his first visit to Bradford.

John Hustler originally proposed the road in conjunction with an appeal for increased market facilities. The lord of the manor, John Marsden, was reluctant to invest capital on the scheme, and Edward Leedes, through whose property the road would pass, strongly objected. On Leedes' death in 1787 work on the road immediately went ahead. It ran along the edge of the alluvium bank of the Bradford Beck, passing in front of the Piece Halls. It was appropriately named New Street and subsequently Market Street (Fig.29).

It was within this small urban nucleus of less than half a square mile that the majority of the town's inhabitants lived in the late eighteenth century. Of the 4,506 Bradfordians counted in the unofficial census of 1780, over twenty five per cent (1,604) lived in Westgate.[7] Thomas Jeffrey's map of the county of 1771 suggests some ribbon development along the approach roads from Horton, Manningham, Laisterdyke and Bowling. Merchants like John Hustler and John Buck had purchased estates close to these roads and built detached houses within spacious grounds.[8] However, lesser merchants continued to live within the heart of the town, usually in Westgate or Kirkgate, where their houses also served as workshops and warehouses 'The manufacturers of stuffs, who resided in this town had warehouses near their houses, in which they shewed their pieces'.

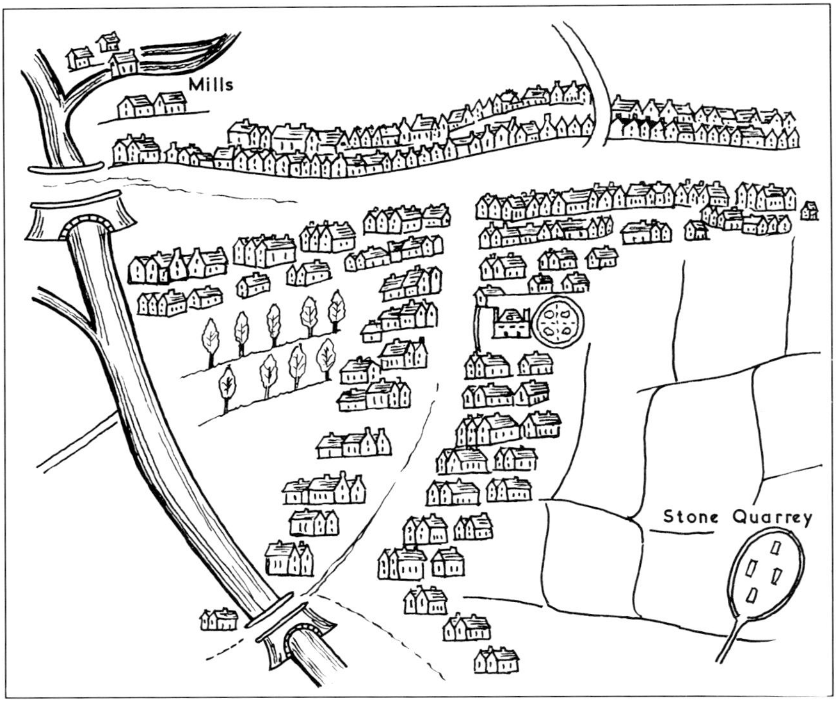

Figure 28 Bradford in 1722

Benjamin Piele, Richard Sclater and Robert Milligan, all future millowners, all had property in Westgate, and Kirkgate housed entrepreneurs like John Preston and John Hardy (Low Moor Ironworks), James Marshall (Bierley Ironworks), Joseph Priestley and James Garnett.

Kirkgate, dominated by the Manor Hall built in 1705, consisted mostly of 'large and old-fashioned houses, standing apart from each other'. The back of Kirkgate, on both sides, was made up of meadows, landscaped gardens, avenue walks and a great rookery. James stated that 403 Bradford households paid the window duties in 1781 and estimated that at least half of the township were above the condition of cottagers. For those who were not, housing consisted of one roomed cottages of poor quality and low value, dropped piecemeal into the garths and folds of the ancient tofts and crofts. Antecedent property boundaries profoundly affected Bradford's subsequent urban plan. At least 66% of the township was freehold as early as 1311.[9] This medieval freehold tenure accounted for the distinctive smallholding of the long narrow croft in Bradford. As population rose steadily after 1780 Bradford increased its accommodation accordingly by the economic 'in-filling' of these garths and

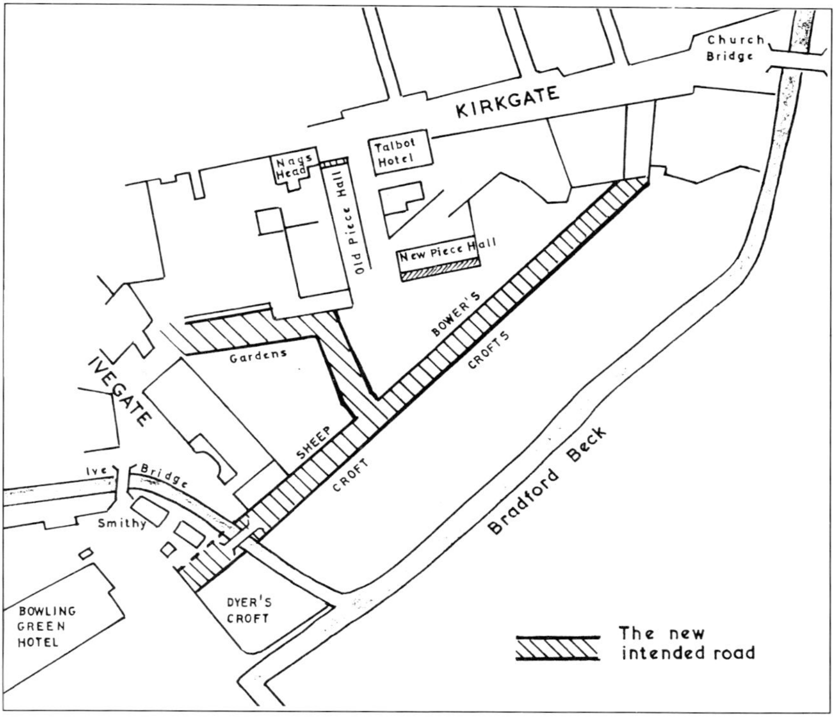

Figure 29 Bradford Town Centre in 1787

folds noted for their 'absence of water and sanitation. Nor were the proprietors put to the charge of road construction, pavage and drains, since the houses were sited behind thoroughfares'.[10]

These houses were built along one or both sides of the garth, and usually adjoined similar properties in the adjacent yard, access to the main road was through a covered alley. Bower's Crofts, adjoining the Beck between Ivegate and Kirkgate was transformed between 1782 and 1840 by this kind of development (Fig.29). Similarly at Naylor's Yard between Ivegate and Millbank there was considerable piecemeal in-filling of yard property with cottages backing on to similar terraces in the next croft (viz Fig.30). By 1845 this locality was highlighted by the town's woolcombers in their report on the sanitary conditions of Bradford,

> 'behind the Sun Inn stables it is filthy in the extreme; the street is narrow, drainage bad, stagnant water suffered to accumulate.... The foul atmosphere which exists in this locality is augmented to a fearful extent by the crowded state of the apartments in which the parties live and follow their occupations....'[11]

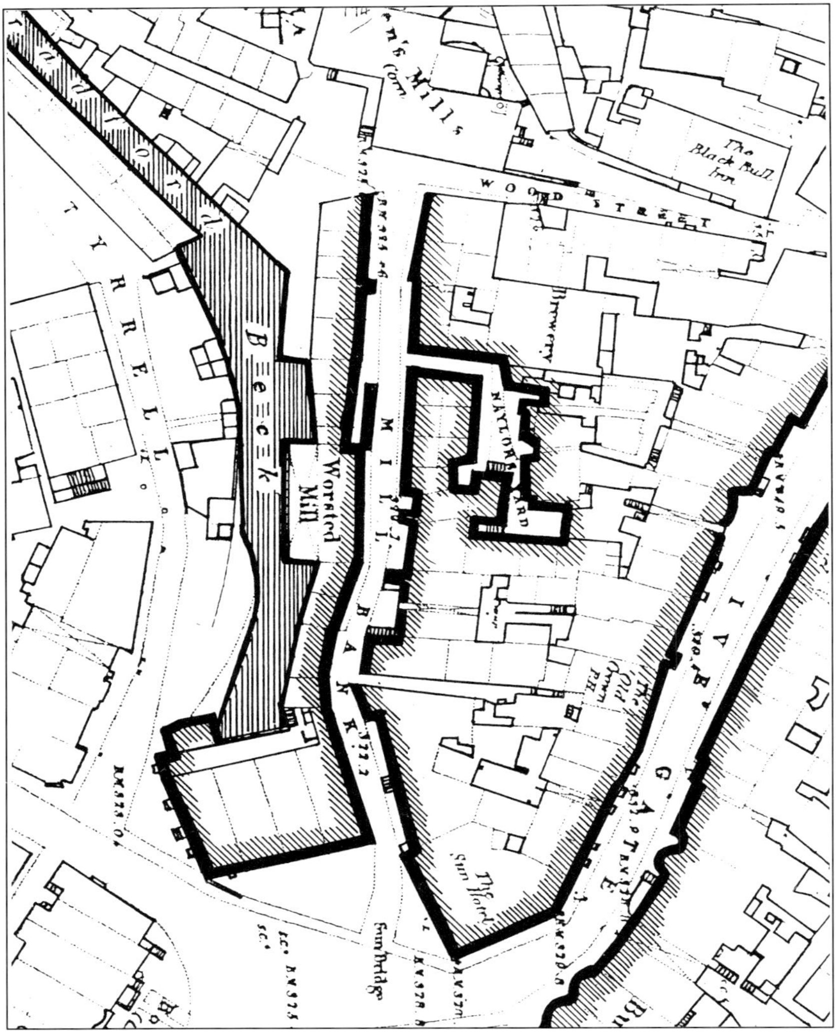

Figure 30 Naylor's Yard, Mill Bank, 1845

The high density housing and human congestion following upon the acceleration of the town's population brought early problems of environmental decline. The smells of factory chimneys, chemical works, open markets and thousands of unwashed bodies eventually forced out of the town centre the merchants, manufacturers and well-to-do. As early as 1793 James Buckley attempted to build a steam-powered spinning mill on the Tyrls, an open rural area, but was pressed by Bradford's leading inhabitants to take his scheme elsewhere. In June 1807 the Improvement Commission concerned themselves for the first time with the nuisance of smoke pollution from Richard Fawcett's mill. Developments such as this were inevitable as Bradford took on the mantle of industrialism. As the noise and smell of city life intensified, the town's wealthier families moved to the outskirts where they purchased property with substantial surrounding estates. Thomas Mann, the first stuff merchant to live in Bradford, erected Mannville House in Great Horton Road. Dr. John Simpson noted in 1825 'Mannville is as nice a place as any in the neighbourhood of Bradford but there is no water and soon the place will be built up.' Richard Fawcett purchased Randal Well Close (site of the later Alexandra Hotel) and built the impressive Westbrook House with its fine 'westerly prospect and an uninterrupted succession of green fields'. In 1797 Edmund Peckover purchased part of the Vicarage lands to create a private parkland around Eastbrook House.

A map of the township of Bradford in 1834 illustrates clearly the large number of private mansions and estates peripheral to the nucleus of the town centre.[12] In 1845 the German George Weerth could write,

> 'one finds a second housing estate on the half of the hilltops which were likewise originally given up to private dwellings...within a few years the industry had sequestered the whole valley and pursued the fugitives up the hills too...the whole town...looks like an enormous crater which is continually fermenting and boiling and once a year breaking through its side walls and pours out a portion of its insides into the neighbouring fields'.

The centre of the town between 1800 and 1836 began to attract the new units of production, the mills and factories of the worsted trade. They transformed the nascent urban geography surrounding Ivegate, Kirkgate and Westgate. Much of the activity in these years occurred in four main areas. The largest development area was to be found between Westgate and the Bradford Canal with Kirkgate as its southern boundary. Secondly the development of the land between Tyrrel Street and Bridge Street was attributed largely to John Wood and the firm of Illingworth & Murgatroyd. A similar urban change came to the land between Westgate and the Bradford Beck where Richard Fawcett, Matthew Thomspon and Thomas Hollings all provided the entrepreneurial initiative. Finally, there was some development of the land between Leeds Road and Bridge Street to the east of Vicar Lane, primarily as residential rather than industrial property. These four areas of urban growth all showed a partiality for the town's limited watercourses. The water supply was an important prerequisite for the location of a textile mill. Water was just as important as an agent for cleaning and scouring wool as it was for the steam engines of the mills. In the years after 1820 there was a great competition for sites alongside Bradford's watercourses,

> 'On the occasion of a transfer of such property, these parties measured and sold off half of the bed of the stream.... Hence

buildings were erected either in or over the beck thus strengthening the watercourse and materially increasing the reliability of floods'.[13]

To the north west of the town the water supply was more reliable and this accounts for the proliferation of mills there during these years:

Table XLIII Number of Steam Powered Mills in Bradford Borough 1810–1834

Year	*No of Mills in borough*	*Total h.p.*
1810	5	120
1815	10	250
1820	20	538
1825	26	706
1830	31	862
1834	34	1,148

These mills were situated close to the watercourses of Bradford along the valley bottom where the flatter land was more conducive to buildings of some scale. The beck and goit also acted as sewers for the disposal of effluents, another reason for the high concentration of mills, foundries and factories in the lower parts of the town.

It was the millowners and manufacturers who set the pace of Bradford's urban growth in the first half of the nineteenth century. By 1830 Cheapside and Bermondsey had developed as a well defined warehousing precinct of small stuff warehouses. A plan of property, formerly belonging to Henry Leah in 1849, demonstrates the nature of early stuff warehousing in Bradford.[14] This was located in Piccadilly and close to Darley Street where vestiges of these warehouses have survived. The building surrounded a cobbled yard, access to which was through an arch. Delivery was made through loading doors beneath a crane which fronted Piccadilly. Such warehouses kept pace with the increasing number of small family mills and factories which emerged to meet the demands for West Yorkshire worsted cloth. Thus the spatial patterns of the town centre were determined by the go-ahead industrialists who pressed inner city landowners to benefit from rising land values and sell their estates for industrial purposes. When seeking land for a new Dispensary, Dr. J. Simpson noted in 1825,

> 'The price of land has increased most surprisingly in the immediate vicinity of the town within the last few years. It is now impossible to purchase land adjoining the town by acre, everything is sold by the yard.... Land within half a mile of the town will sell for three to seven shillings a yard. Land adjoining the town from six shillings to one guinea and in the town from one guinea to even three per yard. This arises partly from some of the best building ground being locked up at present in entail but it arises principally from the rapid increase of the town and the consequent great rage for building'.

In the first instance it was the small freeholder, in a preponderance in the western part of the township, who gave up his land in order to take up full time employment, 'The land about Bradford is possessed by small proprietors and occupied by small farmers and manufacturers....'[15] Such estates were ideal for the tentative and small scale building schemes and limited resources of the smaller builder.[16] After 1835 several of the larger estates, formerly the suburban villas, came up for sale. Rev. Godfrey Wright was the largest inner city landowner and in 1835 converted five acres of grassland to warehouses. A year later Wright sold valuable land between the Goit and Beck at Thornton Road to a number of small industrialists.[17] In 1837 the highly valued land in Hall Ings, formerly the estate of Charles Swaine Booth, was sold for warehouses and subsequently was laid out in the form of a gridiron of Charles Street, Swaine Street and Booth Street. Francis Duffield, another representative of Bradford's squirearchy, sold his estate at Albion Court in 1847 for warehouses and offices.

In 1837 Samuel Hailstone sold off an extensive estate and villa in several lots. This was located between the Bradford and Wakefield Turnpike road and Bowling Lane. It included a prestigious mansion, Croft House, surrounded by pleasant parkland.[18] Rural enclaves like this began to disappear in these years as their owners yielded to the demands of the street builders. Hailstone's estate 'opened up a large area of inaccessible land near the Bowling Beck...this new highway, Croft Street, later became a vital link between the great mills and dyeworks of Manchester Road and the warehouse precinct of Little Germany'.[19] Another fine estate to succumb to the urban sprawl was Eastbrook House and its grounds, owned by the Harris family. Charles Harris sold several plots alongside the new roads of Well Street and Leeds Road. In the following year, 1825, he sold to the Methodists the site on which they subsequently erected Eastbrook Chapel. Harris Street and Chapel Street soon followed.

The purchasers of these estates were usually speculative builders with small amounts of capital. Land in the town centre cost almost one pound per yard and as a result these men were able to undertake only piecemeal development with housing of poor quality. Houses were jammed into the tightest corners and cellars converted into separate dwellings, all to increase the profit margin. In addition, the proliferation of small plots and the ineffective regulations of local authorities, contributed to the serious deterioration of Bradford's urban environment at that time.

The poor living conditions brought about by this in-filling of the ancient yards and folds of Bradford was compounded by new developments and the second stage in working class housing after 1810. The small holdings which became available for development after that time included a considerable number of plots which were formerly open field selions, the crofts of the middle ages. These long narrow fields had been acquired by numerous individual farmers at the time of enclosure and were ideally suited to the building of terraced back-to-back houses. Several of these plots, tenter-grounds of domestic manufacturers, were acquired by Matthew and William Thompson with their purchase of land between Silsbridge Lane and the Mill Goit in 1800. Close to the mill which they had built there they had also erected, by 1821, thirty three cottages and were in the process of building fourteen more (Fig.22). As early as 1823 there is evidence of overcrowding and multiple occupation in these houses, as Isaac Brear and Samuel Clegg were each charged two shillings for their occupation of a single room in Thompson Buildings.[21]

Figure 31 Goitside. Now covered in but this is the line of the old mill goit or beck which runs parallel to Thornton Road and adjacent to Tetley Street. The archway in the centre carried the Goit under Silsbridge Lane (Grattan Road). *Photo: Ian Beesley*

Later reports of the Borough Surveyor reveal that these early working-class houses were without basic sanitary facilities, a fact confirmed by the Woolcombers' Report of 1845,

> 'This locality is situate on an eminence at the foot of which runs a filthy beck impregnated with the refuse of dyehouses, manufactories and dwellings contiguous to it. The streets are narrow and filthy and the general arrangement of the dwellings unfavourable to health'.[22]

Thompson's Buildings were without drains and privies and lacked an adequate supply of water. There was a lack of ventilation and family privacy, particularly in the back houses. Such basic services were ignored by speculative builders who had sufficient capital for the development of one, at the most two, of the smallholdings. Piecemeal building on individual plots discouraged the provision of drains and water supplies and contributed to the evil social consequences of the 1840s.

In 1839 land adjoining Bowling Lane and Horton Lane, belonging to John Bower, was sold off in forty two lots by the land agent Thomas Dixon. The arrangement of these lots was ideally suited to the construction of back to back accommodation. On Lots 28 and 29 at Hannah Gate (viz Figs.32 and 33), the purchasers built twenty seven houses, six privies and two ashpits covering 1,530 square yards of which only 150 square yards were used as common yards or open spaces. The rent for each of these houses was 3s.2d. per week inclusive of rates.[23]

The plots in Hannah Gate and Bower Street were acquired by small builders who worked on a small scale and often lacked the capital to adequately develop the small freehold tenure which suited their requirements. Their numbers increased as the town grew.

Table XLIV Number of Building Workers in Bradford 1792–1829

	Architects	*Masons/ Builders*	*Joiners*	*Glaziers*
1792	–	–	2	1
1809	–	–	2	2
1822	–	4	14	5
1829	3	10	23	6

Private building was possible through building societies although the monthly payments, heavy deposits and the inability to withdraw capital discouraged many workers. The town's first known society was the Bradford Union Building Society formed in January 1823.[24] Each member had to pay 10/6 per month for the thirty three back-to-back cottages in George Street, Ebenezer Street and Vicar Lane. The houses were finally conveyed to the individual owners in 1833 when the society was dissolved. A precedent had been set and by 1825 other building societies were established in Bradford.

As a result of the activity of millowners, speculative builders and building societies the typical form of working class house by 1840, 'had changed from

Figure 32 Hannah Gate. A square or yard of back to back cottages built in the 1840s. Hannah Gate was built on land adjoining Bowling Lane and Horton Lane.

yards of crowded cottages to long ranks of terraces...the back to back dwelling had become established as the accepted way of housing the working man....'[25]

The segregation of Bradford's population into different areas according to social status was well under way by 1840. The social distinctions between the different groups of the working classes was established. The lowest orders, including many of the immigrant Irish, lived in the slums and ghettoes of the heavily congested areas close to the mills in Goitside, Wapping and White Abbey. Most urban workers inhabited two storeyed houses built in terraces or around courts with an

> 'insufficient number of privies and ashpits, their improper situation within a very few feet of the doors and windows of the houses, the wane of ventilation and fresh air, especially in back houses, whereby the privacy of families was almost entirely destroyed and habits of decency were made almost impossible'.[26]

Skilled workmen rented or owned larger houses, often terraced, with individual yards and privies and comfortable interiors. Early housing of this kind was completed in 1852 at Listerhills, when a group of artisans built Cobden Street and Villiers Street. Housing for the better-off was built in open streets and squares like Victoria Square and Hanover square. George Weerth noted in 1845 that

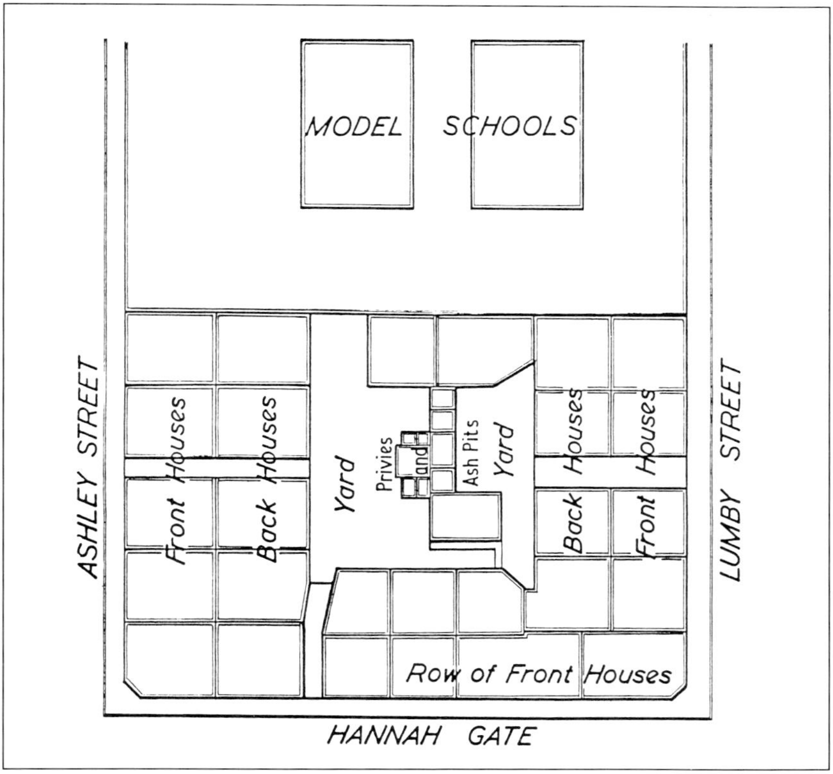

Figure 33 Hannah Gate

> 'The new Bradford squares...are built by capitalists and are occupied by the middle class and workers who are somewhat favoured by fortune. Factory overlookers, shopkeepers who have their shops in town, petty officials and clerks, these are the people who have possession of these Bradford squares'.[27]

The built-up area of Bradford was transformed in the first half of the nineteenth century when the original medieval urban nucleus was in-filled and expanded by industrialisation. By 1833 there were thirty four mills in Bradford and its immediate environs. These mills and other centres of production required an accessible workforce and consequently new working-class housing was built close by (viz Table XLV).

This sharp increase of Bradford's urban fabric matched the massive population growth in these years and as a result the central urban area had almost trebled by 1840 when the township was linked to the outlying towns of Horton and Manningham. This dramatic change in the township's urban

Table XLV Occupied Housing in Bradford Borough 1801–1841

Year	*Borough Population*	*Borough houses*	*(Township houses)*	*Average Occupation*	*Density (Persons per acre)*
1801	13,264	2,890	(1,368)	4.5	2.0
1811	16,012	3,223	(1,622)	4.9	2.4
1821	26,309	5,225	(2,626)	5.0	4.0
1831	43,527	8,193	(4,150)	5.3	6.6
1841	66,715	14,004	(7,246)	4.7	10.1

geography came about at a time when the town's affairs were run by an outdated and inefficient administrative system. The social consequences of this problem for many Bradfordians were far reaching as the disorder of urban society expressed itself through deteriorating standards in public health, law and order and community life. Much of the social disharmony and 'the propensity to riot' which marked the years after 1820 can be attributed to the uncoordinated and haphazard development of Bradford's streets and buildings in the first half of the nineteenth century.

The Government of Bradford

The oldest administrative body, and one much in decay by 1780, was that of the ancient manor of Bradford. The Lordship of the Bradford manor was exercised through the Courts of Baron and Leet, for civil and criminal cases respectively.[29] These courts exerted little influence over the affairs of the town in the eighteenth century although they continued to play a minor part in law and order. The Bradford Court Leet of 1792 for example remained anxious to determine, 'how the constables have discharged their duties in detecting felonies, hawking of hues and cries, and apprehending rogues, vagabonds and sturdy beggars'.[30]

They were the channels through which the manor lord might exert his power and privilege and hold back the progress of an expanding commercial and industrial community. By 1835 they were anachronistic vestiges of a manorial system long since irrelevant and their survival constituted an obstacle to the progress of Bradford. Not until 1866, nineteen years after its formation, was the Corporation of Bradford able to purchase outright the manorial title.[31]

Vestry Government and the Magistrates

The manorial courts had long since yielded their authority to the parochial vestry, which, until 1803, was the most important body of local government in Bradford. Parochial ratepayers were entitled to attend and vote at the annual meeting of the vestry, usually held at Easter. Legislation in 1818 had permitted a system of plural voting whereby one extra vote was allowed for every £25 rateable value over the nominal £50.[32] The authority of the vestry was exercised through a small group of officers; the churchwardens, constables, surveyors and the overseers of the poor. Their duties included the levying and control of the poor and church rates; the management of common property; the relief of the parochial poor; the maintenance of order and the upkeep of local roads. These officers functioned as a closed institution and were able to retain this strength by the system of co-optation which meant, in effect, the oligarchy renewing itself over and over again.[33] However, this did not necessarily mean that each and every parish was ruled by a set of local 'tyrants'. In most cases these were the men who understood the problems and difficulties of their area. They were the principal inhabitants, usually gentry, whose knowledge of local customs and practices and whose personal contact with the people of their vicinity, were of considerable value.[34] In Bradford these men were by no means wealthy and their small estates placed many of them in the humblest ranks of the landed classes. The duties which they fulfilled were not paid, another vestige of the medieval system of vocational organisation and the will to serve.

Another important element of local government before 1835 was the Justice of the Peace. The system of county justice which acted for the town before 1847, represented a very narrow class interest of the ancient families and squirearchy of the region.[35] There was an exclusiveness about their oligarchic control of regional power which lead to their subsequent decline. In addition to their duties as county magistrates, the justices ratified the election of vestry officials and provided the county context within which the vestry system might function. In the West Riding, the Quarter Sessions were held at several of the large towns like Pontefract, Leeds, Skipton, Sheffield and Bradford. However, when an extremely special or localised matter arose, the court met at an Adjourned Sessions. These courts were often held in the main public house of the town. The Bradford Quarter Session was the Midsummer Session and, from 1760 to 1835 was held during July at the Court House in Westgate or the Justice Rooms at the New Inn.

Much of the day-to-day business was dealt with out of sessions, usually in the magistrate's own home. There, he made decisions relating to local highways or poor relief and, from there, the moral tone of an area could be determined. Edward Leedes, the last of the ancient Rookes family which had been manor lords of North Bierley and Wibsey for over two centuries, was such a justice who preferred to administer from his home at Royds Hall, Low Moor. He was known at the time to be a 'bench in himself'. A little eccentric, his was the type satirised in the novels of Henry Fielding and Tobias Smollett, for incongruous tales and legends surround his dispensation of justice.[36]

Fortunately, Leedes and his type were not wholly representative of eighteenth century justice. Nevertheless, his preference for working at home was typical of the county magisterial system. E.C. Lister was another magistrate who held regular petty sessions in an extension of his home, now the Spotted House in Manningham Lane (viz Fig.34). These men knew their own area and the

Figure 34 The Spotted House. This old farmhouse (later in 1840 a pub) was originally part of the Lister estate at Manningham. The photograph shows distinctly the extension of the original house to adjoin the Keighley–Bradford road. This wing was added by E.C. Lister of Manningham Hall in his capacity of justice of the peace. It served as his justice room for the regular petty sessions but here, in 1895, it is the home of the Airedale Cycling Club.

characters within it. They were allowed four shillings per day for expenses which was insufficient on most occasions and encouraged their working from home. It was this localisation which helped brand them as close oligarchies, powerful within their own areas. Representing the local landed interest, they were able to monopolise the control and the handling of local policy. This habit of working only in their own districts meant that the Quarter Sessions were irregularly attended. In some cases the area of administration was far too large, but the infrequent attendance was usually caused by the negligence of the justices themselves.

The eighteenth century justice has frequently been accused of bribery and corruption; and of making himself a profit by his decisions in lieu of a salary. No doubt there were individuals guilty of such acts but generally it seems that the office of J.P. suffered more from the inconvenience of travelling and a general indolence on the part of many justices, than from corruption and malpractice. It was within this framework of magistracy and vestry that the affairs of Bradford were administered in the eighteenth, and early nineteenth centuries. Yet these were years when population increase and economic growth exacerbated social problems to an unprecedented degree and strained the existing political and administrative institutions of the town. Demographic and economic change after 1780 provoked crises in the areas of public order and poverty and later, in the public health of the town.

Firstly, in the eighteenth century the greatest responsibility that any parish had, was to its poor.[37] Since the Restoration there had been little recourse to central government and more vestry meetings were convened on account of the poor than for any other issue. In 1795 Eden noted the gravity of the local situation when he noted 'that money expended on the poor in Bradford in 1773 was £278; in 1775 about £530; in 1793 about £560 and 1794 near £700'.[38] The vestry appealed to the inhabitants in that year, 1794, for assistance in the maintenance of Bradford's Poor House in Barkerend which accommodated mostly women, children and the aged.[39] It was scrubbed and whitewashed three times each year and its floors washed each week. If the pauper was employed then he or she might receive two pence from every shilling earned. On entering the House the paupers brought their own bedding, utensils and apparel which stood forfeit in case of death. The meals were very similar, with the same basic ingredients each time, although every care was taken that 'everyone have a sufficiency and that no waste be made'. Breakfasts consisted of water, porridge and milk and bread served each morning at seven. At the same time each evening the same was served (sometimes broth) as supper. The main meal of the day was as follows,

'Sunday	New milk and Bread or Beer, Porridge and Bread.
Monday	Yeast Dumplings, or boiled Puddings with Vinegar Sauce, Beer.
Tuesday	Meat, Broth Vegetables and Beer.
Wednesday	Broth, Fat Dumplings and Beer.
Thursday	Meat, Broth Vegetables and Beer.
Friday	Broth Puddings, Dumplings and Beer.
Saturday	Meat, Broth, Vegetables and Beer'.[40]

Not exactly a gourmet's delight, but nevertheless a substantial improvement on starvation.

The Vestry Committee insisted on compulsory church attendance and did its best to uplift the moral standards of the inmates. Cleanliness was maintained and 'all those who smoke tobacco be allowed an ounce per week but none be suffered to learn'. Swearing and fighting were punished by a term in the House of Correction. The committee was anxious to find employment for each of the able bodied paupers even if it was in their own kitchens. However, the vagaries of the textile trade and the growing number of immigrants in the town after 1800 strained the resources of this outdated vestry system. In times of real stress their finances and facilities were too limited to accommodate the increasing numbers of those who clamoured for relief.

A wet spring in 1800 caused the harvests of the northern counties to be very poor and there was little alleviation from foreign imports owing to the French war. Corn prices in the town soared and there were riots outside Wilson's, the main corn dealers in Bradford at that time. The town vestry had no answer to this kind of crisis and eventually the poorer people of Bradford formed their own subscription, 'either at once or by installments and every subscriber to be supplied by the Society (which is to be called the Corn Society) with the flour and meal which they want for the consumption of their family'.[41]

The Bradford Corn Society of 1800 was a temporary and voluntary remedy to a crisis situation. In subsequent years similar 'ad hoc' bodies were set up to meet 'pro tempore' a difficult community problem which the archaic Vestry could not handle. A Parochial Benefit Society was founded in 1818 to confront the distress of the post-war years and similar groups were established at various times to police the town and maintain civil order.

Equally at county level similar voluntary institutions were set up to resolve the growing vagrancy problem. In that same year, 1818, a Central Committee on Vagrancy was formed in the Wakefield–Bradford vicinity by a number of concerned West Riding justices. A special committee, chaired by Sir Francis Lindley Wood of Hemsworth and late of Bradford, was convened for the actual 'suppression of vagrants'. Aware of the growing number of vagrants, the justices offered only to repress rather than reform this disorder,

> 'How increasing this evil has been of late years the Riding accounts afford ample proof but it is not merely a measure for economy but still more so of morality for a more worthless tribe of habitual vagrancy can nowhere be found, productive of the greatest mischief....'[42]

They were able to offer little in the way of a constructive policy for vagrancy. The number of vagrants at any one time cannot really be stated; many cases of vagrancy were not dealt with in the Quarter Sessions court.[43] The treatment of vagrants was entirely primitive and no distinction was made between the sexes. Both men and women were publicly whipped and when the country was at war the males were automatically put into the navy. Vagrancy was a field to which the judiciary brought little enlightened thinking and within which they made no significant progress.

In Bradford the vestry fared no better with the problem of vagrancy. The aftermath of the weavers' and woolcombers' strike of 1825 had left thousands unemployed and destitute as late as autumn of the year following.[44] Vestry minutes for 1826 testify to the frantic activity of its members to overcome the numbers of idle and poor within the town. Bradford's poor and unemployed repaired the local roads and one hundred and fifty men were employed, at one shilling per day, to clean the Bradford Beck.[45] Finally, vestry officials decided upon founding a Vagrancy Office, where vagrants and disorderly persons were examined and registered by the Constable. A Vagrant Master was appointed at an annual salary of thirty pounds. He was responsible to a special Vagrancy Committee and was able to check the growing numbers of lodging houses for strangers and remove them from the township if they had no right to be there.[46] This was a pathetic attempt to implement the Act of Settlement and the Bradford vestry, like so many others, did little to attack the root cause of pauperism. In 1834 they were largely relieved of their poor law responsibilities with the introduction of Poor Law Unions and their administrators, the Board of Guardians.

The failure of vestry officials to contend with the administration of poor relief was matched by their inability to provide adequate police facilities for the town. As early as 1759 Bradfordians acknowledged the impossible task of the single parochial constable:

> 'Whereas several dwelling houses, shops, warehouses, outhouses and buildings within the township of Bradford have lately been broken open in the night time and large quantities of diverse sorts of goods, plate, linen and other things of considerable value have been feloniously stolen'.[47]

Several leading townsmen decided to create a fund for the employment of three constables who were to detect felons and bring them to justice before the magistrate. The fund was for expenses only, although each received a half crown for inconvenience incurred throughout the year. John Crosley, Benjamin Peile and William Tetley were the first of these voluntary constables. Dissatisfied with the inadequate policing of the growing town through its vestry system, a number of wealthier townsmen in 1790 organised a private system of watchmen ('charleys'). There were six in all and they were supervised by a committee of the subscribers to the scheme.[48] Only the houses of subscribers were inspected (207 from a population of 6,300 in 1802). 'Any watchman discovered watching any of the premises of non-subscribers (intentionally) they shall be dismissed from the service'.[49] By 1825 the number of watchmen had been increased to thirteen but one can only sympathise with watchman Squire Knowles who was dismissed in December 1828 'on account of a robbery having taken place on the premises of Mr. Thompson which are in his round without his detecting it'. Several of the leading townsmen in March 1817 formed the Association for the Prosecution of Felons.[50] This private body of law enforcement was a common expedient for growing towns and is indicative of the general dissatisfaction with the incompetent efforts of the Vestry and the Commission to police the town. During the 1830s there were frequent letters of complaint in Bradford's new press of 'the number of intoxicated men who have been staggering about the streets since the advent of Christmas.... The want of an organised body of police is severely felt at this time and is much to be regretted'.[51]

The Vestry did not entirely abrogate its responsibility in the field of law and order and by 1830 could record,

> 'In consequence of the large and increasing population of the town and neighbourhood arising partly from the great influx of strangers from every part of the kingdom it appears...that a more efficient police is necessary for personal protection and for the safety of property as the present establishment is very defective and totally inadequate for these purposes....'[52]

They decided to form a working committee which was to visit and observe police management at Leeds and Manchester, towns facing similar social problems as Bradford. Nine months later, the Committee reported to the Vestry meeting that the police system in Bradford, 'was decidedly inferior to that of any other of the towns referred to...whilst the population and commerce of the town have rapidly increased, its moral and municipal discipline is on the decline'.[53] They called for an entire reformation of the system, advising the selection of men of high calibre. As a result, a new office was created, beneath the traditional constable, the deputy constable. Henceforth, he was responsible for the actual police work. The town was divided into districts each one having a number of special constables. The committee stressed the importance of the Workhouse Master as part of their crime fighting force. By 1835 there had begun in Bradford what one historian has recognised as 'the cutting edge of a larger and wider effort in northern industrial towns to improve new standards of urban discipline'.[54] The committee had at least recognised how social distress was responsible for a large amount of urban crime, but their remedy was inappropriate for a town the size of Bradford.

The failure of the parochial vestry in these two important areas of pauperism and public order was all too apparent by 1800 when the town began to adapt itself to the needs of an expanding industrial community. Moreover, new entrepreneurs and manufacturers were demanding well paved thoroughfares; efficient systems of drainage and waste disposal; regular systems of sanitation and policing. As a result, at a meeting of the Vestry in January 1803, a decision was taken by those present to apply to parliament for an act of improvement.[55] Short of money, and essentially conservative in outlook, the Vestry had a short time earlier refused demands for the development of new roads within the township. The men who had made those demands were the 'new' men, the merchants, the entrepreneurs and the business men. Bradford, by 1803, was ready to step into the great business world and these men wanted the best possible start. The efforts of local squires and yeomen farmers were no longer sufficient, for they had shown themselves incapable of keeping up with change, as new voluntary organisations in poor administration, crime control and morality had emerged. These members of the lower gentry and yeomanry who had carried the burden of local government for several centuries, found themselves faced with problems of unprecedented scale. The pace of economic life had gone too fast for them and they were slowly replaced by the industrial entrepreneurs. The Firths, Balmes and Duffields gave way to the Thompsons, Fawcetts and Hailstones of the new industrial world.

It was men like these who subscribed almost £500 for the new Improvement Act at the meeting in January 1803. There were fifty four original subscribers whose industrial and commercial interests were represented in parliament by Henry Lascelles.[56] At a later Vestry meeting Edmund Peckover, treasurer to the Commission, made a further call on subscribers which raised £469. In spite of this support, an opposition group emerged in February 1803, consisting largely of the ancient yeomen families of the town.[57] They feared the heavy expenditure of the bill and the increased rates which would ensue. Their protests were swept aside as the bill became law in 1803.[58] It allowed for the appointment of fifty eight commissioners who qualified by ownership of an estate value of at least £1,000. Their duties were to ensure that, 'the streets, lanes, entries and other places were well and sufficiently cleansed, lighted and watched, improved and regulated and the causeways and footpaths thereof effectively flagged and all nuisances, annoyances and obstructions, removed and prevented and a nightly watch established'.[59]

The boundary of the act encompassed the town of Bradford and part of the hamlet of Little Horton, a locality soon to be overtaken by the urban sprawl of Bradford.

The first meeting of the Improvement Commissioners convened on 1st July 1803, with John Jarratt, iron and coal merchant, as Chairman.[60] Peckover remained as treasurer and the first committee (which had the honour to determine a location 'for depositing the manure arising from the cleansing of the streets'), comprised Peckover, Hustler jnr. and Samuel Hailstone. Hustler, whose father had been a principal pioneer of Bradford commerce, was the proprietor of a woolstapling concern. Samuel Hailstone, an established attorney, had been representative of the Worsted Committee since 1801, and was in partnership with John Hardy, attorney and ironmaster, who was also a commissioner. At that first meeting, there was a strong indication of the kind of individual behind the scheme. The list of fifty eight commissioners more than suggests that the Improvement Act had been used by the new entrepreneurs and merchants, as a means of gaining a greater share in the running of local affairs. At subsequent meetings, the commissioners who were present were mostly from the growing industrial and commercial sectors of the town. They included, Hustler, Jarratt, Pollard, Peckover, Hailstone, Garnet, Aked, Maud and later Thompson, Fawcett and Crosley, all men of commerce and industry.

Their influence changed the ethos of local government in Bradford. The principles of parochial obligation were overtaken by the new capitalist approach. The commissioners initially acted in the interests of the joint improvement of their property, their public responsibilities taking second place. The affairs of the commission were handled along the lines of a joint-stock company. Tenders for street cleaning were put out immediately and the lowest offer accepted. Their obsession for cheapness led them in March 1812 to the offer of a contract for scavenging to the Vestry Overseer. The cleaning of the streets by the poor was deemed to be, 'highly advantageous to the town and will operate as a terror to idle and dissolute persons from craving relief of the town'.[61]

A similar mercenary approach was taken in the commissioners' attempts to illuminate the main thoroughfares of the town. The commissioners' minutes are littered with references to lighting schemes which were considered too expensive and an efficient means of illumination did not materialise until the formation of the Bradford Gas Company in 1822. Even then, the commission was reluctant to accept the terms offered and haggled for over a year before settling upon an agreed sum.

By 1835 the Improvement Commission had a poor track record in civic affairs. They had failed miserably in fulfilling the fundamental duties of the act.

The declining standards of public order, a problem inherited from the Vestry, continued to fall. A townsman could remark in 1825, 'Even the most sober walk through the streets of Bradford after dusk, is such a perilous undertaking'[62]

Moreover, the same individual condemned the decay of the town's expanding urban environment, 'Bradford of which I have now for some years been an inhabitant, is proverbially one of the dirtiest and worst regulated towns in the West Riding'.

The editor of the town's newspaper went further and described Bradford 'as the worst regulated town in the Empire'. The problems of the pre-industrial township, of public order and poverty, had been exacerbated by the growing issue of public health. There had been early bye-laws against roving livestock and open slaughter and there were unsuccessful attempts to dissuade inhabitants from using the Beck for the disposal of waste. As early as 1807 the commission made unsuccessful efforts to control the smoke pollution from the increasing number of chimneys which were beginning to appear on the Bradford skyline.[63] Nor did the commissioners take advantage of the town's geographical position and build an effective system of sewers. All this inactivity occurred at a time when the town was undergoing the embryonic stages of intense urbanisation and when the number of its inhabitants increased dramatically.

This catalogue of failure was brought about by a number of factors. Firstly, from the very beginning the commissioners had not taken their responsibilities and duties seriously. Attendance was poor after the initial meeting and in 1817 the commission failed to meet for two thirds of the year. This apathy continued throughout the 1820s and in 1834 an early correspondent to the recently founded *Bradford Observer* could write, 'Allow me to call your attention to the neglect of the Commissioners under the Lighting and Watching Act...where is there a town of equal importance where those duties are more sadly neglected?'[64] A second weakening influence was the legal limitations forced upon the Commission. The act had never completely superseded the work of the vestry constable and surveyors and as a result of this dichotomy of responsibility, initiative was lost and work never done. Joseph Ellison testified to the Select Committee on the Health of Towns in 1840, 'they do not possess the power to take down a single building or widen a street, or put down a drain'. Four years later the Bradford Board of Surveyors underlined the Commission's lack of authority in street encroachments, refuse collection and building regulations. Health hazards proliferated as the town expanded beyond its medieval urban geography and according to the editor of the *Bradford Observer*,

> 'the blame belongs to the Commissioners for continuing to hold office without legal power or authority. If they voluntarily assume the direction of local politics they ought to procure those powers from parliament...needful for the due administration of municipal affairs....'[65]

The inability of the Improvement Commission to provide adequate sanitation, water supply and regulated buildings, and the failure of the Vestry to attack the deteriorating problem of public order, prompted the movement for the incorporation of Bradford. That story has been told elsewhere and is beyond the scope of this book.[66] By 1835 the ancient vestry and the more recent Improvement Commissioners had become ineffective, closed oligarchies of local administration and were, in consequence, vulnerable to the 'reformist ideas of the aspiring Liberal middle-class'.

The changing nature of urban local government in the early nineteenth century was not unique to Bradford. Many towns, particularly those in expanding industrial economies, were all ill equipped to meet the needs of a rapidly growing and fast changing society. Even those communities, like Leeds and Liverpool, which were favoured with an ancient charter of incorporation, struggled to resolve the problems of an emerging urban industrial society. Furthermore, the twin forces of urbanisation and industrialisation had raised the more important issue of where, and with whom, in the new industrial cities, did the power and authority lie? After the town's Tory magistrates had refused to confirm the appointment of an overseer of the poor elected freely by the ratepayers, one Bradfordian could write in 1832, 'it is high time for us to inquire by whom is the town of Bradford to be governed.... Shall a junta composed of ten or a dozen individuals trample upon the liberties and rights of all ratepayers?' The take-over of first the Vestry and then the Improvement Commission in the early 1840s, led to the establishment of a municipal corporation and more importantly, prompted a dramatic change in Bradford politics.

Bradford Politics 1760–1835

It was not until the great Reform Act of 1832, that Bradford was able to send two of its own representatives to the House of Commons. By that time, its commercial prosperity and industrial growth had warranted its representation as one of the new parliamentary boroughs. Consequently, in the years before 1832, Bradford, like many other West Riding towns, held no election of its own but looked to the county contests for its political arena. However, the county seats numbered only two (four after 1826), and these were usually directed into the hands of the more substantial landowners.[67] Within Bradford, political influence over the affairs of the town was exercised through the Church Vestry and, after 1803, the Improvement Commission. For the greater part of the period 1760 to 1835 political affairs in Bradford tended to be controlled by an oligarchy of Tory landowners and merchants. By 1825, however, the economic expansion of the worsted and iron industries had produced new manufacturing and merchanting men to challenge the traditional authority of the Tory oligarchy. Many of these 'new' Bradfordians 'were Dissenters in religion and Whig Liberals in politics' and in the two decades after 1832 they were to transform the nature of Bradford politics through the politicisation of the town's institutions, and raise the level of the town's political consciousness.[68] This section of the book will examine the period of High-Church Tory predominance and the emergence of a politically conscious Dissenting group, eager to assail the traditional position of the established Church.

Since the seventeenth century Bradford had had a tradition of political radicalism and was one of the 'populous and rich towns which depending wholly upon the clothiers naturally maligned the gentry' during the Civil War. Thereafter, many Bradfordians continued to be characterised by their philosophy of liberty, competitive individualism and their belief in property rights.

However, the radicalism which prompted Bradfordians into an almost ecstatic celebration of the release of John Wilkes in 1770 had given way, by the early 1790s, to a fervent backing of Pitt's new Toryism.[69] In spite of Bradford freeholders' support for Rev. Wyvill's Yorkshire Association for parliamentary reform, the rapid socio-economic change that was taking place in the West Riding after 1780 produced new political patterns. In addition, the events of the French Revolution alarmed the emergent urban middle-classes into acquiescence in the existing political order. Thomas Paine's *The Rights of Man* was well received by a number of Bradford artisans, many of them woolcombers. On the first day of January 1793 a Political Book Club was established in the Bradford Market Place.[70] It was run by William Firth, with a relatively cheap subscription. It aimed 'to pursue truth, investigate opinions and examine,compare and deduce immutable principals...while truth is the object sought, it is no objection what party the books...favour...it is sufficient that they relate to affairs of government and politics'.[71] Other 'seditious clubs' of Painite artisans met secretly in those hectic months of 1792/3 but theirs was a minority voice.

In December 1792 many principal inhabitants, including several of the town's entrepreneurs like Jarratt, Rand, Hardy and Balme, had met to condemn those 'wicked and designing men who are endeavouring to overturn and subvert the constitution....'[72] As the Association against Levellers and Republicans they appealed to the Tory magistracy of Bradford to convene a public meeting at the Piece Hall. This took place on 20 December when an effigy of Paine was imprisoned, drawn round the town, hung outside the Piece Hall and torn to pieces. The meeting was 'attended by all ranks and denominations with the most signal marks of loyalty and affection to our present happy constitution... In the Church there were 3,000 persons...not backward in showing their attachment to government and their abhorrence to Paine and his principles....'[73] In January 1793 a select committee was appointed to enforce more rigorously the resolutions determined at the December meeting. The committee included local gentry like Wickham, Busfeild, Hodsden, Sharp and Field; the town's commercial interests were represented by Jarratt, Sturges, Skelton, Hardy, Balme, Rand and others, Tories to a man. This very strong 'church and king' group persecuted the likes of William Firth and other Painite sympathisers who 'should be avoided and guarded against as incendiaries and dangerous subjects'. They seem to have had some success for John James noted 'that a few respectable individuals who had "imbibed" Paine's opinions were forced to leave the town'.[74]

It was the same committee, a year later and under the secretaryship of Samuel Hailstone, which agreed to organise and promote a Volunteer Corps. This decision was taken at a meeting held at the Sun Inn, 7 April 1794. Twelve years earlier, the Volunteer Act had resulted in the founding of the first Bradford Volunteers Corps.[75] The main promoter, and later its commander, was J.A. Busfeild who, long before the 1782 statute, had initiated a similar movement to deal with domestic riots and discontent. There had been a shortage of oatmeal and corn in the North in 1779 and several violent disturbances occurred. In fact sixty Bradford traders, fearing the ugly mood of the poorer people, decided to form an alliance for the purpose of 'learning the use of arms' and protecting themselves for when the storm broke. Busfeild, writing from Myrtle Grove, Bingley, in October 1779, informed the Secretary-at-War, Charles Jenkinson (later Lord Liverpool) that he was quite willing to organise a semi-military corps to deal with the trouble. The Volunteer Movement thus became more than a military reserve and civil police force, it was 'the deliberate creation of a party of order', commending patriotism and loyalty to church and king.[76]

Busfeild's application of 1779 was refused but in 1794, under the threat of a French invasion, Busfeild was permitted to command a Volunteer Corps of three hundred men.[77] Assisted by John Sturges and John Hardy the corps was frequently drilled and trained in the use of arms. The Bradford Corps was mocked by a contemporary rhymester.

> At Gomersal renowned will be the day,
> When in huge heaps the ale-puffed warriors lay.
> Oh! What a worthy subject for your pen!
> To see in bold array three hundred men.
> Here they storm fort tankard with the greatest ease,
> There mount the ramparts of a Cheshire Cheese.
> Here draw a sword – for what? it mocks belief
> To cut a slice off from a round of beef!
> With bayonets fix'd the Alehouse door assail
> And crown their labours with a jug of ale....'[78]

Bradford's principal inhabitants did not see the corps in this derisory light and, as the threat of a French invasion receded, the corps was retained to control civil disorders. The events of the early 1790s in Bradford were a triumph for the hierarchical politics of the 'old society' and Pittite Toryism, as a member of the Bradford Corresponding Society, confirmed in 1795,

> 'Bradford where I have lived about three years, may be ranked with the first in the West Riding of Yorkshire for a domineering aristocracy.... A society had been organised in this town about four months when the suspension of Habeas Corpus took place...we have many Patriots but there appears to be a majority of aristocrats'.[79]

By the end of 1795 it was clear however that the 'aristocrats' of Bradford were divided in their attitude to constitutional reform. While the majority of Bradford's leading citizens accepted the political 'status quo' there was a small number prepared to speak their mind on the issue of parliamentary reform. Between 1795 and 1797 a number of personal rows became public and in consequence, the town's political consciousness at that time was raised. Since the political crisis of 1793 'party feuds...have prevailed in this place'.[80] They were fuelled by the actions of Bradford's leading constitutional reformer, the Rev. Edward Baldwyn, who was master of the grammar school. To his dismay Baldwyn had not been appointed by the Rev. John Crosse to the traditional position of Lecturer at the parish church, which had gone to the Rev. William Atkinson, an Evangelical and like Crosse a supporter of John Wesley. Between 1786 and 1791 Baldwyn made several public attacks on both Crosse and Atkinson, details of which need not detain us here.[81] Baldwyn, in 1795, gave a number of political lectures in which he condemned Pitt's policies. The Tory attorney, Samuel Hailstone, wrote of Baldwyn, 'Political quacks, both sacred and profane should no longer be permitted to vend their sixpenny doses of sedition, to poison the minds of the ignorant and unwary....' It was Baldwyn's friendship with the medical practitioner George Mossman which led Hailstone to suspect the latter's constitutional principles when, acting as steward, he ejected him from Bradford's Constitutional Ball in 1795.

> 'Instead of joining the Country Gentlemen and inhabitants of Bradford to check the progress of seditious and republican principles, (Mossman) stood aloof...ridiculed their attempts to preserve peace and tranquility...was the advocate of Paine and his Disciples'.[82]

Mossman, however, had been converted by Busfeild in 1794 from the 'enigmatic wilds of DEMOCRACY and placed on the sure and solid ground of Constitutional Liberty'. Hailstone and others found his sudden conversion hard to accept and by October 1795 had further cause to revile him. Mossman engineered the resignations of Hailstone, John Hardy and William Bolland from the Volunteers Corps in which he himself had received a commission from Busfeild. They left the Corps resignedly but determined to 'neither forsake nor lose sight of that cause in which we are all still united'.[83]

Despite these divisions in the Tory dominated Volunteers Corps, the cause of 'king and church' in Bradford was upheld by Rev. William Atkinson who produced a number of pamphlets tracing revolutionary tendencies and the ways to avoid them. Atkinson's adversary in religious and secular matters, Edward Baldwyn, attempted, in 1797, to persuade the Rev. Christopher Wyvill to revive the County Association of earlier years. Baldwyn had steadfastly supported the cause of parliamentary reform, despite the fact that,

> 'in this part of the country the great body of the people continue to think that opposition is a desperate faction whose only aim is, by getting into power, to introduce French principles and bring about a Revolution and that the only way to prevent this horrid design from being carried into execution is to support Mr. Pitt.... This is

the doctrine they imbibe weekly from the Leeds Intelligencer...and they believe it as implicitly as they do the gospel....'[84]

Wyvill thought it imprudent to proceed in reconvening County meetings of freeholders at that time. Baldwyn's efforts to revitalise the county association and his continuous attacks upon Pitt led to his being voted out of the town's Coffee Room in June 1797. Baldwyn's open letter on this issue was offensively directed at John Struges, the Tory ironfounder, for Baldwyn believed him responsible for his dismissal, and consequently his attack was personal and insulting. Sturges' response, several hundred copies of which circulated the town, refuted many of Baldwyn's insinuations and let it be known that Sturges had actually voted for Baldwyn in the Coffee Room ballot,

> 'As to your interspersed insinuations that my political principles are regulated by motives of self-interest, they are equally unfounded with your other informations. It is well known that I entered into the military association in which I am now engaged a very considerable time before I made any contracts with Government. Long before the war broke out with this country, and consequently before I could possibly have any view of contracts or any military office from governments my political sentiments were exactly the same as they are at this moment'.[85]

Baldwyn had, by 1797, offended the greater part of the Bradford Tory oligarchy and his relations with the Anglican church had never been anything but hostile since his arrival in 1784. Henceforth there was a concerted effort by Rev. Crosse and Rev. Atkinson, as well as many leading townsmen, to get rid of him. Their excuse was the quality of his teaching at the grammar school. He resisted their attempts and remained headmaster until 1802 when he retired to Shropshire.

During the years before Baldwyn's departure from Bradford, the local political temperature was heightened by the massive rise in the price of provisions. The economic background of the crisis of 1800–1801 has been detailed elsewhere.[86] Wet summers and poor harvests forced grain prices to rise astronomically. This coincided with a severe recession in the regional textile trades as a result of a marked decline in domestic demand for cloth. The results were widespread disturbances across Northern England.[87] In Bradford there was rioting and looting. However, in the political atmosphere of the period, social and economic tensions of this nature became increasingly politicised.[88] The response of the government to the deteriorating situation was a reiteration of earlier policies, the repression of riots and the insistance upon the free market economy (no price-fixing). This short-sighted view of the situation provoked a widespread crisis of confidence in Pitt and his ministry. In 1797 Wyvill had refused Baldwyn's request for a relaunching of the County Movement,

> 'I am very well satisfied with having done what, in the present situation of the Country, Public Duty deems to require, but I can see no prospect that any good can be done by pressing a meeting in Yorkshire at present... be content to acquiesce a little longer a state

of inactivity, however zealously they may wish for a favourable opportunity, as I also do, to call a County meeting to accelerate a Peace with France'.[89]

By 1800 the opportunity for reconvening the County Association had presented itself once again, but by February 1801 Wyvill's prevarication meant that the petition to parliament requested only peace; there were no references to constitutional reform. In the West Riding of Yorkshire the peace petitions sprang from the industrial and commercial groups of the larger towns. In Bradford such men met at the Piece Hall, 29 January 1801 and blamed the war for the 'decay of the trade of this town...the great and rapid increase of our Poor Rates and of our Taxes...great numbers of workpeople being now totally destitute of employment....'[90] In a letter to Lord Fitzwilliam, Colonel J. Dixon described the Bradford petition as 'a pretty strong one'.[91] It was too strong for ultra-royalist Tories like the Rev. William Atkinson, who led the opposition to the Bradford petition. Atkinson had written a number of political tracts throughout the 1790s which had attacked dissenters, radicals and republicans. Atkinson was brother to Bradford's leading Tory magistrate J.A. Busfeild (who had taken the family name of his wife upon marriage) and both were conservative and anti-reformist, advocating,

> 'aristocracy...as secure a check to the licentiousness of democracy. While you continue faithful to the constitution, we have nothing to fear, the aristocrats can never oppress, the democrats can never produce anarchy. There is wisdom amongst you clearly to ascertain the fallacy of republican schemes, and resolution enough to set them all at defiance'.[92]

The petition of 1801 was, for Atkinson and High Church Tories like him, a confirmation of the 'strong dissenting element among the manufacturers and merchants with radicalism...a dissenter-cum-democrat ploy'. Atkinson's worst fears were confirmed when the economic crisis was given a sharper political edge through the activities of West Riding radical groups.

The radicals seized the opportunity of using the crisis to involve the masses in their political ideals and their demand for universal suffrage. The worsening economic situation became attributed directly to an outdated system of government; democracy was to be the panacea for all economic ills. In the spring of 1801, all kinds of political 'creatures' crawled out of the woodwork. In Bradford, Zaccheus Robinson, a weaver of Great Horton, led a small but fanatical sect of 'New Jerusalemites', who certainly perturbed the local magistracy.[93] More serious, in April 1801, was the threatened attack, by local democrats, upon the arms and ammunition of the Bradford Volunteers Corps.[94] In addition, several hundred bills had been posted inviting 'oppressed brethren' to attend a mass meeting at Steeton Moor, 20 April 1801, in order to consider,

> 'the exorbitant price of provisions...to expose fraud and every species of Hereditary Government, to lessen the oppression of taxes, to propose plans for the education of helpless infancy and the

comfortable support of the aged and distressed...to make peace...to break the chains of political suppression, to raise degraded man to his proper rank.... And you will suffer yourselves to be thus imposed upon by a Majority of Mercenary Hirelings, Government Pimps, Corndealers, Place Men, Pentioners, Paracites, etc and yourselves starving for Bread'.[95]

The gathering at Steeton Moor was one of several meetings throughout Yorkshire designed to promote a mass movement for radical parliamentary reform as well as peace with France. The movement was nipped in the bud by a swift but moderate counter-attack from the magistracy who possibly exaggerated the nature and scale of the disturbances. J.A. Busfeild had summoned the 10th Light Dragoons to Bradford and had insinuated a number of informants into the Steeton society by 17 April 1801.[96] By the end of the month Portland wrote to Fitzwilliam, pleased 'at the happy failure of this attempt to disturb the public tranquility'.[97]

It was clear however that several local magistrates had overreacted throughout the crisis. The assignees of the Bradford circular may have expressed their feelings in violent language but their intent was to petition parliament not to precipitate insurrection,

'How can the commonality expect any redress for their grievances when our cotton manufacturing magistrate declares he had rather die gloriously on the field of battle than at home in bed, I wonder where that oppressing idiot will find his glory, except he rightly suffer before the commanders of a Noble Revolution.'[98]

This reference to J.A. Busfeild confirms the exaggerated fears of local magistrates as well as the peaceable intent of the democratic movement of 1801. Gradually, throughout the rest of that year prices fell and employment was increased in the textile trades; Pitt was replaced by Addington and peace with France was agreed. These factors ended the economic crisis and in turn relieved some of the political tension in the town.

Several Bradford radicals, disillusioned by the peaceable methods of 1801, turned to the adoption of more militant tactics thereafter and in July 1802, the Bradford magistrates requested troops to suppress the nightly meetings 'for the mischievous purposes of sedition and insurrection'.[99] The extent to which trade unions influenced the politicisation of working men in this period has been the subject of a keen debate since the publication of Edward Thompson's thesis on the making of the English working class. The development of trade unions in the Bradford worsted trade has been examined elsewhere but there is local evidence to support Thompson's view that there was some overlap between trade unions and the movement for popular democracy. Changes in the structure of the worsted industry, the repressive Combinations Acts of 1799 and 1800, the work of the Worsted Committee, all made a number of Bradford working men antagonistic to the established political system, and convinced them of the relevance of democratic political principles. The events of 1801–02 and the highly organised counter-offensive of the magistracy and

Tory oligarchy in Bradford, drove underground the movement for democracy. For two more decades the majority of Bradford's workers and small masters tolerated a social and political system in which paternal protection was no longer given in return for deference and paternal discipline.

The events of 1792–1802 served to confirm the power and resilience of Toryism in Bradford in the period with which this book is concerned. In the wider parliamentary sphere both county seats had gone to Tories in 1796, to William Wilberforce and Henry Lascelles. Both Whig candidates, Duncombe and Fawkes, had withdrawn and consequently as in previous county elections since 1761, there had been no contest. However, those Bradfordians who were able to vote, involved themselves closely in the electioneering of 1806 and 1807.[100] The town's electorate of one hundred and eighty freeholders was given the customary lead from the local gentry. Francis Lindley Wood, by reputation 'an advanced Whig', was active in the cause of his friend the Whig candidate, Walter Fawkes of Farnley Hall. Wood ordered his land steward Isaac Wells to generate Whig support in Bowling and Bradford. The indifference of Henry Lascelles to the condition of the Yorkshire textile trade in 1805 lost the Tory party some votes. Moreover, Bradford's growing Dissenting community (Baptist and Independent rather than the traditional Quakers and Unitarians) increasingly gave their support to Fawkes, 'the Presbyterians to a man are all with Fawkes'.[101]

However, on 23 October the Tory cause in Bradford was reaffirmed when a meeting at the Talbot Inn was chaired by John Jarratt, the colliery owner. Aided by John Sturges, J.G. Paley and Thomas Mason of Bowling Ironworks, Jarratt was soon 'very active in getting votes for the Old Members'. Their efforts were encouraged by a personal visit from Wilberforce seven days later. Like Fawkes before him, he gave 'a pretty good speech' from the steps of the Piece Hall in Kirkgate. Lascelles, very much in the shadow of Wilberforce, was not as active and his success would depend upon a party vote. Walter Spencer-Stanhope, a life-long Tory ordered his land steward John Hardy, 'to wait upon all the Freeholders immediately and inform them that it is your wish that they should give their votes for the Older Members and to take down the names of those who promise and those who do not'.[102]

His efforts were in vain, as Lascelles withdrew in November. Fawkes stepped in and once again the county election went uncontested.

The county election of 1807 proved a memorable exception to this rule. Parliament had been forcibly dissolved by George III over the problem of catholic emancipation. Walter Fawkes had been so disgusted with the king's decision that he did not put himself forward as the Whig candidate.[103] Wilberforce, the county M.P. for almost a quarter of a century, sought re-election and Henry Lascelles returned as the second Tory candidate. The Whig interest was represented by Lord Milton, son of Earl Fitzwilliam, who only reached his majority in the middle of the campaign. The contest began in earnest and in early May the candidates were in Bradford where the Tory interest was once again promoted by the Tory ironfounders, Sturges and Jarratt. Wood whipped up support for the Whig cause.

Figure 36 Talbot Hotel. In the early nineteenth century this ancient hostelry was the headquarters of the Bradford Tories, patronised by such famous local 'blues' as E.C. Lister and Frank Duffield. It was an important coaching house, the 'Union' coach called here daily on its runs from Leeds to Kendal. It was considerably rebuilt in 1879.

Wilberforce was off to a poor start in the polling but soon picked up whilst Milton and Lascelles remained neck and neck throughout the contest. Wilberforce made liberal use of the £65,000 collected for him by subscription but was unable to equal the extravagance of the other two candidates. Legend has it that the contest cost Fitzwilliam and Harewood £100,000 each. Wilberforce, on the much smaller budget, was easily returned, along with Milton, in a close finish.

Table XLVI Voting in the County Election 1807

Candidate	*No. of Votes*
Wilberforce	11,808
Milton	11,177
Lascelles	10,990

The victory had been one for the Fitzwilliam electoral machine.[104] Milton's father had brought together a central committee of leading Yorkshire Whigs. Chaired by William Wrightson, this committee had delegated responsibilities to a number of area sub-committees, each with its system of agents. On the eleventh day of the poll, Wilberforce was safe with 10,000 votes and it was expected that Lascelles would sweep up any superfluous Tory votes. On that day Milton was heading for defeat until it was realised that the West Riding clothing districts 'had not been completely roused till they found Lascelles was likely to be returned'. Fitzwilliam had the organisation ready to exploit the clothiers' dislike of Lascelles and on each of the last four days Milton polled a hundred more votes than his Tory counterpart.

It was the vote of the smaller clothiers which swung the election Milton's way. Of his 11,177 votes, 69% came from the West Riding (7,625). From the wapentake of Morley, Milton received 1,538 votes or 14% of his total vote. In Bradford township Milton polled seventy eight votes to the ninety five of Wilberforce and eighty three of Lascelles.[105] As Elliott points out,

> 'With three candidates, two of them Tories, contesting two vacancies, it is clear...that most Whigs "plumped" for Milton, only using one of their votes'.[105]

John Crosley, Fitzwilliam's Bradford agent, had failed to break the Tory influence in what was to become the future parliamentary borough of Bradford but by comparing Milton's 148 votes with the 163 votes of the popular Wilberforce, it is clear that Tory supremacy within the town was under threat. In Bradford in 1807 the influence of the established church prevailed but elsewhere in the region, several townships came 'to be regarded as hot-beds of radicalism' and eventually succumbed to Whig policies. Great and Little Horton and the closely linked communities of Shipley, Idle, Eccleshill, Bolton and Heaton were all strong Dissenting towns. In each of them the Whig cause was given a massive vote of confidence (at Idle and Eccleshill the Tories were outvoted by 114 votes to sixteen). Of the thousands of migrants who poured into Bradford in the early decades of the nineteenth century, many were Dissenters. Their influx coincided with a period of Anglican decline and complacency.

One has but to examine some of the scandalous remarks made by both Rev. Baldwyn and Rev. Atkinson in their prolonged public feud,[107] to understand the weakness of the Anglican church in Bradford at this time. It was from the ranks of the Baptists and Independents that the Whig-Liberal challenge to the political leadership of the town would emerge in the 1830s and 1840s.

County politics continued to be controlled by the large county families and was concerned primarily with the interests of the landed classes. Increasingly after 1807 an urban and middle-class consciousness was inadequately politically represented at county level and consequently the moderate parliamentary reform movement was revived at the end of the Napoleonic Wars. Sir Francis Lindley Wood, who had been a sympathiser of constitutional change for thirty years, turned his back on the movement in 1817.[108] Resolutions passed by Whig radicals at a Yorkshire county meeting in that year were too extreme for Wood and many others. Walter Fawkes, conscious of the growing economic status of towns like Leeds and Bradford, was eager to give the new urban middle classes the political representation which they merited. To Wood, Fitzwilliam and others 'a more efficacious means of overturning the liberties of the county could not be devised. What more certain mode of introducing either despotism or anarchy'.[109] When the Leeds banker J.W. Becket stood as candidate in the county election of 1817, Fitzwilliam anticipated that,

> 'the contest henceforth will not be between Whig and Tory but between the Yard and the Acre – between the Banker's back parlour and the Gentleman at large – between the boro' of Leeds and the County, – between the monied and the landed interest'.[110]

Becket's effort in 1817 failed but nine years later the county families 'were willing to allow a townsman, John Marshall, the flax spinner, to take one of the four county seats....'[111] By that year, 1826, the commercial and industrial employers of Bradford were uneasy about the threat of organised labour and the economic conditions which had created it. They turned to Edward Baines and the parliamentary reform movement.

> 'Contingents from Bradford attended the county meetings ...organised by the "Bainesocracy" during the later 1820s, as well as cooperating with Baines in holding free trade, and anti-slavery meetings in both Bradford and Leeds'.[112]

The issue of parliamentary reform split the Tories of Bradford. Fawcett, Wood, Thompson and other members of the old business elite were now in favour of mild reform. Other 'church and king' Tories led by John Rand remained unconvinced.[113] This division in the Tory ranks was evident in 1829 and widened after the Whig party introduced their proposals for reform in 1830. There was a massive demonstration for reform in Bradford in March 1831, attended by many of the town's bankers, merchants and manufacturers, although John Rand and a hundred other ultra-Tories petitioned Lord Harewood to protest, on their behalf, against the Bill. Four days earlier, a reform meeting at the Piece Hall in October 1831 had been attended by the older families of Anglican Tories as well as by the new capitalist elite, the Dissenting families of Salt, Forbes, Milligan and Townsend. This was an uneasy alliance. Both sides, doubtless cringed as they heard E.C. Lister criticise that the bill 'did not extend the elective franchise to the lower classes which in his opinion it ought to do'.[114] They strongly opposed the working-class activists led by Peter Bussesy and John Dawson who, through the Bradford Political Union, advocated universal male suffrage and the secret ballot. Equally both Tory and Whig middle-class Bradfordians demanded economic reforms like the abolition of the East India Company monopoly. They realised the inefficacy of county representation for their economic and political grievances.

This middle-class unanimity was undermined in 1830 when Richard Oastler, an Evangelical Tory who believed in the pre-industrial paternalism of the squirearchy, began his crusade for factory reform. Subsequently, this movement united the extreme Tory right with the extreme left of the working class movement whose members were alienated by the discipline and culture of the new urban mills. Moreover, factory reform appealed to the larger well established manufacturers, many of them Anglican and Tory, who feared the economic and religious competition of the new generation of dissenting radical entrepreneurs. Their fears were justified, for behind the Dissenting-Whig demands for parliamentary change lay their true intent, of securing their rightful position in the political arena.

The confusion at the interfaces between the political parties in Bradford in the early 1830s is demonstrable in the first borough election of 1832. George Banks was introduced by Rand's extreme 'church and king' Tories but proved too liberal for them. E.C. Lister was a member of the local gentry and had certainly voted Tory in 1807. John Hardy, the second so called 'Whig' candidate had been a firm Pittite at the Pontefract election of 1830. Once elected for Bradford, his Toryism was increasingly apparent.

> 'In moderate placing all my glory
> The Tories call me Whig, and Whigs a Tory'.

And so it was with Hardy who was elected as a reformer in 1832, he had denied his Tory principles in 1834 but by 1837 was firmly in the ranks of the 'blue cockade'. The new borough voters themselves exercised an inordinate amount of cross-party voting in 1832, as many as thirty per cent of their votes were cast in this way (c.f. Leeds 5.9%).[115] This lack of politicisation was remedied in the years after the 1832 election when a number of important political institutions were developed.

There had been two attempts to provide Bradford with its own newspaper in 1825, but their ownership reflected the confusion of cross-party loyalties at that time. Of the *Bradford Courier*, John Simpson noted in his diary,

> 'The politics of the paper were to be mild but those of the present Ministry, more particularly those of Mr. Canning and Mr. Robinson...we are three Whigs and three Tories, the present Ministry is extremely popular with all parties, there being very little political difference in the country, the only dispute being whether the Whigs have turned Tories or the Tories turned Whigs'.[116]

Within nine days of the appearance of the *Courier*, the *Bradford & Wakefield Chronicle* was printed, which described itself as 'moderately Conservative' but in reality was Whig. Both papers were short-lived. By 1834 party lines were more clear cut and a group of nonconformist Liberals determined that Bradford should no longer rely for its news upon the Leeds press. The group included Titus Salt and his father Daniel, Edward and Henry Ripley, Robert Milligan, Henry Forbes and Christopher Waud. The *Bradford Observer* was edited by William Byles and soon began to prescribe a liberal policy on the Corn Laws, Church Rates and the franchise. The paper sharpened the political focus within the town often with an inevitable bias, as Byles became an ardent Liberal.

Bradford's politicisation was extended in 1835 when the parties established local institutional frameworks. The Whig-Radical alliance of 1832 had collapsed on several issues and the Whigs were violently attacked by some Bradford working men in the election of 1835. In consequence, the Whigs established a number of organisations to strengthen their position and win

Figure 36 Robert Milligan. Of Scottish peasant stock Milligan was born in 1786. In 1819 he settled in Bradford as a wholesale draper but soon developed a successful career as worsted merchant. He began an illustrious career of public service in the 1840s. He was elected first mayor of Bradford following its incorporation in 1847 and became Liberal M.P. for the town in 1851. Following his death in 1862 he received the distinction of a public funeral. He is buried in Undercliffe Cemetery.

back popular support. One of these was the Bradford Reform Society founded in February 1835 which 'marks the emergence of a thrusting brand of Liberalism, associated with the new Nonconformist manufacturers, in place of the moderate Whiggism, which was hardly distinguishable from the Toryism of

Wood, Fawcett or Hardy'.[117] Its membership was dominated by nonconformist liberal manufacturers who subsequently became prominent in the affairs of Victorian Bradford. The society offered facilities for social intercourse and political education but in May 1836 turned its attention to active politics, when its members became involved in the elections for the poor law guardians.

The Bradford Tories were already institutionalised through their control of the magistracy, vestry and Improvement Commission. Yet in the newly elected offices for parliament and the Board of Guardians, the Tories would need to recruit popular support like their Whig counterparts. Oastler's factory reform movement went some way towards this but in 1837 the Bradford Tories formalised their links with the recently enfranchised working men of Bradford by the establishment of the Bradford Operative Conservative Society. This was modelled on a similar society founded at Leeds in 1835 and was patronised by many of Bradford's leading Tories. As a result several of Bradford's working-class voters supported the Conservative policies of Robert Peel after 1837.

The majority of working class radicals, however, followed Peter Bussey into the Bradford Radical Association, founded in January 1836. They campaigned for an extension of the suffrage, the rejection of the new poor law and factory reform. These issues ensured their separation from the Whigs and the Reform Society. However, the Bradford Radical Association was divided in 1837 when Bussey led its extremists into the Bradford Northern Union which was noted for its 'strong denunciation of the Whigs and the appeal to physical force Chartism'.[118] The more moderate members of the Radical Association, led by Christopher Wilkinson, ultimately aligned themselves with the middle-class Reform Society which conceded on the divisive issue of an extension of the vote.

Thus by 1835 the political lines had been drawn in Bradford. The Tory oligarchy of gentlemen, merchants and manufacturers still clung to control of local affairs in spite of the arrival of new manufacturing families, many of whom were Dissenters in their religion and Whig in their politics. Increasingly, after 1828 the latter challenged the authority of Bradford's traditional Tory elite over the day to day running of a growing industrial town. The two groups eventually entered the political fray on the issue of the parochial collection of church rates. The levy was condemned by nonconformists who maintained their own chapels and obtained no benefit from the Church of England. In 1835 it was moved that the Bradford Vestry adjourn its decision to raise a church rate, a precedent continued in later years and one which, with the development of party organisation, precipitated profound change in the political and administrative development of Bradford in the early Victorian period.[119]

Middle Class Cultural Developments in the Town

The greater part of this book has been taken up in considering the ways in which Bradfordians developed their community through industry, commerce and politics in the period of the Industrial Revolution. This final section is about the ways by which those who had created wealth and acquired power put them to enjoyable use by the promotion of art, music, theatre and literature and other cultural forms which are considered as uplifting to the human spirit.

This creative contribution to Bradford's cultural development came largely from the new middle class taking shape in these years. They also included a small number of landed families verging on gentry status who had retained, if not increased, their wealth by their industrial and commercial diversification. These 'principal inhabitants of the town' included families like the Hodgsons of Kirkgate, the Skeltons of Hall Ings and men like Henry Dawson and Nathan Jowett of Good Man's End. This traditional middle class elite was, during these years, joined by the 'new wealth' of merchants and manufacturers like John Hustler, Abraham Balme, Richard Fawcett and John Sturges. The Bradford middle classes also included a growing group of professional men, lawyers, doctors and parsons, men like Joseph Priestley, Samuel Hailstone and George Mossman M.D.[120]

Below them in Bradford's social hierarchy and officially part of the 'middle' orders of society were a variable number of tradesmen, shopkeepers and well-to-do artisans.[121] Collectively these people gave the lead to Bradford's cultural maturity after 1780, either by taking part as spectators or, as in the case of some, by organising creative activities and cultural events within the community. If their motive was not simply one of personal pleasure but 'a defence against those who criticised them as money makers....'[122] then they had little success, for Scruton in 1891 could write 'of private money-making enterprise there was plenty but of noble philanthropic spirit, alas! there was but little'.[123]

Several contemporaries also thought that the social and intellectual climate of the town had not kept pace with its industrial and commercial expansion. Dr. John Simpson was bored with Bradford in 1825,

> 'I am at a loss what to do for there is no kind of Society here, every one being engaged in trade and thinking of nothing else. There are no pleasant rides, no pleasant walks, all being bustle, hurry and confusion'.[124]

An opinion, confirmed by Jacob Behrens thirteen years later, who 'found Bradford greatly lacking in comforts and facilities.... All machinery of social intercourse was lacking. The only thing approaching a club was a toddy drinking meeting of manufacturers.... I had to give up a circle of cultivated friends in Leeds and go to, what was then, no more than a large village'.[125] Despite such criticism of Bradford's cultural institutions, the town's middle classes did make some headway in the promotion of science, art, literature, music and theatre in the period 1780 to 1830. There were several members of the Bradford bourgeoisie, albeit a minority, who made an important contribution to the raising of the town's cultural consciousness. Initially they were motivated by the need for personal entertainment and social intercourse. Yet as the ranks of the middle classes swelled in the nineteenth century, the development of high culture became the answer to attacks of bourgeois commercialism and the lust for financial success. George Weerth, a German agent living in Bradford in 1843 noted,

> 'The coarse, barbarian taste of the English bourgeoisie betrays itself in everything they do.... Nothing is more amusing than a ball given by a millowner. The tendency of most people on such an occasion is to display in words and movements the highest propriety, the most wonderful pomp which becomes so desperately funny....'[126]

This section of the book will examine the ways in which some of the Bradford middle-classes put their wealth and influence to work in order to raise the cultural standards in the town. By 1850 their cultural achievements were not significant but the efforts which were made in the years preceding laid the foundations for the cultural zenith of late Victorian Bradford.

Cultural life in most provincial towns in the eighteenth century was often narrow and limited particularly in those towns where the respectable classes had few connections with landed wealth and were indebted for position or status to aristocratic patronage. Increasingly, in the years after 1780, there was little wealth or culture in Bradford which was not mercantile or industrial in origin. Most of the gentry in Bradford were in decline and their social graces increasingly challenged. Art, literature and music consequently retreated to the privacy of old family homes and manorial halls. For most of the 'newly-risen', church and chapel offered the major opportunity of cultural enhancement. Listening to sermons and sacred music were important cultural pastimes in eighteenth-century Bradford. As late as 1825 John Simpson's diary records weekly the quality of the sermon at Bradford Parish Church and by April of that year he noted,

> 'I was at Church this afternoon and heard the Vicar preach, but was not particularly pleased with him. The congregation at the church evidently decreases every year. It arises in my opinion from our having men of no talent in church. Mr. Heap is a good kind man but very ignorant.... He is not a member of any University.... I don't suppose as long as he is Vicar that there will be any popular Clergymen in Bradford consequently the congregation of the church will run off and those of the dissenting chapels increase.[127]

In addition to the sermons, church and chapel provided public musical performances. Bradford was probably influenced by the strong musical tradition of Halifax in the 1780s. It was in March 1785 that Rev. John Crosse obtained permission from the church authorities for an organ to be installed in the Parish Church.[128] Payment for the instrument and the organist was to come from subscriptions and from the sale of pews in the new galleries that were to be built for the audience and congregation. The organ was inaugurated in May 1786 with a grand oratorio. Thereafter, Bottomley the organist played sacred music for public entertainment as well as for the religious service. There was a performance of 'sacred music to be performed in Bradford Church on Wednesday June 26th 1799: chiefly from the works of F.G. Handel Esq.'[129] The programme included recitations, airs and choruses from a selection of Handel's major works. Handel's 'Messiah' had been popular in the West Riding since 1766 and Bradfordians had heard performances of it before the installation of the church organ. Abraham Balme recorded in his journal at Christmas 1774. 'There was the oratorio of the Messiah at the Piece Hall in Bradford to which I and Miss Isles and Mrs. Hodgson went'.[130] Much of the music in Bradford before 1815 featured the oratorio to which vocalists and instrumentalists from far and wide were invited. In June 1802 the Parish Church was the venue for the Bradford Musical festival, a massive jamboree of sacred music.

The event was followed in the evening by a concert of miscellaneous music and dancing. Occasional concerts had been held in the Piece Hall since 1773 but from 1801 were performed in the Assembly Rooms, on the first floor of the Market Hall built in that year.[131] The larger public houses also provided musical entertainment. In January 1825 John Simpson attended a ball at the Sun Inn, not getting home until three in the morning.

> 'Our dances have been very pleasant ones and very well attended.... The subscription for the three dances for Gentlemen was one guinea and Ladies fifteen shillings. Out of this we found the room, lights, music, tea and attendance. We had four musicians....'[132]

The provision of popular music was increased in the 1840s when the Gentlemen's Glee Club was formed (1840) and a number of German residents established the Bradford Liedertafel in the same year.[133] A number of Germans, also helped Samuel Smith and Joshua Mann begin the subscription concert movement in Bradford in 1844. The first concert was given in the Exchange Rooms in December of that year. At a lower cultural level were the singing rooms attached to public houses, the forerunners of the music halls and variety theatres. One of the best liked in Bradford was that attached to Mrs. Dunn's Old Bermondsey Hotel, in Broadstones. Customers purchased checks which could be spent on entrance or refreshments. General manager at the Bermondsey was Henry Pullan who eventually built the Coliseum Music Hall in Westgate in 1849.[134]

In spite of the increase in secular music, hymns and anthems dominated the local musical scene as more and more religious groups brought their musical talents together in what were called 'sittings-up'. These frequent festivals of sacred music led to the formation of the first choral society in Bradford, the Bradford Musical Friendly Society. The first meeting took place in the Assembly Rooms in 1821 and thereafter, quarterly performances were given. In 1843 the name of the society was changed to that of the Bradford Choral Society.[135] Another institution which carried on the tradition of good choral music was the Philharmonic Society founded in 1831. Like its rival it comprised both vocalists and instrumentalists and was sponsored by many of the leading families of the town. Concerts were held in the upper room of the Exchange Buildings and some of the finest names in the country sang and played there.

Reading was a central cultural activity in the late eighteenth century and the Bradford Literary and Library Society was founded as early as December 1774. Much of the initiative for the establishment of the library came from the

Unitarian Minister, the Rev. John Dean, but its early committee tended to be dominated by Anglican Tories like John Rand and Dr. Outhwaite.[136] In the first year there were seventy two subscribers each of whom paid one guinea and an annual subscription of five shillings. The range of works was wide although Dean's prejudice for Dr. Joseph Priestley's works was much in evidence in the early years.[137] Books were purchased from the Bradford booksellers, Dudley Rocket and John Smith. The society's accounts provide a clue to the arrival of Bradford's first printer. Before 1781 the catalogues of the society were printed in Leeds but in that year John Nicholson established his printing business at the top of Albion Court. The same John Nicholson became librarian to the society in 1814 when the library was moved to Chapel Court in Kirkgate. By that time the membership had increased to 112. Many of the leading merchants and manufacturers as well as the town's professional men were members of the library. Initially the membership in 1774 had comprised the local gentry and leading merchants, the majority of whom were Tory and Anglican.[138]

Another library society with a similar political flavour was that attached to the Literary and Philosophical society. Scruton suggests that the first philosophical society was founded in Bradford in the 1790s under the auspices of the Unitarian scientist Dr. Joseph Priestley. A fanatically loyalist 'King and Church' group in Bradford probably explains the brief existence of this society. When it was resurrected in 1808 it no longer speculated in political philosophy but gave primacy to scientific investigations.[139] Politically respectable Tory Anglicans were in control, and its first committee included Samuel Hailstone, Joseph Priestley, John Jarratt, Richard Fawcett, Benjamin Thompson and Henry Leah. The object of this association was the 'acquirement of Science and improvements in Arts and Manufacturers'. At its first meeting at the School of Industry, 9 November 1803 it resolved to admit members at three guineas and associate members at half a guinea. The latter were to number no more than twelve and,

> 'shall have no part in the management of the business of the society...it being the intention of forming this class to encourage the exertions of deserving persons who have a taste for science and arts but whose circumstances may render it inconvenient to contribute to the extent of full membership....'[140]

It was the local iron industry rather than the worsted manufacture which promoted the scientific culture of this society. Many of the early lectures were given by the town's iron manufacturers. The first lecture, read in January 1809, discussed the nature and properties of oxygen gas. Joseph Priestley succeeded Joseph Dawson as president in 1810 by which time the society had purchased a library of books on natural philosophy, mechanics, physiology and mineralogy. Several members contributed a whole range of scientific instruments including a microscope given by Samuel Hailstone. By 1814 the society emphasized its role as a library,

> 'For a place like ours where machinery and manufactures are daily increasing, to be possessed of those recent publications and of

> other scientific treatises would be highly useful and would lead to the introduction of many improvements....'[141]

For a number of years the activities of the Philosophical society lapsed but in September 1822 Samuel Hailstone was once again instrumental in re-establishing it. Forty two merchants and manufacturers each subscribed fifty pounds towards the building of a public hall.[142] Unfortunately, the Rev. Henry Heap preached a sermon 'in which he enlarged on the irreligious tendency of a philosophising spirit' and as a result many potential subscribers withdrew and the society was not formed. It was Heap's successor as Vicar of Bradford, William Scoresby, an ex-whaling captain and a scientist of some repute who helped to found the next philosophical society in 1839. Much of the initiative, however, came from William Sharp, a surgeon, whose departure from the town in 1844 led directly to the society's sudden demise.[143]

Each of the abortive Lit. and Phil. societies established in Bradford between 1791 and 1839 had come from the town's new middle-classes. It was, however, from the ranks of the operatives that the initial idea of forming a Mechanics Institute emanated. In 1822 a Mechanics' Friendly Union Institution met in Bradford and within three years a campaign was under way to establish a proper institute. It began in February 1825 when handbills circulated the town, summoning a meeting of operative mechanics in the Parish Church Sunday School room.[144] Seventy two members enrolled and a committee was formed to draw up a constitution. Edward Baines attended, as did Joshua Pollard and several local clergy.[145] Three local radicals, Benjamin Berry, Squire Farrar and the bookseller and free thinker, Christopher Wilkinson, were all elected to the first committee which resolved 'that a majority of the committee so formed shall always be artisans'.[146] This rule was intended to secure artisan control over the institute and its affairs. Another rule of this society stated that 'No book of controversial divinity or party politics shall be admitted to the library'. Despite this safeguard, the political flavour of men like Farrar and Wilkinson was sufficient to discourage middle class support and finance.

> '...the strict aloofness observed by both churchmen and dissenters in Bradford, the promoters of the movement being known as men of pronounced sceptical opinion and Mr. Squire Farrar's personality being particularly obnoxious'.[147]

Few of Bradford's leading merchants and manufacturers backed the institute and as a result it was never launched. The political implications of the Great Bradford Strike in that year doomed the scheme, and when it was resurrected in 1832 control of the institute was in very different hands.[148] Henceforth, its affairs and the kind of cultural contribution it made to Bradford were influenced largely by middle-class Nonconformists.[149] By 1837 it provided a variety of public lectures and classes under well-qualified masters as well as a well stocked library of 1,800 volumes. Gradually the premises of the Mechanics Institute (at the junction of Well Street and Leeds Road) served the town's recreational as well as its educational needs. Demonstrations of mesmerism and phrenological delineations were succeeded by concerts, horticultural exhibitions and variety entertainment like that of the New York Male and Female Seranaders who visited Bradford in October 1847.

Like other provincial towns, Bradford in the eighteenth century had no fixed theatre of its own but was visited, particularly on fair days, by travelling players who set up their stage in public houses and at inn courtyards. These dramatic pieces, interspersed with music, were advertised as concerts and thus obviated the need for a licence. In the last quarter of the eighteenth century Bradford followers of Thespis were few.

> '...legitimate drama had small chance of success in Bradford. For so large a population playgoers were not numerous. There was no regular theatre. The few gentry living amongst us...for the most part discountenanced the stage. Working people were too illiterate to enjoy and too ill paid to support it'.[150]

In spite of this lack of support and the outright condemnation of both church and chapel, Bradford's first permanent theatre was erected in a barn in Southgate in 1810 by L.S. Thompson. He moved later to the rear of the Kings Arms Inn, Westgate and by 1820 was established at Bartles Corner in Market Street. There, Bradford's theatre-going public were offered Shakespeare, restoration comedy and occasionally melodrama from local writers like John Nicholson. Thompson rarely filled the seven hundred seats which his theatre provided but he introduced some talented actors and actresses to Bradford.[151] Dr. John Simpson visited Thompson's theatre on three consecutive nights in 1825:

> 'July 11th — At seven o'clock I went to the Theatre. It was very much crowded and being a very poor, small, inconvenient place was intensely hot....
>
> July 12th — After tea we went to the Theatre to see Miss Clara Fisher. She was Shylock in the Merchant of Venice. Afterwards The Actress of all Works.... The house was not so full as last night and quite a different kind of company'.[152]

Dismayed by lack of patronage Thompson vacated the theatre and moved to London, which left Bradford without a permanent theatre for fourteen years.

Several travelling theatres visited Bradford in that interval including Old Wild's and Mrs. Chatterton whose players offered 'The Wife of Seven Husbands', 'Sweeney Todd' or the 'Spectre Bridegroom'. The cultural level was lifted in 1836 when Mr. Smedley built a permanent theatre in Peel Square. His theatre was respectable, comfortable and possessed imaginative scenery and a good regular cast. The quality of Smedley's theatre did much to improve the public's opinion of drama in Bradford, and by 1841 a fine stone building was erected as the Theatre Royal in Duke Street.

Art and Sculpture fared no better than theatre in Bradford before 1840. William Scruton suspected this stemmed from the 'employers who were too busy or too sordid to care for such things while the employed were too ignorant or too poor to feel any interest in such trifling things as pictures'. However there was some local demand for the portrait or landscape painter as wealthier families sought to capture for posterity favourite views and faces.[153] Until the 1820s, Bradfordians looked to Leeds artists for these services and for any artistic stimulus. Dr. John Simpson and several of his medical friends visited Leeds in July 1825,

> 'After we had taken luncheon we went to the exhibition which is in Albion Street. There were some very fine pictures there...on the whole I was very much pleased. There was a good portrait of the present Earl of Harewood by Sir Thos. Lawrence....'[154]

Two years later Bradford's own small community of artists established the Bradford Artists' Society of Painting and Sculpture. They hired rooms in Darley Street and from July to September 1827 held an exhibition of one hundred and fifty paintings and several pieces of sculpture. Several 'old masters' were loaned by local gentry from their private collections; other items included the products of artists from Leeds and neighbouring towns but a large number were exclusively of their own work. The local press encouraged their support.

> 'There are three or four young artists in Bradford of considerable talent whose works are little known to the public.... Mr. T.M. Richardson will exhibit a view of Edinburgh Castle: Mr. J. Wilson Anderson two sea views; Mr. J. Clayton Bentley, an excellent portrait of his father and Mr. W.O. Geller has several pictures which do him credit as a self-taught artist'.[155]

The exhibition was a failure and a financial disaster for the group. They were all young men, Bentley was only eighteen at the time of the exhibition. He left for London in 1832 and made his name as an engraver. Geller, born in 1804, also moved to London and became proficient as an engraver although his skill as a painter was never lost. He helped to refound the Mechanics' Institute in 1832 a year before his departure from Bradford. J.W. Anderson came to Bradford in 1818 and was apprenticed to Goodchild, a painter and decorator. Throughout the 1820s he advertised his work in the Bradford press and became a portrait painter of considerable merit. He remained in Bradford and was patronised by local merchants and manufacturers for family portraits. Anderson was also renowned for his scene-painting in the early Bradford theatres. These men were not famous artists but they acquired a regional reputation as painters and teachers which attracted the custom of the new men of wealth and as a result they were able to make a living from their work and heighten the cultural achievements of the town. By 1840 the Mechanics Institute had mounted several art exhibitions which were patronised by an increasing number of manufacturers.[156] Low entry fees encouraged working class attendance as part of the programme of national recreation to promote class harmony and self improvement. This account of middle-class culture in Bradford after 1780 has been primarily concerned with cultural forms and the societal or institutional framework in which they were expressed. For many people, cultural and leisure pursuits were conducted in the privacy of the home. Dr. John Simpson dined with friends in May 1825. 'Sherwin showed us several new books he had just got in from London. Mann played us several tunes on the piano'. Throughout the period individuals had access to an increasing number of retail outlets for music, books and pictures. In spite of the inconsistencies of data provided by local directories there was a general upward trend in the number of retail outlets which reflects the growing demand for cultural improvement.

Table XLVII Retail Outlets in Bradford for Literature, Art and Music 1792–1850

	Printers	*Booksellers and Stationers*	*Music Sellers*	*Artists*
1792[1]	1	3	–	–
1809[2]	1	3	–	–
1829[3]	4	9	2	–
1837[4]	4	12	5	–
1841[5]	10	11	5	–
1850[6]	23	18	14	3

Sources:
1. *Universal British Directory 1792*
2. Holden's *Triennial Directory 1809–11*
3. Pigot & Co. *National Commercial Directory 1828–9*
4. *History, Directory & Gazeteer of West Riding* W. White 1837
5. Pigot 1841
6. Ibbetson, *General & Classified Directory 1845*

John Nicholson is thought to have printed the first book in Bradford in 1785. By 1800 Nicholson and his sons were joined by Richard Sedgewick who was both printer and bookseller. The first Bradford periodical, the *Bradford Instructive and Entertaining Miscellany*, was published by John Blackburn in 1818 but lasted only one year.[157] Henry Wardman of Chapel Lane specialised in printing children's literature and Sunday School tracts. John Stansfield became the most respected printer and typographer in Bradford between 1793 and 1835. From his Westgate works came the published poems of John Nicholson, Poet of Airedale,

> 'A poor man of the name of Nicholson, Poet of Airedale, known by the name of the Rombalds Moor Poet has by the advice of some friends published by subscription a small collection of poems. The book has come out today and the price is six shillings. I think the work very creditable indeed to the poor fellow and I hope it will repay him for his trouble'.[158]

remarked Dr. John Simpson somewhat patronisingly in his journal for 1825. A later entry in the journal identifies Simpson as a co-founder of the first Bradford newspaper, the *Bradford Courier and West Riding Advertiser*. It was printed and published by Thomas Inkersley and first came off the press 14 July 1825. It lasted three years and served the Tory cause well but it was a financial disaster for its shareholders. Within nine days of the appearance of the *Courier*,

Bradfordians were faced with a choice of newspapers when the *Bradford Chronicle* was printed by John Stansfield. Simpson's view that 'the Editor by attempting to please all sides has made the paper so tame and insignificant that it has pleased none' was well founded and the *Chronicle* lasted a mere nine months. For six years Bradfordians depended, as before, upon Leeds newspapers but in 1834 a syndicate of Bradford Liberals raised shares to finance the *Bradford Observer*. Under the editorship of William Byles it became one of the leading provincial journals of the nineteenth century.

Perhaps more relevant than individual culture and personal entertainment was the status and social position to be gained from participating in those cultural activities regarded by others. The middle class elite of industrial Bradford became increasingly aware of the need for culture as an outward show of their social standing. The compulsion to present visible evidence of their developing cultural taste can best be found in their efforts to provide a central forum for culture in Bradford. Before 1770 rooms to the rear of the Kings Arms Inn, Westgate, had served as the town's public rooms until the erection of the Piece Hall. Accommodation in the Market Hall of 1802 had thereafter functioned as Bradford's Assembly Rooms. None were appropriate for the expanding community and in 1825 Dr. John Simpson noted,

> 'We have long felt at Bradford the want of public rooms. We have no regular assembly rooms, a very bad news room, a wretched room for the public library and no decent billiard room. A paper was drawn up by Outhwaite...proposing to build a set of public rooms by subscription in shares of £25....'[159]

Dr. Outhwaite's proposal got the backing of several leading townsmen. The cost was estimated at £7,000 and a site at the junction of Piccadilly and Kirkgate was chosen as the most central. The rooms were finally opened in October 1828 as the Bradford Public Rooms. So popular was the building with the town's millocracy that it subsequently became known as the Exchange.[160] Eventually it catered for the News Room and the Subscription Library as well as many balls, assemblies, concerts, exhibitions and public lectures. Scruton notes that the Exchange and its affairs were dominated by a small group of master manufacturers and professional men, a fact which gave rise to a spirit of rivalry between what were then styled the 'aristocracy' and the 'shopocracy of Bradford'. It was the influence of this 'old order' with its essentially aristocratic nostalgia for the past which led to the architectural style of the Exchange.

> 'We particularly recommend to the committee to hold fast to the models which have been handed down to us from the days of Greek excellence. Gothic is of course out of the question for an erection of this nature and no mongrel or nondescript style which we have ever seen is at all comparable with the unadorned chastity of the Doric or the Ionic'.[161]

The value of Greek Revival architecture as appropriate for civic and commercial buildings was continued in the Court House (1834), Piccadilly warehouses (1830–34) and St. Georges Hall (1853). The last building

Figure 37 Court House. This public building stood in Hall Ings. It was built in 1834 as part of the Classical revival of that period. From the balcony beneath the portico, parliamentary candidates addressed the electorate of Bradford after 1835. Prior to that time the steps to the Piece Hall in Kirkgate had been used for that purpose.

superceded the Exchange rooms as the cultural centre of Victorian Bradford and remains one of the finest concert halls in the whole country.

The cultural achievements of Bradford's middle classes by 1840 may not have complemented their industrial and commercial progress. In art and drama they had advanced little from the cultural wasteland of a late eighteenth century market town. The musical, philosophical and literary life of Bradford was less bleak although John James having published at a loss the town's first history in 1841 noted 'The people of Bradford are not remarkable for their encouragement of literary effort'. However by that year Bradford's bourgeoisie had laid the foundations upon which the city's rich and varied cultural life in the later nineteenth century was subsequently built.

By 1850 Bradford was no longer the remote rural backwater it had been a century before; transport changes and a quickening of economic activity in addition to the comings and going of many thousands of people, all had played their part in making Bradford's regional economy an important new link in the national economic network. So too with the town's cultural development. By 1850 Bradford was part of a national culture and, owing to its worldwide trading links and its migrant German and Irish communities, it could even be considered as part of an international culture. What was true of J.B. Priestley's Bradford in

1895 had its origins in the early part of that century, Priestley wrote, 'Bradford became...at once one of the most provincial and yet one of the most cosmopolitan of English provincial cities. There was, then, this odd nature.... A dash of the Rhine and the Oder found its way into our grim runnel – t'mucky beck. Bradford was determinedly Yorkshire and provincial but some of its suburbs reached as far as Frankfurt or Leipzig'.[162]

By the end of the nineteenth century Bradford had become the world centre of the worsted trade, a true Worstedopolis and a far cry from the sleepy remote market town which it had been a century earlier.

1. J. James, *Continuation and Additions to the History of Bradford* p.88
2. 2nd Report of the Commissioners for Inquiring into the State of Large Towns P.P. 1845 XVIII (602) p.150
3. J. James, Ibid
4. J. Burnley, *Old Streets of Bradford*, (Bradford 1883), and P. Ross, Old Roads of Bradford, *Bradford Antiquary* N.S. VI 1912, pp.297–311
5. W. Cudworth, *Historical Notes on Bradford Corporation*, p.24
6. J. Burnley, *Old Streets of Bradford*, p.6
7. B.C.L. Scruton Ms. 10/18/13 and Misc. Ms 27/16
8. W. Cudworth, *Historical Notes* pp.35–47
9. J. Lister, Survey of the Manor of Bradford in 1342, *Bradford Antiquary*, Vol. II (1895) p.57
10. D. Fraser, (ed). *History of Modern Leeds*, (1980) pp.75
11. *Bradford Observer* 12 June 1845 and B.C.L. Selected Extracts from the Writings of George Weerth, 1845
12. J. Johnson, *Map of the Township of Bradford* 1802; L. Atkinson, *Plan of the Town of Bradford* 1825; J. Wood, *Plan of Bradford from an Actual Survey*, 1834
13. 2nd Report. State of Large Towns, p.150
14. B.C.L. Maps & Plans. PIC 1849 BRA
15. J. Aitkin, *A Description of the Country 30–40 Miles around Manchester* (1795) p.569
16. M.J. Mortimore, Landownerhsip and Urban Growth in Bradford and its Environs 1850–1950, *Transaction of Institute of British Geographers*, 46 (1969)
17. B.C.L. Maps & Plans BRA 1824 and BOL and BLA 1837 PEA
18. B.C.L. Ibid BRA 1837 PEA
19. J. Roberts, *Little Germany* (Bradford 1977) p.21
20. J. Simpson, *Journal*, (Bradford 1980) p.5
21. B.C.L. Rate Books 1819–23
22. *Bradford Observer*, 12 June 1845
23. B.C.L. BRA 1839 DIX and N. Whitehead, Report of Building and Improvement Committee on the Operation of the Building By Laws, Braford 1864
24. E. Naylor, *Bradford Building Societies from 1823*, (Bradford 1903)
25. C. Richardson, The Irish in Victorian Bradford, *Bradford Antiquary* NS XLV (1971)
26. J. Hole, *The Homes of the Working Classes* (1866), pp.36–39

27. G. Weerth, op. cit. *The Government of Bradford*
29. W. Cudworth, Courts Baron and Leet, *Bradford Antiquary*, Vol.II (1895) pp.185–9
30. W. Cudworth, Bradford in 1795, *Bradford Antiquary* Vol.II (1895) p.216
31. S. Webb and B. Webb, *English Local Government, The Manor and Borough* (1908), and K.B. Smellie, *A History of Local Government*, (1968)
32. S. Webb and B. Webb, *The Development of English Local Government 1689–1835*, Reprint (1963) pp.3–8
33. B.C.L. Bradford Cathedral Records, Vestry and Township Book, 1687–1824
34. H.E. Wroot, Bradford Parish Churchwarden's Accounts, *Bradford Antiquary*, Vol.II (1895), pp.260–270
35. J.S. Cockburn, North Riding Justices 1690–1750, *Yorkshire Archaeological Society Journal*, 41, (1966), pp.481–516
36. W. Cudworth, *Round About Bradford*, (Bradford 1876), pp.36–7
37. J.D. Marshall, *The Old Poor Law 1795–1834* (1968); D. Marshall, *The English Poor Law in the Eighteenth Century*, (1926), pp.225–54
38. F.M. Eden, *The State of the Poor* (1795), pp.810–1
39. B.C.L. Vestry Minute Book, 8 Jue 1795
40. Y.M.L. Hailstone Ms. G3 Poorhouse Rules
41. B.C.L. Spencer-Stanhope Ms. 2168 4 June 1800
42. Ibid. Ms 1170, 28 February 1819
43. W.Y.C.R.O. West Riding Quarter Session Order Books, 17 July 1762 and 14 July 1803
44. *Bradford Courier*, 11 August 1826
45. P.P. Home Office 40/19/752. 6 May 1826 and B.C.L. Vestry Minute Book 2 August 1826
46. B.C.L. Vestry Minute Book 2 August 1826
47. W. Cudworth, *Bradford in 1795*, op. cit. p.216
48. W. Cudworth, *Historical Notes*, p.24
49. B.C.L. Improvement Commission Ms. Minute Book 8 December 1828
50. W. Cudworth, *Historical Notes*, p.20
51. *Bradford Observer* 12 December 1836
52. B.C.L. Vestry Minute Book 11 February 1831
53. Ibid. 23 November 1831
54. R.D. Storch, The Policeman as Domestic Missionary, *Journal of Social History* Vol. 9, (1976), pp.481–509
55. W. Cudworth, *Historical Notes*, pp.22–5
56. Y.M.L. Hailstone Ms. 2/1/49
57. Ibid 2/1/43
58. Gt. Britain Statutes. 43 Geo. III cap. 90 1803
59. W. Cudworth, *Historical Notes*, p.19
60. B.C.L. Improvement Commission Order Book 1803–24 1 July 1803
61. Ibid 25 March 1812
62. *Bradford Courier* 5 September 1825
63. B.C.L. Improvement Commission Order Book II November 1814 and 8 June 1807
64. *Bradford Observer*, 17 April 1834
65. *Bradford Observer*, 18 September 1834

66. A. Elliott, The Incorporation of Bradford, *Northern History*, XV (1979) pp.156–175 Bradford Politics 1760–1835
67. G.R. Park, *The Parliamentary Representation of Yorkshire* (Hull 1880), pp.28–36
68. D.G. Wright, A Radical Borough – Parliamentary Politics in Bradford 1832–41, *Northern History*, Vol. IV (1969) pp.132–166
69. J. James, *History of Bradford* op. cit. p.155 and *Leeds Mercury* 24 April 1770.
70. B.C.L. Misc. Ms 3/7/3
71. Ibid 37/6/10
72. *Leeds Intelligencer* 17 December 1792
73. *Leeds Intelligencer* 24 December 1792
74. J. James, op. cit. p.156
75. H.J.M. Maltby, The Early Volunteer Movement in Bradford, *Bradford Antiquary*, New Series, IV (1918) pp.335–46
76. A. Mitchell, The Association Movement 1792/3, *The Historical Journal* Vol. IV No. 1 (1961) pp.56/77 and J.R. Western, The Volunteer Movement as an Anti-Revolutionary Force 1793–1801 *English Historical Review* (1950) pp.603–14
77. *Leeds Intelligencer* 17 April 1794
78. B.C.L. Pamphlets. P. Pindar, *Advice to Juvenis or a Squeere for His Touch*
79. B.M. Add Mss 1795, Minutes of London Corresponding Society
80. Y.M.L. Hailstone Ms G3
81. Ibid and Rev. Edward Baldwyn in *Bradford Antiquary* Vol. 1 N.S pp.41–2
82. Hailstone HH6 Pamphlet, 'A Dose for the Doctor or a Bitter Pill for G. Mossman', (1796), I am indebted to J.M. Hagerty for this information
83. B.C.L. Misc. Ms 3/17/3 24 October 1795
84. N.Y.C.R.O. Wyvill Papers 11/1–3 26 April 1797
85. Y.M.L. Hailstone Ms G3
86. K. Wells, *Dearth & Distress in Yorkshire 1793–1802*, Borthwick Papers No. 52 (1977)
87. K. Wells, op. cit. p.24
88. E.P. Thompson, The moral economy of the English crowd in the Eighteenth Century, *Past and Present*, No. 50 (1971)
89. N.Y.C.R.O. Wyvill Papers 110/1/3
90. *Leeds Intelligencer*, 3 February 1801
91. S.C.L. Wentworth-Woodhouse Muniment. F45/29. 1 February 1801
92. W. Atkinson, *Four Addresses to the People of England on the Subject of Reform* (Bradford 1798) p.14
93. Wentworth-Woodhouse F45/8
94. Ibid F45/10
95. Ibid F45/12
96. Ibid F45/13
97. Ibid F45/16
98. F45/12
99. F45/50–3
100. E.A. Smith, The Yorkshire Elections 1806–7, *Northern History* II (1967) pp.62–90
101. W. Cudworth, *History of Bolton & Bowling* (1891) p.176
102. B.C.L. Spencer-Stanhope Ms 2206. 22 October 1806

103. E.A. Smith, op. cit. p.72
104. Y.A.S. Ferrand Ms Busfeild Diaries M.290 Box 14
105. Leeds Central Reference Library, 1807 Poll Book, Morley Wapentake
106. A. Elliott, Unpublished Ph.D Thesis University of Bradford 1976, The Establishment of Municipal Government in Bradford 1837–1857
107. Y.M.L. Hailstone Mss G3
108. Hickleton Papers A19/5 28 January 1817
109. Ibid A4 19/1 12 August 1822
110. Ibid A4 19/3 22 June 1818
111. D. Fraser (ed.) *History of Modern Leeds* (M.U.P. 1981) p.275
112. D.G. Wright, op. cit. p.136
113. B.C.L. Misc. Mss 16/4/9
114. *Leeds Mercury* 1 October 1831
115. A. Elliott op. cit. p.33
116. B.C.L. *Diary of John Simpson*, 6 May 1825
117. Elliott, p.33
118. A.J. Peacock, *Bradford Chartism* 1838–40, Borthwick Papers, No.36, (1969), pp.13–14
119. A. Elliott, The Incorporation of Bradford, *Northern History* XV (1979) 'Bradford and Middle Class Culture'
120. W. Cudworth, *Historical Notes on the Bradford Corporation* (1881) p.14
121. J. Reynolds, *The Great Paternalist* (1983) p.15
122. R.J. Morris, Middle Class Culture 1700–1914 in D. Fraser *History of Modern Leeds* (1980)
123. W. Scruton, *Pen and Pencil Pictures of Old Bradford*, op. cit. p.233
124. B.C.L. *Diary of John Simpson*, p.11
125. H. Behrens, *The Unpublished Memoirs of Jacob Behrens* (1925?) p.8
126. G. Weerth, *Selected Writings*, op. cit. p.4
127. B.C.L. *Diary of John Simpson*, 24 April 1825
128. W. Cudworth, *Musical Reminiscences of Bradford* (1885), pp.114–5
129. Ibid, p.36
130. B.C.L. Ms 6/1 Daybook of Abraham Balme, 26 December 1774
131. W. Hustwick, Old Market House, *Journal of Bradford Textile Society* (1953–54) p.82
132. *Diary of John Simpson*, op. cit. p.2 7 January 1825
133. W. Cudworth, op. cit. pp.40–42
134. *Bradford Corporation Centenary Brochure 1847–1947*
135. W. Cudworth, op. cit. pp.5–12
136. W. Scruton, op. cit. pp.5–45
137. B.C.L. Ms 42 D81/1/1/1
138. Ibid
139. B.C.L. Hailstone Ms 204
140. Ibid Ms 194/106 2 November 1808
141. Hailstone Ms 204. 13 November 1814
142. B.C.L. Scruton Papers 5/47/1
143. W. Scruton op. cit. pp.91–2
144. *Leeds Mercury*, 12 February 1825

145. *Diary of J. Simpson*, 13 February 1825
146. *Leeds Mercury* 26 February 1825 and B.C.L. Rules of the Bradford Mechanics Institute, 1825
147. C. Federer, *The Bradford Mechanics Institute* (Bradford 1906)
148. J. Farrar, *The Autobiography of Joseph Farrar* (Bradford 1889) p.46
149. J.F.C. Harrison, *Learning and Living* op. cit. p.
150. Quoted by Ben Preston in W. Scruton op. cit. p.126
151. B.C.L. Scruton Papers 5.32
152. *Diary of J. Simpson*, July 1825
153. R.J. Morris, Middle Class Culture 1700–1914 in D. Fraser (ed.) *A History of Modern Leeds* (M.U.P. 1981), pp.200–222
154. *Diary of J. Simpson*, 1 July 1825
155. *Bradford Courier*, 17 July 1827
156. B.C.L. Reports of the Bradford Mechanics Institute 1833–41
157. W. Scruton, *Old Bradford*, pp.233–4
158. *Diary of J. Simpson*, 14 April 1825
159. Ibid. 5 February 1825
160. W. White, *History, Directory & Gazeteer of West Riding*, (1837)
161. *Bradford Courier* and W. Scruton op. cit. p.121
162. J.B. Priestley *English Journey* (1934) reprint (1984) p.124